WORLDS /

Nassau Adams was born in 1932 in Kingston, Jamaica. He was educated at Queen's University, Canada and Harvard, USA, where he received his PhD in Economics in 1962. The following year he joined the United Nations in New York where he has since had a long and distinguished career working on a variety of economic problems. He participated in the various UN teams which made pioneering contributions on such issues as the problems and techniques of development planning, the use of econometric models for assessing trade prospects and capital needs of developing countries, and techniques for measuring the development effort in these countries.

He has been closely involved with the work of UNCTAD ever since its inception, specialising in programmes relating to the least developed countries, primary commodity exports, and economic cooperation among developing countires. Since 1989 he has been the head of UNCTAD's Division for Data Management.

Over the years, Dr Adams has travelled extensively in the South advising on problems of international trade and economic development. In addition to a year spent teaching at the University of the West Indies, he was twice in the 1970s a member of ILO Employment Advisory Missions – one led by the late Professor Dudley Seers to Colombia and the other by Professor Hans Singer to Kenya. During 1974–76 he headed a UN Advisory Team on regional integration in the Commonwealth Caribbean.

In addition to a large body of reports and papers which he authored within the UN system, he has contributed articles to learned journals, including, *inter alia*, the *American Economic Review*, *Economic Development and Cultural Change* and *Social and Economic Studies*.

NASSAU A ADAMS

Worlds Apart

The North-South Divide and
the International System

ZED BOOKS

London & New Jersey

Worlds Apart: The North-South Divide and the International System
was first published by Zed Books Ltd, 57 Caledonian Road, London
N1 9BU and 165 First Avenue, Atlantic Highlands,
New Jersey 07716, USA in 1993

Cover designed by Andrew Corbett

Typeset by Martin Best
Printed and bound in the United Kingdom by
Biddles Ltd, Guildford and King's Lynn

A catalogue record for this book is available
from the British Library
US CIP is available from the Library of Congress

ISBN 1 85649 165 X Hb
ISBN 1 85649 166 8 Pb

Contents

Preface

The rapidly growing disparity in incomes and living standards between the rich countries and the poor is a striking feature of life today. In a world which is being brought ever closer together by the revolutions in transport and communications, this situation must be a cause of grave concern. In fact, few would dispute that, with the associated problem of growing poverty in the South, it is now the most pressing global issue that the world faces as we approach the end of the present century. This is especially so now that the East–West conflict has drawn to a close and is no longer on the international agenda.

In trying to understand the immense and seemingly unbridgeable economic gap that now separates the countries of the North from those of the South, I have found it useful to bear in mind a number of historical facts. These include: the relatively recent origin of the gap when viewed in the perspective of history, having its roots in development only over the past two hundred years or so; the part played by almost arbitrary circumstance in planting the seeds from which the gap has sprouted; the contrasting roles of positive and negative 'spread effects' in determining which countries would stand on either side of the divide and, finally, the explosive widening of that divide which has taken place in the few decades since the end of World War Two, when compared with all that took place before.

Over the years, much has been written on these disturbing issues of the widening North–South income gap and the growing spread of poverty in the countries of the South. There is, however, one aspect that I have long felt should be more fully brought into the picture if we are to understand adequately the dynamics of the increasing income gap and the contradictions which it poses. I refer here to the role of the international system which sets the framework for economic relations among states. While this aspect has not been entirely neglected in the literature, it is seldom given the emphasis it deserves. It is around this aspect, therefore, that the discussion in this book primarily revolves, as it examines the interplay between the ability of states to influence the nature of the system and to benefit from it, and as it recounts, in particular, the efforts of the countries of the South over the past half-century, unavailing as it turns out, to bring about, through negotiation, dialogue and international debate, changes in a system they considered unjust and heavily stacked against them. What we have witnessed so far suggests that, in these matters, negotiation and dialogue have only a limited role to play when pitted against the realities of power. Nevertheless, given the dire consequences for all concerned of the continuation of current trends, we can only hope that reason will in the end prevail, and that somehow a more accommodating international system will finally take shape before it is too late to avoid tragedy.

It is now my hope that the analysis and conclusions contained in what follows will help all those interested in the future of North–South relations to understand better the role that the international system has played in sustaining the rapidly increasing economic divide that separates the North from the South, and that this in turn will help foster awareness and stimulate action to reverse present tendencies.

This book could not have been written without accumulating a heavy debt to many, both known and unknown to me. Perhaps my greatest debt is to those writers who have contributed to the vast literature on which I have liberally drawn in crystallising my ideas, including those with whose views I sometimes sharply differ. I am also indebted to all those, including former colleagues, with whom I have discussed these matters over the years, particularly the late Sidney Dell, whose writings on the IMF I have found most illuminating. My special thanks go to Havelock Brewster for reading through the entire manuscript and for making many useful suggestions. My special thanks also go to Geraldine Maden and to Martin Best for expert assistance in preparing the manuscript for publication. Needless to say, the author alone remains responsible for all shortcomings.

Nassau. A. Adams

Introduction

It is now going on half a century since the end of the Second World War and the birth of a new era which seemed to open new horizons to mankind in his pursuit of economic security and betterment. After countless millennia of economic stagnation and subsistence living, mankind had, during the previous two centuries or so, discovered the means of applying technology and organization to achieving continuous increases in income and economic well-being. This process started in Western Europe, particularly in the British Isles, and by the Second World War had spread to and economically transformed a small group of countries. The great bulk of mankind, however, was up to then largely untouched by this process and remained economically underdeveloped.

This new era which dawned with the end of the war was characterized by a heightened and widespread recognition of two important truths: the possibility of promoting, on a continuous and long-term basis, and as a conscious purpose of policy, the economic betterment of mankind; and the inadmissibility of colonial rule of one people over another, a nefarious institution that had taken root and spread through the previous centuries. A process of decolonization was therefore soon to unfold that would see, in less than a decade, the freeing from colonial rule of hundreds of millions of people, representing over a half of mankind and occupying the great land masses of Asia and Africa and sundry territories elsewhere, and their constitution into independent states. These peoples and states would join the ranks of the underdeveloped and constitute its core.

In the new era, governments everywhere, in both developed and underdeveloped countries, were to set as an important objective of policy the promotion of the economic development of their countries and improvements in the economic well-being of their peoples. The outcome, after more than four decades of this new era, is well known: while those countries already industrially developed at the end of the war have prospered, and over the succeeding years have made great strides in attaining ever rising income levels, the countries which at that time were still underdeveloped have made much more patchy progress, if not stagnated, with the result that the gap between the developed and underdeveloped countries has greatly widened, and on present trends shows every sign of continuing to widen in the years ahead. This stark fact is a matter of great concern in a world which, as a result of the process of economic development itself, has become culturally and politically smaller and more compact, and in which events and developments at one point on the globe are of growing concern and interest to all.

Our main purpose in the present work is to examine the role of international economic policy in the evolution of these events. In doing so we will trace the development of the international system during the post-war years, probe into the various forces that have been brought to bear in influencing its evolution, and assess the way in which the system as it has evolved has impacted on underdeveloped countries and affected their development prospects. The international debates and discussions are reviewed in order to help understand the motivations and forces at work, and the policy developments are examined and discussed in the context of their relevance to and bearing on the economic development problems of developing countries. The issues surveyed and the period covered embrace a wide expanse. It has therefore been necessary to paint with a broad brush on a wide canvas. The main theme that emerges from the discussion is that of an international system heavily stacked against the underdeveloped countries, of a growing effort by these countries during the first three post-war decades to bring about beneficial changes in the system, with limited success, and of a major turning of the tide in the 1980s which saw them no longer able to sustain such effort, facing now a bleak future in an ever more hostile international economic environment.

The plan of the book is as follows. In Chapter 1 we place in the perspective of history the economic gap between developed and underdeveloped countries at the start of the post-war period, discuss the developments leading to this gap, and examine the statistical data on the evolution of the gap in the subsequent decades. Chapter 2 centres on the international policy framework which emerged in the aftermath of the war. The focus there is on the influences and considerations which determined its design, the purposes it was intended to serve, and the question of its relevance to the problems of the economic development of underdeveloped countries. In Chapter 3 we try to give the flavour of the dramatic change of mood in the international political climate that occurred during the 1950s as former colonies were set free and a host of new states, all quintessentially underdeveloped, entered the political arena and began to demand beneficial changes in the international system with which they were confronted. The discussion examines the demands made, the reactions elicited, and the impact on the system of any resulting concessions. Chapters 4 and 5 deal with the evolution of dialogue and confrontation between North and South during the 1960s and 1970s, and the impact of this on the international system. These were decades when developing countries were becoming bolder, better organized and better able to articulate their views and present their demands, and which saw them able to achieve some modest success. Chapters 6 and 7 deal with the period of the turning of the tide, when developing countries were no longer able to press their case for change, and indeed found themselves in retreat. Chapter 6 examines the forces which led to this turnaround, while Chapter 7 discusses the nature and implications of the reversal. In Chapter 8 the various strands of the discussion are brought together in the context of our assessment of future prospects.

Some brief comments and explanations on a number of matters may be helpful here. First as to terminology. Following established practice, we have used interchangeably throughout the expressions 'underdeveloped', 'less developed', 'developing', 'third world', and 'the South' to refer essentially to the same group of countries whose constituent members are evident from the discussion in the text. Similarly, 'the North', 'developed countries,' and 'industrial countries' are used interchangeably to refer to the capitalist developed countries. Second, while for obvious analytical reasons the discussion focuses on relations between 'North' and 'South' as defined above, and in considerable measure proceeds almost as if these two groups constituted the entire universe, we were not unaware of the existence during the period under review of the large communist bloc which, however, because of its minimal participation in international economic relations, could to a large extent be conveniently left out of the picture. But with the recent breakdown of communism in Eastern Europe and the Soviet Union and the present efforts by these countries to join the capitalist world, the parameters of the North-South problem will clearly change. We can only hint at some of the implications here.

1. The Development Gap in Historical Perspective

Historical antecedents

As the 20th century draws to a close and we reflect on world economic developments during the past 100 years, two aspects stand out - the seemingly inexorable process of worldwide economic growth and accompanying economic transformation, and the progressively increasing gap between the rich and the poor, the industrial and the non-industrial, the developed and the underdeveloped countries. It is noteworthy, however, that these two features, which we take so much for granted today, are a unique and exceptional feature of history. They derive from the phenomenon of modern economic growth whose origins date back scarcely 200 years.

It is true that earlier times had seen the emergence of great states and empires in Egypt, China, India, Central America and the Mediterranean, among others. But the wealth of these states was based on traditional production methods that did not contain the seeds of dynamic long-term economic growth. These pre-industrial states therefore achieved a certain greatness and relative wealth, but soon stagnated and failed to generate a process of long-term economic growth.

It is also true that the pre-industrial phase of European economic history spanning the 14th to the 17th centuries also saw the accumulation of considerable wealth. This wealth resulted, in particular, from the profits earned in the great seafaring activities connected with the exploration and conquering of new lands in the era of merchant capitalism and European geographical expansionism. The exploitation of the technologically backward peoples of Asia, Africa and the Americas with whom the explorers and traders came in contact, the slave trade, and the trade in spices, precious metals and other exotic goods found in these faraway lands, were all sources of tremendous profits to the Western European countries involved.[1] But during these centuries the economic structure and modes of production of these European economies remained basically unchanged, and there was very little movement towards economic transformation and higher living standards for the masses of their peoples.

1

In fact, it is probably safe to say that this accumulation of wealth was used for the most part either to fight wars, to promote the more intensive exploitation of these mercantile activities, or to support extravagant patterns of consumption of the rich. Production methods remained relatively unchanged, and very little of this new wealth was ploughed back into productive investment for economic transformation and growth. It was not until the coming of the industrial revolution, which began in England in the late 18th century and quickly spread to other European countries and elsewhere, that modern economic growth, combining technological innovation, capital accumulation, economic transformation and income growth as one dynamic process, became a reality.[2]

Origins and spread of modern economic growth

To fix our attention, 1820 may be taken as the date of the beginning of the period of modern economic growth. By the end of the Second World War, therefore, the process of modern economic growth would on this basis have been under way for about a century and a quarter. It was only a relatively small group of countries, however, mostly European or of European stock, that effectively participated in this first major phase of modern economic growth. It has been estimated that these countries averaged rates of *per capita* income growth in excess of 15 per cent per decade over those years, implying that in the century or so leading up to the 1950s the level of *per capita* income in these countries more than quadrupled. During those years these countries also experienced substantial increases in their populations, averaging about 10 per cent per decade. The result has been an enormous increase in total output and income in these countries at rates averaging over 25 per cent per decade, and this has meant a massive increase in their economic size.[3]

By the early 19th century, wealth and incomes in Western Europe and the European offshoots in the 'areas of recent settlement' (i.e. North America and Australasia) were already significantly higher than elsewhere. Nonetheless, the wide differentials in *per capita* income and in levels of development that were to become evident by the middle of the 20th century were largely a result of the differences in growth rates experienced during the subsequent century and a quarter of modern economic growth. This is reflected in Kuznets' calculations, which show that about three-fifths of the difference in *per capita* income between developed countries and low-income underdeveloped countries observed by the middle of the 20th century was due to differences in *per capita* income growth over the preceding 100 years.[4]

Why the locus of growth was restricted to a particular group of countries during this critical initial period of modern economic growth and why therefore some countries moved forward while others stood still, is a question of immense importance about which much can be written. The question is nonetheless much too vast and involved to be treated here. Kuznets, who has perhaps given as much thought to this question as anyone else, stresses the importance of the distinctive historical heritage of the pioneer countries and of those participating in the early spread of this process of economic growth. This heritage included a long stretch of common history shared by the Western European countries, a number of similar institutions, and a not too dissimilar tradition of views and values.[5] Geographic proximity facilitated communication and social intercourse, and the spread of ideas and economic impulses among these countries.

This heritage also included the accumulated wealth and other economic benefits derived from the previous centuries of expansionism, merchant capitalism and exploitation of faraway lands and peoples. Apart from other obvious ways in which this wealth made its contribution to the growth process, it is of interest to note that the age of geographic expansionism spanning the 14th to the 17th centuries coincided with the age of European Renaissance and Enlightenment which saw the explosion of intellectual, scientific and artistic achievements and advances in political ideas, setting the stage for the advent of the industrial revolution and the subsequent phase of modern economic growth. These processes are clearly interrelated, since the wealth generated in this process was of key importance in providing the economic surplus required to maintain the intellectual elite, without whom these achievements would not have been possible.

There is also the other side to this age, which helps to explain further the restricted geographical scope of modern economic growth. We refer here to the disastrous impact of this expansionism on the native peoples with whom the Europeans came in contact. This point is well emphasized by Adam Smith who, in explaining how this expansionism greatly contributed to the wealth and prosperity of Europe 'considered as one great country', goes on to add:

> To the natives, however [of these distant lands], all the commercial benefits which can have resulted from these events have been sunk and lost in the dreadful misfortunes which they have occasioned. At the particular time when these discoveries were made, the superiority of force happened to be

so great on the side of the Europeans, that they were enabled to commit with impunity every sort of injustice in those remote countries.[6]

The pattern of exploitation of the technologically backward peoples of Asia, Africa and the Americas during the three or four centuries of merchant capitalism, and the system of colonialism and imperial rule to which this gave rise, thus severely circumscribed the potential of these non-European peoples to participate effectively in the initial process of modern economic growth. Apart from the 'dreadful misfortunes' to which Adam Smith alludes, it did so in a number of ways. The slave trade, which flourished for over 300 years as a major source of European wealth creation, is a good example here. From the European point of view, this was simply profitable trade by which great wealth could be amassed, but for the African societies affected this was social violence of a most destructive kind, seriously disrupting the economic and social fabric of society at its very core, and thereby making it that much more difficult to acquire the attributes required to participate in the process of modern economic growth.

Deliberate policies designed to stifle industrialization and modern economic growth and to perpetuate economic dependency on the metropolitan countries also played their part in restricting the geographical locus of growth.[7] The case of India provides as good an illustration as any. Romesh Dutt, the Indian economic historian writing at the turn of the 20th century, long before our present-day concepts of developed and underdeveloped countries had crystallized, lamented the extent to which the scope for wealth creation and economic growth in India had been narrowed under British rule. As he pointed out, India in the 18th century was a great manufacturing country and an important supplier of textiles to markets in Europe and Asia. However, to quote Dutt,

It is, unfortunately, true that the East India Company and the British Parliament, following the selfish commercial policy of a hundred years ago, discouraged Indian manufacturers in the early years of British rule in order to encourage the rising manufactures of England. Their fixed policy . . . was to make India subservient to the industries of Great Britain, and to make the Indian people grow raw produce only, in order to supply material for the looms and manufactories of Great Britain. This policy was pursued with unwavering resolution and with fatal success; . . . prohibitive tariffs excluded Indian silk and cotton goods from England; English goods were admitted into India free of duty or on payment of a nominal duty.[8]

In the other colonies and territories the details were probably different, but the broad pattern was much the same. Colonial policy would always be designed to provide markets in the colonies for the manufactures of the metropolitan countries while promoting the colonies as a source of raw produce. Industrialization, the driving force of modern economic growth, could therefore find no fertile soil in the colonies.

There is no need to deny here that in some respects (though not necessarily in all cases) contact with the technologically more advanced European countries had positive modernizing effects on the more backward colonial territories. And indeed Romesh Dutt, in lamenting the debilitating effect which British imperial rule had in stifling the scope for industrialization and modern economic growth in India, acknowledged the positive side of British rule in introducing modern education, modern thought and sciences, and modern institutions including systems of modern administration and justice. But this does not in any way detract from our main conclusions above.

Be that as it may, the fact remains that by the end of the Second World War the world was well and truly divided into rich and poor, developed and underdeveloped, industrial and non-industrial, colonizers and colonized. And while these categories did not always coincide exactly, they were largely representative of the same phenomenon and could be used to identify the same groups of countries. Broadly speaking, the rich, industrial, developed countries, i.e. the colonizers, were represented by the European countries and their offshoots, the largely European settlements of North America and Australasia, while the poor, underdeveloped, non-industrial countries - the colonized - were represented by the peoples of Asia, Africa and the rest of the Americas.

This classification is not exact, and there are some anomalies. Thus Japan, a non-European, Asian country, had before the war already virtually qualified to be included in the developed category, as evidenced by her ability to engage the leading industrial and colonial powers in a major war. It is significant, however, that Japan, unlike most other Asian countries, had been able to avoid the yoke of being colonized by the imperialist powers, a factor of undoubted importance in accounting for Japan's peculiar experience. But one only needs to compare the Japanese experience with that of China to realize that it is not possible to explain a phenomenon as complex as the capacity to initiate and sustain a process of modern economic growth by any single factor. China, like Japan, also escaped the yoke of colonialism. And China, like Japan, also had to face the aggressive expansionism of the Western imperialist countries, the former in the context of the Opium Wars and the imposition of unequal treaties, the latter in the context of the 'opening up' enforced by United States' warships under Commodore Perry. But the somewhat similar experience of these two Asian countries did not prevent the subsequent evolution of events from differing markedly between them as regards success in carrying forward the process of modern economic growth.

The South American experience was also something of an anomaly. This region, also settled by the colonizing Europeans, did not share in this process of modern economic growth, and therefore found itself at the beginning of the post-war period in the category of low-income underdeveloped countries. Here, the significant point to bear in mind is that the South American colonies were established in lands in which there existed highly organized and populous native communities. They were therefore much closer to the classical European colonial systems which evolved in Africa and Asia than to the European colonies established in North America and Australasia. The latter were established in areas in which there existed only weak and thinly populated native communities spread out over vast territories. These native populations could therefore be conveniently exterminated or otherwise driven from the land, and wholly European settlements established. We therefore had two very different types of European colonization, with very different end results - one involving the wholesale migration of native Europeans to settle new lands, the other the super-imposition of European rule on native peoples. And it was the latter system that was the breeding ground for stagnation and underdevelopment. The South American colonies were something in between, and ended up in the category of the colonized and underdeveloped.[9]

A world divided: the income and development gap at the start of the post-war era

We now wish to give a summary picture of the way in which the world was divided in the early post-war years, and of the differences in incomes and levels of development which then separated these groups in the aftermath of the process described above. One way to go about doing this is to compare the shares of the relevant country groups in world population and world income, using data conveniently put together by Kuznets for 1958. These show the developed countries (USA, Canada, the countries of Western Europe, Australia, New Zealand and Japan) accounting for 20 per cent of the world's population and for 65 per cent of world income. On the other hand, the countries of Asia (excluding Japan), Africa and Latin America accounted at that time for 67 per cent of the world's population but for a mere 18 per cent of world income.[10] These statistics dramatically highlight the vast gap that separated these two groups of countries in the early post-war years.

A peculiar feature of these years was the predominant position occupied by the United States, accounting by itself, with just 6 per cent of world population, for over one-third of world income. There were thus important differences in income levels among the countries included in the developed group, with the United States *per capita* income in the mid-1950s being more than three times the average for Western Europe. Similarly, important differences in income levels existed among the underdeveloped countries as well, at least as great as, if not greater than, those among the developed countries. In general, income levels were significantly higher in Latin America than in Asia and Africa, and indeed some Latin American countries, for example Venezuela and Argentina, enjoyed income levels in the early post-war period higher than or equal to those of a number of West European countries. As a rough guide, it may be said that income levels varied by a ratio of about 10:1 among the developed countries and by a somewhat greater proportion among the developing countries. The gap was probably of the order of 50:1 or more between the highest-income developed country and the lowest-income developing country.[11]

While the level of income is still the main tool used for classifying countries into development categories, it is, as the above discussion illustrates, by no means a perfect one. An important characteristic that helps to define the level of development is the degree of industrialization attained. This is perhaps what, more than anything, distinguishes the developed from the underdeveloped country. The share of the industrial sector in total output is often taken as an index of the degree of industrialization attained, and the important differences between developed and less developed countries in this sector's share confirms the relevance of this index.[12] Industrialization and the pattern of resource use are important indicators of the level of development in that they provide evidence of the necessary structural transformation of the economy without which the process of long-term, self-sustained economic growth cannot become a reality. Thus a relatively high income level (which may for example be achieved by windfall gains from export earnings) may not necessarily be evidence of a corresponding level of economic development, if the necessary structural transformation has not been (and is not being) made.

The post-war experiences: a statistical analysis

As we have seen, the century-and-a-quarter or so leading up to the Second World War witnessed the successful take-off into modern economic growth of those countries which by the middle of the present century could be classified as being among the developed. During this century-and-a-quarter these countries made great strides in increasing their *per capita* incomes and levels of development, with the result that by the middle of the 20th century vast differences separated them from those who failed to participate in this process of economic growth during those years. The extent of these differences was brought out in the previous section.

In the four-and-a-half decades which have elapsed since the end of the war, this process has continued and indeed intensified resulting in even greater increases in levels of income and consumption. The impressive progress achieved in the post-war years reflects, apart from anything else, the purposeful manner in which official policy world-wide has made the pursuit of high rates of economic growth a major objective. We now seek to throw light on the question of the extent to which the process of modern economic growth has since spread beyond the group of countries who were the main participants in, and beneficiaries of, the pre-Second World War phase of this process, how even and wide has been this spread, and whether there has been any tendency in the post-war period towards a narrowing of the gap in incomes and levels of development.

Taking the four decades up to the end of the 1980s as our period of reference, it appears that the economies of the developing countries as a group expanded at an average rate in excess of that for the developed countries (4.9 per cent per annum for the developing countries compared with 3.5 per cent for the developed countries).[13] But in view of the much higher rate of population growth in the developing countries (2.4 per cent per annum, compared with 0.8 per cent for the developed countries), *per capita* incomes grew at a somewhat lower rate in the developing countries than in the developed over these post-war years (2.4 per cent compared with 2.6 per cent). While the differences in growth rates may not seem great, the data nonetheless suggest a continuing widening of the gap in income levels between developed and developing countries in the years since the end of the Second World War.

This widening can be measured by comparing the ratio of average *per capita* income of developed countries to that of developing countries in the early post-war period with the ratio in a recent year. The comparison shows that

Table 1.1

***Per capita* income of developed countries, 1957 and 1987: Rankings of individual countries and shares in total GDP of developed countries**

	1957	1987	1957	1987
A. *Per capita* income		(US$)		Ranking
United States	2577	18429	1	6
Canada	1947	15849	2	11
Switzerland	1428	26772	3	1
Luxembourg	1388	16715	4	9
Sweden	1380	19323	5	5
Australia	1316	12180	6	15
New Zealand	1310	10357	7	18
Belgium	1196	13999	8	14
United Kingdom	1189	12123	9	17
Norway	1130	20103	10	2
Denmark	1057	19763	11	3
France	943	16047	12	10
W. Germany	927	18402	13	7
Netherlands	836	14581	14	13
Finland	794	18103	15	8
Austria	670	15577	16	12
Ireland	550	8024	17	19
Italy	516	13167	18	15
Greece	340	4637	19	21
Japan	306	19453	20	4
Spain	293	7412	21	20
Portugal	224	3607	22	22

B. Shares in total GDP of developed countries (%)

	1957	1987
United States	58.0	36.0
Japan	3.6	19.0
EEC	17.9	25.0
United Kingdom	8.0	5.5
All others	<u>12.5</u>	<u>14.5</u>
Total	100.0	100.0

Source: Figures for 1957 based on Mikoto Usui and E.E. Hagen, *World Income, 1957*, Massachusetts Institute of Technology, Cambridge, Massachusetts (1959, mimeo). 1987 data based on UNCTAD, *Handbook on International Trade and Development Statistics*, 1989. *Per capita* income in current values.

this ratio, which was about 10:1 or 11:1 in the earlier period, had increased to over 15:1 by the late 1980s.

Another approach is to look at the extremes in income levels reflected in a comparison of the highest-income developed country with the poorest of the developing countries, similar to the comparison done above for the early post-war period. In 1987, the highest *per capita* income among the developed countries was recorded for Switzerland, at more than US$26,000. Among the developing countries, there were several in Africa and Asia for whom *per capita* incomes of well under US$200 were recorded. Using US$200 as the lower limit to allow for possible biases in the data, this gives a ratio of 130:1, compared with a ratio of about 50:1 noted for the immediate post-war period. This comparison therefore confirms our finding that the gap between the richest and the poorest countries has widened over the past 40 years.

So far we have been discussing the experience of the developed and underdeveloped countries as if they were homogeneous wholes. But these groups are composed of individual countries whose experiences may be far from uniform, and hence important changes may have been taking place within the groups themselves. It is therefore now necessary to give a flavour of the heterogeneity of experience within the two groups to get a fuller picture of how the spread of economic growth during these post-war years has been proceeding. Among the developed countries there have, during the post-war years, been significant differences among individual countries in long-term average rates of growth leading to major changes in their relative standing in respect to income levels as well as economic size. Table 1.1 summarizes some relevant data for the developed countries, comparing the 1950s with recent years. The most notable features are the fall of the United States from the top of the list in terms of *per capita* income in the earlier period to sixth place in the late 1980s, the meteoric rise of Japan, the outstanding performance of Switzerland, now standing far ahead in first place, and the very creditable performance of the continental European countries, particularly the original six EEC member states. On the other hand, one cannot help but notice the significant fall from grace of Australia and New Zealand, once near the very top in the income scale, as well as that of the United Kingdom.

This reordering with respect to income levels has been accompanied by a corresponding reordering with respect to economic size. Thus the United States, which accounted for close to 60 per cent of the aggregate income of the developed countries in the early 1950s, saw its share fall to 36 per cent by the late 1980s, while Japan's share rose phenomenally, from a mere 3.6 per cent in the mid-1950s to 19 per cent by the late 1980s. The share of the original six member states of the EEC also recorded a substantial rise, from 18 per cent to 25 per cent over this period. It is interesting to note, however, that notwithstanding these major changes in relative shares among the developed countries, the developed countries as a group appear to have about maintained their share in world income at least over the early post-war decades.[14]

A significant point to note is that among the developed countries there appears to have been a distinct narrowing of the gap in income levels between the country with highest *per capita* income and the country with the lowest, the ratio of the one to the other falling to about 7:1 in the late 1980s, from about 11:1 in the mid-1950s.[15]

Among the developing countries the post-war years have witnessed an even wider diversity of experience than among developed countries in terms of differences in rates of economic growth, resulting not only in significant reorderings of countries in respect of income levels but also to widening gaps among developing countries in incomes and levels of development. Thus cumulative long-term average rates of growth in *per capita* income recorded for individual developing countries during this period have ranged from negative figures (meaning, if the figures are to be believed and taken literally, that *per capita* incomes and standards of living have actually been falling over these years), to rates of up to 6 and 7 per cent per annum for some countries. The magnitude of these differences can be more fully appreciated if we observe that a 7 per cent cumulative average growth-rate over a 30-year period implies nothing less than an eight-fold increase in *per capita* income.

Table 1.2 summarizes some pertinent data reflecting this diversity of experience of individual developing countries. It will be seen that of the 106 developing countries for which the relevant data are available, 26, or about a quarter, actually experienced negative average growth-rates over the period covered in the table. On the other hand, 43 countries had low but positive growth rates of up to 2 per cent per annum, while 26 experienced moderately high growth-rates ranging between 2 and 4 per cent. At the same time 11 countries, about 10 per cent of the total, experienced exceptionally high growth-rates, in excess of 4 per cent per annum. As may be expected, the great majority of the countries with negative *per capita* income growth-rates are in Africa (19 out of 26), while Asian countries predominate among the high performers (8 out of 11).

The table also shows the proportion of the developing countries' total population accounted for by the countries falling within the various ranges of

Table 1.2
Annual average rates of growth of *per capita* GDP of
individual developing countries, 1960-1989

		<0%	0-2%	2-4%	>4%	Totals
a.	No. of countries with growth rates falling within designated ranges	26	43	26	11	106
b.	Breakdown of countries by major geographical regions:					
	Americas	4	13	11	0	28
	Africa	19	20	6	3	48
	Asia	3	10	9	8	30
c.	Share of total population* accounted for by countries in each growth range (%)	7.0	56.4	30.7	5.0	100

Source: Based on data in UNCTAD, *Handbook of International Trade and Development Statistics*, 1989.

*Total population of countries covered in the table.

growth-rates. While these proportions tend to be dominated by the position of a few large countries, they nevertheless allow a fuller grasp of the significance of the data on the distribution of countries within the various growth ranges. Thus it is of interest to note that the relatively large number of countries experiencing negative growth-rates account between them for only 7 per cent of the total population of developing countries, implying that these low performers are predominantly the smaller countries. Exceptionally high growth-rates (above 4 per cent) were also achieved by countries representing only a small proportion (less than 6 per cent) of the total population of developing countries.

In terms of the main geographic regions of the developing world, the highest average growth-rate of *per capita* income over these years was achieved by Asia (at 3.2 per cent per annum), followed by Latin America (at 2.0 per cent), with Africa in the rear with a mere 1 per cent. And it is of considerable interest to note that the particular group of some 40 countries classified by the United Nations as 'least developed' because of their extreme poverty and general economic backwardness averaged, as a group, virtually zero growth in their *per capita* income over this long span of post-war years. As may be expected, most of these least developed countries are in Africa.

With these large disparities in growth-rates it is to be expected that the income gap has been widening among the developing countries, especially so since, as we have just seen, it is the poorest of these countries that have made the least progress in terms of income growth. It was suggested above that in the early post-war period the gap in income levels among developing countries (i.e. comparing countries at the extremes in the income range) was about 10:1 or 11:1.[16] By the end of the 1980s the order of magnitude of this gap was very much greater than this. Even excluding the very rich oil emirates like Qatar, United Arab Emirates and Brunei with *per capita* incomes rivalling those of the rich developed countries, there are now a number of developing countries with moderately high *per capita* incomes of $5000 and above (Singapore, Bahamas, Barbados, Taiwan, Saudi Arabia, Libya, among others), and thus with income levels twenty-five times or more those of the poorest countries.

While it is true that, in general, the poorest countries at the dawn of the post-war period remain the poorest countries today, there have been some significant changes in relative income positions among those countries. A number of Latin American countries that were near the top of the developing countries' income range in the immediate post-war period, such as Venezuela, Argentina and Uruguay, have witnessed a fall in their relative income position, to be replaced not only by the oil-rich sheikhdoms but also by some of the Asian rising stars such as Singapore and Hong-Kong. By and large, however, it is the growing disparities in income levels rather than changes in relative standing that have been the significant feature in the experience of the developing countries group.[17]

On interpreting the post-war experience: falling behind or catching up?

What conclusions are we to draw from this post-war experience relating to the spread of economic growth? The most obvious point to note is the growing gap in income levels between the developed and the developing countries and, equally importantly, among the developing countries themselves. The indications are that nation states have been growing further apart in standards of living and levels of development. But the differences in experience among the developing countries indicate that while many of these countries are standing still or merely crawling, others are moving ahead at quite a clip. Returning to the data summarized in Table 1.2, we may agree that all countries averaging rates of growth of *per capita* income below 2 per cent are to be considered as crawling or standing still. This seems a fair characterization since at such low rates of growth it would at best be many decades before any significant progress is achieved. Of the 106 countries covered in the table, 69, or roughly two-thirds of the total, representing roughly the same proportion of the total population of the developing countries, were in the category of those who may be said to be crawling or standing still, obviously being left behind in this process of economic growth.

But in terms of the catching-up process, we may be a little bit more precise and take as the norm the average rate of growth of *per capita* income achieved by the developed countries during the post-war period, considering all those developing countries averaging growth-rates below this norm as continuing to fall behind, and only those with growth-rates at or above this norm as keeping pace or even catching up. Using this criterion, the data indicate that 83 of the 106 countries, accounting between them for somewhat over three-quarters of the total population of developing countries, have been falling behind during the post-war years, while only 23 countries, representing somewhat less than a quarter of the total population, have been keeping pace or catching up.[18]

One way to interpret these results is to say that there has, over these years, been a splitting apart of the developing countries, with a small sub-group moving ahead at rates that will eventually place them in the ranks of the developed countries, while the vast majority is left falling ever further behind. The question would then arise as to whether and when individual countries in the first sub-group had made the transition from underdeveloped to developed, forcing the issue of appropriate criteria for distinguishing between 'developed' and 'underdeveloped' countries. The issue is a complex one that has never been squarely faced, and we do not intend to do that here.

It is clear, however, that *per capita* income by itself is not adequate, and needs to be supplemented by other criteria indicating whether the necessary economic transformation has thereby taken place laying the foundation for long-term self-sustained economic growth. Thus, a number of developing countries that have attained relatively high *per capita* income levels based on the exploitation of a single natural resource-based export product (e.g. petroleum, tourism) have clearly not achieved the necessary broad-based structural transformation of their economies, and are much too dependent on a narrow resource base, to be considered to have made the transition.

The question may also be raised as to whether the criteria themselves should be taken as fixed, or whether they may need to be changed to keep pace with the times. In other words, would criteria expressed in absolute values be the same today as in 1950, or is there a need to adjust the absolute values of these criteria (and possibly even to introduce new criteria) to take account of all the important changes that have taken place over the past 40 years, in income levels and standards of living in the developed countries, in technologies, products and production methods, in the patterns of international economic relations, to name some of the more obvious. To put the question differently, if US$500 was the appropriate criterion in 1950 for distinguishing between a developed and an underdeveloped country, would the equivalent of US$500 in today's prices be an appropriate criterion today, notwithstanding that in the meantime there has been a several-fold increase in income levels in the developed countries?

Apart from *per capita* income, other criteria to be taken into account in deciding if a country is to be classified as developed should include: an ability to sustain on a long-term basis an adequate rate of growth of income; an ability to generate the required foreign exchange earnings without the need to rely on non-market based loans or other ad-hoc non-market arrangements; a sufficiently large and diversified modern industrial sector; an adequately developed education system and a sufficiently large pool of professional and skilled indigenous workers able to run the key sectors of the economy and to keep abreast of and participate in pushing forward the frontiers of technology in these key sectors; and a sufficiently industrialized agricultural sector. These are among the conditions which seem necessary for a country to qualify as being developed.

Bearing these conditions in mind, it is unlikely that there are many countries classified as 'developing' in the 1950s who could now be considered to have made the transition to 'developed'. Many who could pass the *per capita* income test would fail to meet one or another of the above criteria. And, indeed, only a limited few could pass the *per capita* income test. Only two or three of the large number of countries classified as underdeveloped in the post-war years have, in the light of their economic performance over the past three to four decades, come close to reaching the stage where it may soon be possible (or necessary) to classify them as developed. We would suggest South Korea,

Singapore and Taiwan. Hong· Kong, whose status as a country is unclear, may also fall in this category.

This is not to deny, of course, that some of the oil-rich countries may not in time use their oil wealth to build the physical, industrial and human infrastructure necessary to form the base for a transition to developed country status. And in time other countries might also join South Korea and Singapore in making the necessary transformation. The main point that needs to be stressed here, however, is that in the four decades of post-war económic development there has been a widening of the income gap and virtually no change in the basic division of the countries of the world into the categories of developed and underdeveloped.

Notes

1. This point is made much of by Adam Smith in his remark that 'The discovery of America, and that of a passage to the East Indies by the Cape of Good Hope, are the two greatest and most important events recorded in the history of mankind', contributing greatly to the wealth and prosperity of Europe 'considered as one great country'. See Adam Smith, *The Wealth of Nations*, The Modern Library, New York, 1937, p. 590.

2. An indication of the extent to which world economic developments since the 18th century represent a qualitative break with the past is suggested by data on the size and growth of the world's population. Where incomes are already close to the subsistence level, as they must surely have been for the great masses of the population in the pre-industrial world, significant increases in the population imply corresponding increases in productive capacity, and hence economic growth in the aggregate sense. Kuznets presents estimates of the world's population from the year 1000 onwards. These show that for the 750 years prior to 1750 world population increased slowly, averaging about 1.3 per cent per decade. After 1750, however, there was a marked, and indeed dramatic acceleration, with the rate averaging 7.0 per cent per decade between 1750 and 1960. While this acceleration apparently affected all the major geographical regions of the world (except Africa before 1850, presumably due to the slave trade and the general rape of the continent by the Europeans), the greatest acceleration was experienced by the Europeans, with a growth rate averaging 9.5 per cent per decade (this includes the European out-reaches in North America and Oceania). This acceleration in the long-term rate of growth of population, coinciding as it does with the period of modern economic growth, is clear evidence of the unique character of this period. See S. Kuznets, *Modern Economic Growth: Rate,*

Structure and Spread, Yale University Press. New Haven and London, 1966, Chapter 2, on which the above discussion is based, for a fuller discussion on this issue.

3. To give some examples, between 1840 and 1960 the economic size (total GDP) of the United States increased by a factor of 35; for Sweden the increase over the period 1860-1960 was by a factor of 23; and for Japan over the period 1880-1960 the increase was by a factor of 33. See Kuznets, *op. cit.*, table 2.5.

4. Kuznets, *op. cit.*, p. 394.

5. See Kuznets, *op. cit.*, Ch. 9.

6. See Adam Smith, *op.cit.*, p. 590.

7. See Adam Smith, *The Wealth of Nations*, Chapter VII ('Of Colonies') for numerous examples illustrating this aspect of European colonial policy during this period.

8. See Romesh Dutt, *The Economic History of India*, 2 Vols. (Publications Division, Ministry of Information and Broadcasting, Government of India, 1903, reprinted 1960); the quote is from Vol. 1, p. xxv.

9. It is of interest to note here that Argentina, Uruguay and Chile, the Southern Cone countries which come closest to the ideal European settler type of colony, had by the beginning of the post-war period come closest to qualifying as 'developed'. Perhaps the strong negative pull of their geographic neighbours was the determining factor in tilting the balance against joining the 'developed' club.

10. See Kuznets, *op. cit.*, Table 7.1. Kuznets' estimates of the distribution of world GDP for 1958 are comprehensive in that they include estimates for the communist countries of Eastern Europe and for mainland China. The figures quoted above for the underdeveloped countries of Asia, Africa and Latin America include the estimates for mainland China, but we have made no reference to the estimates for the communist countries of Eastern Europe. In view of the unavailability (and, where available, incomparability) of the relevant data for the communist countries in later years, we will in the subsequent analysis exclude the communist countries from our estimates of, and reference to, world totals.

11. The most comprehensive internationally comparable estimates of *per capita* income for the 1950s are in Mikoto Usui and E. E. Hagen, *World Income, 1957* (Massachusetts Institute of Technology, Cambridge, Mass., Nov. 1959 mimeo). These data show a number of developing countries with *per capita* incomes of US$45 in 1957, which, when compared with the estimate of US$2577 shown for US *per capita* income in that year, gives a ratio of 57:1.

12. See S. Kuznets, 'Quantitative Aspects of the Growth of Nations: Industrial Distribution of National Product and Labor Force', *Economic Development and Cultural Change*, V, No. 4 (July 1957), for an extensive analysis of the statistics relating to this aspect of economic growth, including cross-section analysis comparing data for developed and less developed countries during the 1950s. See also in this connection, H.B. Chenery, 'Patterns of Industrial Growth', *American*

Economic Review (September 1960), and Nassau A. Adams, 'Import Structure and Economic Growth: A comparison of Cross-Section and Time-Series Data', *Economic Development and Cultural Change*, Vol. 15, No. 2, Part 1, January 1967.

13. Consistently prepared estimates permitting a comparison of economic performance between developed and developing countries are available only for the years since 1960. The discussion below is therefore based on data covering the period since 1960. See United Nations, *Handbook of International Trade and Development Statistics* (1989), Table 6.2.

14. This observation is not inconsistent with the previous finding concerning the increasing gap in income levels between developed and developing countries reflected in the post-war data; as earlier noted, higher population growth-rates in the developing countries has meant somewhat higher rates of growth of aggregate income in developing countries.

15. See Table 1.1.

16. See above.

17. The conclusions reached in this section are very similar to those arrived at by Baumol using a somewhat different data base and a more rigorous statistical methodology. Thus his analysis of the data covering the period 1950-1980 shows a marked tendency towards convergence of the incomes of the developed countries, but towards divergence among the poorer developing countries. (See William J. Baumol, 'Productivity Growth, Convergence, and Welfare: What the Long-Run Data Show', *American Economic Review*, Vol. 76, No. 5, December 1986). Baumol's findings of a similar tendency to convergence among the (now) developed countries over the past century or so has been sharply criticized by De Long on statistical grounds (largely in terms of sample bias), and this criticism has been accepted by Baumol. (See Bradford De Long, 'Productivity Growth, Convergence, and Welfare: Comment', *American Economic Review*, Vol. 78, No. 5, December 1988, and the Reply by William J. Baumol and Edward N. Wolff in the same issue of that Journal). In view of the various points of statistics and methodology made by the authors in this debate, perhaps the safest conclusion is that of Baumol and Wolff in their 'Reply' (p. 116), that 'much of the nineteenth century was a period of divergence in standards of living of the leading European economies. Then, sometime towards the end of the century, this process began to erode, and was replaced by convergence among increasingly large sets of the initially (or later) more affluent of the countries.' This conclusion may have some relevance for an understanding of the post-war experience of the developing countries.

18. Calculations based on data in the same source as for Table 1.2.

2. Establishing the Post-war World Economic Order

Planning the post-war international economy

The end of the Second World War saw the establishment of an array of institutions for international economic co-operation never before seen or contemplated. These institutions, near universal in scope and membership, provided the framework for the conduct of international economic policy during the post-war period, and were a major factor in setting the tone of world economic development during this period and in determining the participation of individual countries therein. The development problems and prospects facing the underdeveloped countries could not therefore but be heavily influenced by the existence and role of these institutions. In this chapter we shall take a look at these institutions and the considerations leading to their establishment and examine their relevance to, and bearing on, the development issue.

It was the Second World War and its immediate antecedents which provided the motivation and the occasion for the creation of these institutions. The antecedents concern particularly the economic chaos of the inter-war period and the belief that this chaos was both a result of the First World War and an important cause of the Second.

The United States, in taking the lead and providing the main driving force for the establishment of these institutions, was heavily influenced by the inter-war experience, where US isolationism was widely felt to have contributed to the economic chaos that reigned during the inter-war years. This was reflected, *inter alia*, in the US failure to join the League of Nations and in its attitude of distancing itself from the problems of post-First World War reconstruction in Europe and the associated economic and financial difficulties to which these gave rise. The fact that the United States' economy was so greatly affected by the economic depression of the 1930s, the deepest and longest depression in history, and the most obvious manifestation of the economic chaos of the period, no doubt also influenced thinking on this score.

US policy makers therefore started early planning for a post-Second World War institutional framework that could cope with the problems of transition to

peace-time conditions and could provide a framework for a smoothly functioning international economy. The major issues that needed to be dealt with
included reconstruction finance for repairing the heavily war-damaged economies of Europe, monetary co-operation arrangements to deal with the problem
of exchange rate stability and currency convertibility, and trade co-operation
arrangements to ensure that governmental barriers to trade were kept under
control. These are issues that had all come to plague the international economy
during the inter-war years and had constituted a hindrance to the expansion of
world trade and prosperity.[1]

The thrust of US thinking was reflected in the negotiations surrounding
lend-lease agreements under which the US undertook to provide its allies with
supplies during the war. In consideration, the allies undertook to co-operate in
the post-war reconstruction of multilateral trade through agreed action,
'. . . open to participation by all other countries of like mind, directed to the
expansion, by appropriate international and domestic measures, of production,
employment and the exchange and consumption of goods, . . .'[2] Originally
negotiated with the UK, this language was essentially accepted by 16 other
governments before the end of the war, and formed the basis for the negotiations of post-war international economic institutions.[3]

One aspect of the inter-war experience that had a particularly profound
impact on thinking about post-war policy was the apparent helplessness of
governments in the face of economic chaos. This apparent helplessness gave
rise to a good deal of debate among professional economists during this period
and led to major revisions of accepted doctrine concerning the responsibility
of government for the maintenance of full employment and aggregate demand.
The theoretical underpinning for the new doctrine was provided by the writings
of John Maynard Keynes, whose influence on the theory and practice of
economics was to become so great as to acquire the status of a new paradigm.
Henceforth, governments would be expected to pursue policies to ensure full
employment and a satisfactory level of aggregate demand, and Keynesian
theories would provide the tools to do this.[4] This new-found realization of the
role of government in ensuring macro-economic balance heightened the
urgency of putting in place suitable arrangements for multilateral economic
co-operation, particularly in the areas of trade and monetary and exchange rate
policies, since it was clear that without such co-operation full employment
objectives could not be met without unacceptable losses in efficiency.

Ideas for post-war multilateral economic co-operation focused on two
main areas: monetary and financial institutions to deal with the problems of

exchange rates, currency stabilization, reconstruction finance and international investments; and a trade organization to deal with the problems of commercial policy and to promote the liberalization of trade. The former led to the Bretton Woods Conference and the establishment of the International Monetary Fund (IMF) and the World Bank (International Bank for Reconstruction and Development - IBRD), the latter to the Havana Charter embodying the scheme for an International Trade Organization, which, however, was never ratified and never saw the light of day. Instead, a more limited scheme for trade liberalization, the General Agreement on Tariffs and Trade (GATT), was put into effect.

The United Nations was also assigned an important role in post-war economic planning, particularly in the co-ordination of full employment policies. This role was never allowed to develop, however, and instead the UN became the main forum where attempts were made to deal with the specific problems of the less developed countries. ,

The birth of the Bretton Woods institutions

Concrete proposals for a 'Currency Stabilization Fund' and a 'Bank for Reconstruction' were already being discussed within the US Government in early 1942. In the meantime the British were working on parallel ideas for a 'Currency Union' (the 'Keynes Plan'), and in due course, following detailed negotiations between the British and the Americans, there emerged a Joint Anglo-American Statement on the Establishment of an International Monetary Fund, issued in April 1944. Discussions on the proposals for a Bank also proceeded, if at a slower pace, and basic Anglo-American agreement was also reached.[5]

Following consultations held in early 1944 with a number of other governments on the ideas contained in these proposals, the US President invited 43 countries to attend a 'United Nations Monetary and Financial Conference' to be held in Bretton Woods, New Hampshire, beginning 1 July 1944. This was the famous Bretton Woods Conference from which were born the two pillars of the post-war multilateral financial community, the IMF and the World Bank. The key provisions of the Joint Anglo-American Statement were embodied, with only minor changes, in the Articles of Agreement of the Fund. [6]

It will be evident from the above that the Bretton Woods Conference, the crucial negotiations that preceded it, and the issues that came forth from it, were very much an Anglo-American affair. Moreover, the United States was throughout the dominant partner, not only in the leadership it had shown in developing and promoting the proposals for these institutions, but also by virtue of the fact that it alone had the resources to make these institutions work, and was therefore in a position to impose its views at all critical stages in the Anglo-American negotiations. The part played by the other industrial countries were, for a number of reasons, small or minimal, only Canada appearing to have played any significant role.[7]

It goes without saying that the influence of the underdeveloped countries on these negotiations and on the nature of the institutions that emerged was nil or negligible. Of the 43 countries invited to attend the Bretton Woods Conference, 27 were from the underdeveloped regions of Africa, Asia and Latin America, with the overwhelming majority (19) being Latin American countries. Indeed there were only three African countries present (Egypt, Ethiopia and Liberia) and five countries from Asia (India, Iran, Iraq, the Philippines and China). The bulk of Africa was still under European colonial rule, as was a large part of Asia. Given the complexity of the issues involved, the late stage at which they were brought into the picture, and the minimal real bargaining power that they could in any event exert, it is not surprising that the influence of these countries on the conference and its outcome was minimal.

Changed perception of the role of the Fund and the Bank in the immediate post-war period

As originally conceived, both the Fund and the Bank were to play a major role in the restoration of economic equilibrium after the war.[8] It was not long after these institutions were formally established, however, that it became apparent that they were not to play this role. The Fund was supposed to grant assistance for short-term stabilization, but in the immediate aftermath of the war what was really needed was assistance for reconstruction. And while the Bank made an early start in fulfilling its role, it quickly became apparent that the resources at its disposal were far short of what was needed for the reconstruction of Europe. A major shift in American policy, spurred on by political developments in Europe, thus led to the launching of the 'European Recovery Programme' (or 'Marshall Plan') under which the United States undertook to provide massive reconstruction aid to Europe under bilateral programmes outside the framework of the Bank.[9] The Bank was thus sidelined as far as reconstruction loans were concerned. At the same time, special intra-European payment arrangements were devised to facilitate intra-European trade and to overcome the disruption of trade caused by the dollar shortage and the inconvertibility of most European currencies. The effect was to help equilibrate the balance of payments of the war-torn European countries at higher levels of production and trade, and to help facilitate the transition to convertible currencies and unrestricted trade.[10]

The upshot of all this was that the post-war problems of reconstruction, currency stabilization and trade restoration which had figured so heavily in the thinking behind the creation of the Fund and the Bank did not rely on these institutions for their solution. This aspect is well summed up by Gardner when he says: 'With the beginning of the European Recovery Programme the Fund practically ceased exchange operations and the Bank left the field of reconstruction lending. The emphasis shifted from the pursuit of world-wide multilateralism through the Bretton Woods institutions to the more limited objective of the recovery and "integration" of Western Europe.'[11]

It was the threat of communist advances in Europe, and the recognition in the US that without a speedy and effective reconstruction programme the European countries would fall prey to these advances, that spurred the US into action and made it possible for this massive programme of bilateral aid to be put in place. But what is significant here is the by-passing of the Bretton Woods institutions and the use of alternative mechanisms to achieve the specific purpose for which those institutions were originally established, and the reasons for this. In the case of the Bank, the answer is simple. Given the magnitude of the funds required for reconstruction, funding through the Bank would have given rise to an unsustainable debt burden endangering the long-term economic prospects of the war-torn European countries and undermining the commercial viability of the new Bank. Hence the resort to bilateral financing largely on grant terms. In the case of the Fund the answer is a bit more complex, but basically revolves around the questions of conditions of access to the Fund's resources and of the exercise of authority by the Fund over the policies of its members.

A major task that faced the Fund in its early years was how to speed up the return to currency convertibility and multilateral payments. The Articles of Agreement required that this should be achieved within five years of the Fund's establishment. The deadline came and went, however, with currency inconvertibility and payments restrictions still widespread in Europe.

The Fund carried out the necessary consultations with its European members as called for under Article XIV, but was unable to make much headway in speeding up progress towards currency convertibility. In order to get the consultations effectively under way, the Fund had first to overcome a host of definitional problems and to resolve points of principle raised by the European countries eager to ensure that the Fund did not trespass on their sovereign rights. Thus it was soon established (after the matter was first raised in consultations with Belgium and Luxembourg in 1952) that, notwithstanding the language in Article XIV, Section 4, the Fund would not attempt to make any 'representation' to members that conditions were favourable for the withdrawal of any particular restrictions. It was also soon established that the Fund had no authority to 'approve' or 'agree to' the retention of restrictions, lest this implied corresponding authority to disapprove or not to agree to. To avoid the risk of any appearance of encroachment by the Fund on the sanctity of members' sovereign rights on exchange restrictions, it was decided in 1952 that all decisions taken in Article XIV consultations should conclude with the innocuous sentence: 'In concluding the consultations, the Fund has no further comment to make on the transitional arrangements maintained by [name of country]'.[12]

An issue which also received a good deal of attention in the early years concerned the role of the Fund in commenting on the domestic policies of its members. Thus, almost as soon as the consultations got under way, the Fund began urging its European members to pursue 'sound' fiscal and monetary policies in order to overcome or to avoid inflation and to achieve balance-of-payments equilibrium, intimating that the Fund would be willing to underwrite such policies with its resources. But the propriety of the Fund's meddling in domestic fiscal and monetary policies was sharply questioned. These European countries took the view that the restrictions they maintained were necessary for balance-of-payments purposes, and 'as for the Fund's offer of assistance for those who went forward with the work of liberating payments, it was useless for the Fund to expect borrowers on such conditions, as the external imbalance of most countries was too acute for them to abandon protective controls and to accept the obligations which Fund assistance entailed.'[13] As a result, during much of this period the Fund's exchange activities were largely in abeyance, not much use being made of its resources by the European countries still facing serious balance-of-payments difficulties. This was at the time when the European countries were economically at their weakest, suffering serious balance-of-payments problems, and might have been most dependent on Fund resources. Nevertheless, the Fund was kept at bay, unable to exercise any significant influence over these countries' domestic policies or to encroach on their authority in areas where they regard national sovereignty as paramount, such as exchange rate and domestic adjustment policies. The point was well put by the UK Executive Director in October 1948 when he drew the attention of the IMF Board to the 'increasing number of interpretations reading into the Fund Agreement limitations which were not in the text. Because of such limitations the Fund was now of no use to its European members; it carried obligations but no benefits'.[14]

The American influence and the evolution of the Fund's policy on access to its resources

It was clear from the outset that the Bretton Woods institutions would be under American control, notwithstanding the obvious international character of these institutions. The US developed the original ideas for these institutions (with significant British inputs) and brought them into being, and the US would be putting up the bulk of the funds required to make them operational. It was the US, furthermore, who insisted, over the strong objection of the British, that the seat of these institutions should be in Washington, away from traditional financial markets, but right under the very nose of the US Government. US control over these institutions has always therefore been tight, and it has been with regard to policy on the use of the Fund's resources that US influence has been most in evidence.[15]

The major issue that divided the American and British negotiators from the earliest stages in the negotiations concerned the conditions of access to the Fund's resources, the British arguing for a high degree of automaticity as a matter of right, the Americans against. In fact the British view was shared by all the other participants in the negotiations, with the Americans standing alone on the question of conditionality. There appears to have been no real meeting of minds on this issue, and in the circumstances the IMF was established with statutes sufficiently ambiguous to leave the matter unresolved. It would be some time after the IMF came into being that a definitive interpretation would emerge. In the meantime, the two sides continued to cling to their opposing interpretations, and as Dell points out in his penetrating review of the evolution of the Fund's policy on conditionality, as late as September 1947 the British Government continued to believe that the 'battle for "automaticity" may be largely regarded as won'.[16] But this was far from the case, and the Americans, who held the purse strings, simply refused to release funds and to allow access to IMF resources in the absence of conditionality. There was therefore a stand-off, and for the first few years after coming into being the IMF remained moribund, with threatening signs that it may yet be still-born. Gradually, however, the Americans were able to impose their views on the rest of the membership, and by 1951 a policy on conditionality began to evolve on the basis of which the Fund could soon begin meaningful operations.

A significant step in this direction was taken in 1951 when the Executive Board approved a proposal 'designed to ensure that the Fund's resources would be made available to give confidence to members in undertaking practical programmes of action to help achieve the purposes of the Fund Agreement' - such programmes to be the subject of consultations between members and the Fund (Annual Report of IMF for 1951, p. 81). It was not until the following year, however, that the Executive Board adopted a decision which clarified the policy on conditionality. This included the following main elements: in deciding whether a given request for assistance would be granted the Fund would have regard to the economic policies of the applicant and their value in dealing with the deficit; three to five years were to be regarded as the outside limit for repayment; members were to receive 'the overwhelming benefit of any doubt' respecting drawings in the gold tranche; 'standby arrangements' were to be envisaged whereby a member would enter into discussions with the Fund not for an immediate drawing 'but in order to ensure that it would be able to draw if, within a period of say 6 to 12 months, the need presented itself.'[17] This Board decision provided the basic framework on which Fund policy on conditionality has been built over the years.

Concerning the question of degrees of conditionality linked to the various tranches of members' quotas, the matter was clarified in the 1957 report of the Fund's Managing Director as follows: access to the gold tranche is almost automatic; requests for drawings within the next 25 per cent (the so-called 'first credit tranche') are also treated liberally. For drawings beyond that tranche (i.e. beyond the first 50 per cent of the quota), substantial justification is required, including 'well balanced and adequate programmes which are aimed at establishing or maintaining the enduring stability of the currencies concerned at realistic rates of exchange.' It is in these higher credit tranches, therefore, that the full rigour of Fund conditionality will come into play.

Stand-by arrangements, introduced in the policy decision in 1952, and intended to assure a member that, on the basis of prior negotiations with the Fund, drawings up to specified limits and within an agreed period might be made without reconsideration of its position at the time of drawing, were soon to become the centre-piece of the policy on conditionality. From the Fund's point of view these stand-by arrangements offer more effective opportunities for influence and control over the policies of borrowers. As an IMF policy document puts it, under stand-by arrangements

> drawings on the Fund are usually phased between two or more periods, and may be made only while certain specific conditions are being observed. If these conditions are not satisfied, drawings may be resumed only after new understandings are reached. This type of stand-by arrangement provides greater assurance of the proper use of Fund resources than are immediate drawings granted on the basis only of the member's declaration that it intends to follow certain practices.[18]

From the point of view of users of Fund resources (borrowers), the implications of the emerging trend of Fund policies on conditionality are brought out in the following quotation from the officially sponsored Brookings Institution study of World Bank policies (which also included aspects of IMF policies), based on interviews with the staff and on privileged access to unpublished material of these institutions:[19]

> What the Fund is engaged in, through consultation, advice, and persuasion, is a financial programming operation designed to bring into balance externally the supply and demand for foreign exchange with the smallest feasible resort to restrictions on trade and payments . . . The principal instrument relied on to achieve external balance is the exchange rate - in words hallowed by Fund usage, a 'realistic rate of exchange.' The principal instrument internally is the credit ceiling, used to achieve, through control of the quantity of money, an 'enduring stability of the currency.' But there are all sorts of combinations and permutations connected with the use of these basic instruments, and the Fund must necessarily concern itself, in the area of fiscal policy, with government expenditures, the tax structure and tax rates, and the price policies of public enterprises; in the area of income policy, with wage rates and price controls; and with many aspects of capital and foreign exchange markets. Inevitably the Fund is involved in highly sensitive areas of public decision-making.

The implication is that use of Fund resources in the higher credit tranches will necessarily mean very intrusive involvement of the Fund in the most sensitive areas of public policy. And since access to the needed foreign exchange depends on reaching agreement with the Fund, it is easy to see the kind of leverage that the Fund can apply to have its point of view accepted and to influence policy. This is a result that was hardly contemplated by Keynes in developing his ideas about a 'Currency Union'. It was also a far cry from the response of the UK Executive Director to a proposal of the Managing Director in 1950 that would tie drawings to programmes of action by the drawing members. The British Government, he said, objected to 'any suggestion that the right of members to come to the Fund would in any way depend upon their carrying out policies with which they did not agree.[20] We can perhaps understand now why the European countries did not countenance a resort to Fund resources in their time of financial need and balance-of-payments difficulties, even if at that time Fund policies on conditionality had not yet fully evolved.

With regard to Fund dealings with the less developed countries, the policy on conditionality had by the late 1950s also taken a further step. This concerns the practice of making compliance with Fund policies a condition of access to capital from other quarters, a practice begun in the early 1950s at US insistence in order to avoid what the US regarded as the improper use of its public (bilateral) funds (particularly in Latin America) to meet balance-of-payments crises. According to the Brookings Institution study (p. 542): 'There were, at least initially, some misgivings on the part of IMF officials concerning this practice. Some officials questioned whether use by the US Government of Fund conditions as a guide to its lending policies might not injure the Fund's "image" as an international institution. But whatever the strength of these misgivings, they appear to have been temporary.' In fact, the policy was explicitly endorsed by the Fund's managing director in 1958 in language that makes it clear that the Fund was to act as a proxy and policeman for the creditors in enforcing the necessary discipline. It would hardly have escaped the Fund's attention, of course, that if agreement with the Fund (and compliance with Fund conditions) became necessary for the release of needed credit from other sources, this would greatly increase the leverage that the Fund could exert on the suppliant borrower, who now finds himself in a tight squeeze. There is therefore a neat coincidence of interest here between the Fund and other creditors, though it is doubtful if this kind of symbiosis enhances the Fund's standing as an international institution. Be that as it may, from modest beginnings under American pressure, it soon became common practice for European creditors, New York bankers and other would-be lenders to make negotiation of and compliance with Fund agreements a condition of lending to the less developed countries. Renegotiation of short-term debt under the Hague and Paris 'Clubs' also came to be contingent on the debtor country reaching an agreement with the Fund. Access policy and conditionality have therefore evolved a long way from the days when Keynes and the British were advocating automaticity.

The reality of the Fund in practice

The Fund witnessed a remarkable evolution during the first 15 years of its existence. It was conceived originally as a stabilization fund whose main purpose was to promote, through the use of its resources, exchange rate stability and adjustments to short-term disequilibrium in the balance of payments, particularly among its leading members. Yet, during the first ten years of its existence the Fund remained almost comatose while the leading European countries worked out their problems of balance-of- payments disequilibrium and adjustment quite independently of it. Thus, it had little or no role to play in the restoration of balance-of-payments equilibrium in Europe, and was never able to play the role of policeman or to exercise much influence or control over economic policy in these countries. As Harry Johnson puts it,

> Ever since the establishment of the [IMF] there have been strong forces - associated first with the dollar shortage and subsequently with the dollar glut - working to displace it from the central position it was intended to occupy in monetary affairs. The field has been dominated instead by politically motivated and oriented direct relationships between the United States and the major European countries. Partly for this reason . . . the ordinary operations of the Fund have become increasingly concerned with the monetary problems of the less developed countries . . .[21]

By the end of the 1950s, when currency convertibility had been restored in Europe and the dollar shortage had become a part of history, the balance of economic forces had begun to shift, and the political dominance of the US in the Fund to weaken. The Fund could therefore now begin to take on a new life. The US, economically weakened (relatively speaking), would no longer exercise single-handed control. Instead, it now joined a newly formed coalition of the richest industrial countries, the so-called Group of Ten, to assume joint political direction of the Fund. To carry out its stabilization functions the Fund now took on a two-tiered structure. For members of the Group of Ten, short-term resources were to be made available through a special arrangement called the 'General Agreement to Borrow' under which funds were to be supplied by and made available to members of the Group, under agreed rules, as circumstances warrant, this arrangement to operate quite separately from and independently of the Fund's general resources. At the second tier, the Fund's general resources would continue to be available to its ordinary members. It is with respect to the use of these resources by 'ordinary' members that the elaborate conditionalities evolved by the Fund's management during the quiescent years of the 1950s are to apply.

Events here present us with some rather curious twists of history. Unable to play its intended role of supplier of liquidity to its leading members because of their determination not to brook interference from it in their economic policy-making, the Fund has nonetheless gone on to elaborate a most intrusive and meddlesome policy of conditionality for the use of its resources, and, as it happens, these very members now constitute the directorate which oversees the implementation of this policy *vis-à-vis* the others! Also, the countries allocated the largest quotas and drawing rights on the theory that they were likely to have the greatest need for the Fund's resources now have no need whatever for these resources, preferring instead to set up their own private system to take care of their short-term stabilization needs.[22] Thus, as it turns out, the only function their large quota allocations serves is to give them the right to dominate an institution whose purpose has been quietly but decidedly transformed.

The irony of the Bretton Woods system is that it combined a formal symmetry of treatment as regards compliance with rules and obligations with an obvious asymmetry as regards influence and control. Thus all countries, large and small, industrial and non-industrial, are treated on a basis of legal equality in accepting similar obligations, and in principle have access to the Fund's resources on the same legal basis, proportional, of course, to their quotas. But the size of the quota determines not only the size of the member's contribution and its drawing rights, but also its voting rights and share in the government of the Fund. Thus formal equality of rights and obligations coexists with unequal influence and control.

This asymmetry takes on particular importance in view of the fact that the Bretton Woods system involved, for the first time in history, the assignment of tasks to an international organization requiring the exercise of authority over its members, thus encroaching on their sovereignty. Bear in mind also that the Articles of Agreement of the Fund only adumbrate the rights and obligations of members, and that these have to be defined and made operational in the policies and decisions of the management of the Fund. And of course, the less detailed and precise the Articles are in establishing rights and obligations, the more power rests with management for doing this in the framework of its policy decisions. (It is of interest to note, as an example, that on the key question of the conditions for access to the Fund's resources, the Articles of Agreement were peculiarly vague, leaving it to the Fund's management to evolve a policy and thus decide the issue.) Since the Americans had made it clear from the outset that the management of the Fund was to be political rather than technical,[23] it is easy to understand why formal equality in rights and obligations may turn out to be little more than a sham.

The World Bank

In the early conception of the Bank, its main purpose was reconstruction financing, and the earliest drafts did not even make reference to development financing. By the time the Bretton Woods Conference was convened, the concept of development financing as an essential purpose of the Bank had been introduced, but it was only at the Conference itself that the words '. . . and the encouragement of the development of productive facilities and resources in less developed countries,' were added to Article 1, dealing with the purposes of the Bank, largely at the insistence of the Latin American delegations.[24] As it happened, with the abandonment of reconstruction financing in the early years, the emphasis quickly shifted to development financing, and more particularly to the development financing of the less developed countries, and this very soon became the main *raison d' être* of the Bank.

Even more than the Fund, the Bank has always been under tight US control. This control was a consequence not only of the prominent US role in establishing and funding the Bank, the fact that the seat of the Bank is in Washington, and the US having arrogated to itself the right to appoint the President of the Bank (always a US national) without consulting the Bank's other members (notwithstanding the formal requirement in the Bank's Charter that the President be elected by the Executive Board), but in addition, the fact that it was early established that the President of the Bank would have a free hand in running the Bank unrestrained by the Executive Board. As Mason and Asher put it: 'The administrative style of the Bank is unconventional and is particularly disturbing to those nationals of countries other than the United States . . . To them, the Bank's style appears autocratic, quixotic, and distressingly disorderly. The top executive of the Bank dominates the organization and encounters few internal checks and balances.'[25] And while the executive directors must formally approve all loans, Mason and Asher observe (p. 236) that 'a project loan recommended by the president and staff of the Bank has never been rejected.' Hence, from the point of view of its management, the Bank can hardly be said to be an international Bank. And while the top executive may encounter few internal checks and balances in the Bank, he is certainly not free of influence from the US Government, and indeed pays great attention to its wishes and interests.

From the outset the Bank had always taken a very cautious and conservative approach to its lending policies, being much more conscious of the word 'bank' than the word 'development', which both appear in its official name. To some extent this reflected the constraints imposed by its Charter. To some extent it was also a response to the need to establish for the Bank an impeccable credit standing in order to facilitate its ready access to the financial market for the loanable funds it would need.

Under its Charter, the Bank could only lend to governments or with government guarantees, and 'except in exceptional circumstances', only for specific projects, and normally only to finance the foreign exchange costs of such projects (i.e. to cover payments for imported equipment, technical services provided by foreigners, etc.). There was therefore a certain tension or conflict between the requirements of the Charter and the basic philosophy of the Bank's management, which saw private investments and private enterprise as the main actors in promoting economic development. Ways had therefore to be found of supporting government-backed projects while keeping to the underlying philosophy. This was done by focusing Bank lending on the financing of certain basic infrastructural projects considered at the same time both proper areas for government investment and necessary to lead the way for the more directly productive investments of the private sector.

The focus was in fact quite narrow, and during the first two decades or so of its existence as much as two-thirds of Bank lending went to just two sectors: transportation and public utilities, mostly electric power. The rationale for this sector concentration of Bank lending was put very clearly in the Bank's *Eleventh Annual Report* (1955-56) as follows: '. . . most of the Bank's loans are for basic utilities . . . which are an essential condition for the growth of private enterprise . . . whether the loan is to a public or private borrower, the resulting expansion of utility services, particularly of power and transportation, is a prerequisite to the development of private initiative in industrial, agricultural, mining, and all other directly productive undertakings.'

While adhering to its Charter obligations to finance only specific projects, the Bank has nonetheless always held to the view 'that the loans cannot be treated as isolated transactions and that the projects which they finance must be examined in relation to the rest of the development effort . . .. It [also] constantly emphasizes the value of a development programme into which the major projects are fitted.'[26] In other words, a comprehensive long-term strategy incorporating a broad understanding of the development requirements and potentialities of the country as a whole was necessary in order to best determine the most effective contribution that the Bank could make in the financing of individual projects.

Motivated by this kind of consideration, the Bank was to take an early lead in carrying out systematic studies of the economic development problems and potentials of individual underdeveloped countries. The first such study, for Colombia, was published in 1950, and by 1958 the Bank had sent major economic missions to 15 countries, and the published reports of these missions comprised, in the words of one writer, 'the largest single collection of information extant on the problems and characteristics of underdeveloped economies.'[27] These studies were intended, *inter alia*, to lead to recommendations 'designed to assist the governments in formulating long-term development programs',[28] as well as, of course, to assist the Bank in evaluating specific country projects. Thus, notwithstanding the private enterprise philosophy which so strongly underlay its thinking, the Bank was to have an important early influence in encouraging governments of underdeveloped countries to think in terms of comprehensive long-term development programming and planning, a way of thinking that would take root and spread to assume an importance going well beyond what the Bank originally had in mind.

The main criticisms of the Bank during its early years centred on its cautious and conservative approach to development financing. With the restriction of its lending to the financing of specific projects, and given the extraordinary care that the Bank took in evaluating a project from all angles before giving its approval, there were inevitably considerable time-lags between the submission of a project proposal, its eventual approval, and its final implementation. It also meant that the flow of Bank resources to underdeveloped countries remained for some time little more than a trickle relative to need, amounting by the mid-to-late 1950s to only around $400 million per year.

The slow pace of lending reflected the Bank's own assessment of the needs of the underdeveloped countries, of their ability to use investment funds productively, and most importantly, of their ability to repay. It took the position that availability of funds was not the binding constraint on its ability to lend, since it could mobilize as much funds as could productively be used. The constraint was provided rather by the capacity of borrowing countries to use funds productively. Critics, however, saw this as merely an admission that the criteria the Bank used for evaluating the financing needs of the under-developed countries were inappropriate and unduly restrictive. It was held, for example, that if the Bank had been able and willing to extend programme loans (i.e. loans to support broad investment programmes and not tied to specific projects), much greater flexibility would be achieved, and the flow of financial resources to the underdeveloped countries could be speeded up. And in this context it was noted that the early loans to European countries were negotiated not in terms of specific projects, but as programme loans on the basis of the loophole provided by the exception clause.[29]

The requirement that the Bank finance only the foreign exchange costs of the approved projects was also considered unduly restrictive, unhelpful and potentially harmful to the borrower. It introduced a bias towards projects with a high foreign exchange component, as distinct from those in which the local expenditure content is high. The bias operates at two levels: in the choice of projects (favouring those projects with inherently high foreign exchange components), and in the manner of implementing a given project (by encour-aging the choice of methods which tend to maximize the import contents of a given project). The result is that investment planning and development priorities are distorted in a manner favouring growing import dependence. A further result is that it denies contractors from the borrowing country a chance to bid on multilateral contracts for projects in their own countries. Again it may be noted that this somewhat incongruous result did not apply to project loans made to developed countries, at least not in the case of Italy and Japan, where the necessary exceptions were made to by-pass the requirement.[30]

The narrow focus of Bank lending on physical infrastructure, mostly transportation and power, was also seen as arbitrary and unbalanced. For one thing, the Bank had too fine (and perhaps too commercial) a concept of 'productive'. Thus social investments in such areas as education, health services, water and sanitation facilities, housing, etc. were equally necessary as part of the development effort, but were not considered 'productive' investments by the Bank, and hence were not eligible for Bank financing. And for ideological reasons the Bank fought shy of manufacturing industry, and kept its distance from the petroleum and other mineral resources sectors where

US corporations were traditionally heavily involved and which it considered better left to the private sector.

This misgiving on the Bank's part about widening the sector coverage of its lending no doubt reflected, among other things, its preoccupation with its image as a hard-nosed banker. But it left a large gap in development financing needs, and many soon began to argue that the Bank as constituted was not really the appropriate mechanism for the financing of economic development, since what the underdeveloped countries most needed were grants and soft loans, and not the hard commercial loans which the Bank could provide but which the borrowers may never be able to repay if extended in quantities commensurate with their needs.[31] According to one writer, what was needed was 'The admirably simple-minded solution of the Marshall Plan era [which] was to provide 80 per cent of the assistance on a grant basis and end the period of dependence as soon as possible.'[32]

Partly in response to these criticisms and to the various pressures that were brought to bear, the Bank was to see some limited changes along the lines being sought by those who saw it more as a development financing institution. Thus there was the creation in the late 1950s of the International Development Association (IDA), the soft-loan affiliate (see p.57) which, according to Asher, the Bank 'vigorously opposed' until the build-up for a soft-loan agency had become irresistible, when 'the then President of the World Bank, Eugene Black, decided that if there was going to be such an agency, he might as well run it.'[33] And by the early 1970s new guidelines were promulgated which widened the scope for programme lending. An effort was also made to diversify somewhat the sector distribution of Bank lending, this being facilitated by the availability of IDA resources, with investments in agriculture and education, and in providing loans and credits to development finance companies, mostly for on-lending to industry, playing an increasing if still relatively limited role in the Bank's operations.

By and large, however, the basic character and philosophy of the Bank has remained largely unchanged over the years, and it is still much more a bank than a development agency, its basic strength lying in the expertise it has built up over the years in the appraisal, financing and implementation of physical infrastructure projects. But as we shall see in Chapter 6, circumstances have led the Bank in recent years to take on a new and expanded role going well beyond the financing of individual projects, with programme lending (or, as it has become known, 'structural adjustment loans') now assuming increasing importance and leading the Bank into areas of economic policy conditionality where its role now overlaps with that of the Fund.

Institutional arrangements for trade co-operation

Article 1 of the Agreement establishing the IMF states that one of the purposes of the Fund shall be 'to facilitate the expansion and balanced growth of international trade and to contribute thereby to the promotion and maintenance of high levels of employment and real income and to the development of the productive resources of all members as primary objectives of economic policy'. For accomplishing these tasks a separate trade organization was foreseen as an ancillary institution and an integral part of the system. While this sister organization was never brought into being, and thus was never allowed to play the role envisaged for it, it will be of interest here to sketch briefly its intended role in order to give a fuller picture of the international economic order foreseen by the post-war planners, and of the gap resulting from the failure to bring this organization into being.

As in the case of the financial institutions, work on a proposed trade organization started early in the United States Government, and, after extensive consultations and negotiations with the British in the context of the Article VII provisions of the Lend-Lease Agreement (see p. 20), the United States published in late 1945 its 'Proposals for Consideration by an International Conference on Trade and Employment' as a joint Anglo-American undertaking. These proposals were subsequently converted by the Americans into the language of a 'Suggested Charter for an International Trade Organization' which provided the basis for the deliberations at the London Preparatory Committee and the subsequent Havana Conference on Trade and Employment. The outcome was agreement on a Charter for an International Trade Organization (ITO) with objectives and functions of wide scope intended to complement the Bretton Woods institutions in securing the conditions for a stable and prosperous world economic environment.

The Havana Charter negotiations differed from those of Bretton Woods in an important respect. Whereas in the latter case the United States so dominated the scene that it could virtually dictate the terms of the final outcome, in the former the US had to be more accommodating, allowing other countries greater scope to make their voices heard and have their points of view taken into account. This applied particularly to the less developed countries, represented in large numbers at the Havana Conference (with the inclusion of a number of

Asian countries just emerging from colonial rule), which participated more actively there than at Bretton Woods, and which therefore were able to ensure that some of their special concerns were taken into account in the final outcome.

In the broadest terms, the Charter lays down rules of commercial policy, establishes rights and obligations for its members with reference to these rules, and vests the Organization with the authority to monitor, supervise and enforce the application of these rules. Two key principles guide the formulation of these rules: that tariffs are the only legitimate form of protection or government restriction on foreign trade, and that in trade relations among members the unconditional most-favoured-nations (mfn) principle should apply. This meant that there was to be a general ban on all forms of quantitative restrictions as a means of protection. In addition, members were placed under an obligation to engage in trade negotiations among themselves to bring about mutual reduction of tariff rates. A special feature was the obligation assumed by members to seek to achieve and maintain full and productive employment within their own borders, and to seek to avoid measures which would create balance-of-payments difficulties for other countries. The Charter also had a lot to say about the use of quantitative restrictions and exchange controls for balance-of-payments purposes, and calls for appropriate consultations and co-ordination with the Fund in ensuring compliance with the rules laid down in the Charter in this regard.[34]

The special concerns and interests of the less developed countries found expression in the Charter in a number of ways. Thus, one of the general obligations of members was 'To foster and assist industrial and general economic development, particularly of those countries which are still in the early stages of industrial development, and to encourage the international flow of capital for productive investment' (Article 1). Of relevance here also is the obligation of members 'not to impose unreasonable or unjustifiable impediments that would prevent other members from obtaining on equitable terms supplies of capital funds, materials, modern equipment and technology, and technical and managerial skills necessary for their industrial and general economic development or reconstruction' (Article 11). There are also a number of provisions calling on the Organization to assist in various ways in helping to promote the industrialization and economic development of its less developed members.

Of special interest are the exceptions to the general rules relating to commercial policy intended for the specific benefit of the less developed countries. The cover for these exceptions was the explicit acceptance by the Charter of the infant industry argument for protection: 'Members recognize that special governmental assistance may be required to promote the establishment, development or reconstruction of particular industries or branches of agriculture, and that in appropriate circumstances the grant of such assistance in the form of protective measures is justified' (Article 13,1). Among the most important of these commercial policy exceptions is that relating to quantitative restrictions, where the less developed countries were given the (qualified) right to use such restrictions where 'imposed in the interest of programmes of economic development'. Subject to qualifications, less developed countries would also have the right to impose new protective measures affecting imports in the interests of their economic development. And finally, notwithstanding the general injunction against new preferential arrangements, it was recognized that such arrangements between two or more countries in the interest of programmes of economic development may be justified.

The scope of the Charter extended to two areas beyond the narrow confines of commercial policy which were of particular interest to the less developed countries. One of these concerned the special problems of primary commodities, a matter of profound importance to these countries in view of their utter dependence on these products for their export earnings. Recognizing these special problems, particularly the tendency towards imbalances in supply and demand and consequent pronounced fluctuations in prices, and the economic hardships to which these give rise, the Charter made provisions for the establishment of inter-governmental commodity agreements (ICAs) to provide a framework for alleviating these problems. This is not the place here for a discussion of the pros and cons of ICAs, a complex subject about which we shall have more to say below (see p.59ff). Suffice it to say that primary products face serious problems of imbalance and instability in international trade, that these problems were of the greatest importance to the less developed countries, and that the Charter explicitly recognized these problems and tried to do something about them.

The other area of special interest to the less developed countries concerns restrictive business practices. Thus the Charter recognized that business practices that restrain competition, limit access to markets, or foster monopolistic control may have harmful effects on the expansion of production or trade and on the attainment of other objectives of the Charter, and enjoins against such practices where they have such harmful effects. Provision is made for the registering of complaints, and the Charter lists a number of practices which could justify complaints. These include the fixing of prices to be used in dealing with others, the allocation or dividing up of territorial markets, discrimination against particular enterprises, limiting production or fixing production quotas, and preventing by agreement the development or application of technology, all matters in respect of which the less developed countries were likely to be the losers from restrictive policies of the powerful corporations of the developed countries.

A final point about the Charter which is relevant here is a two-fold one: that in order to carry out its functions the ITO was to have far-reaching powers of decision-making and enforcement, and that the decision-making machinery of the organization would not be based on a system of weighted voting (as in the case of the Bretton Woods institutions), thereby making it less easy for one or two countries to dominate the organization and its decision-making powers for their own ends. It therefore seemed to offer the possibility of a rule-based international trading system able to take account of the interests of all countries, large and small, developed and underdeveloped, in achieving the broader objectives of promoting the balanced growth of world trade and incomes.

As we now know, of course, the ITO never saw the light of day, and hence there was never any opportunity to put to the test the hope it held out. It was not long after the Charter document was signed in Havana and the delegates had returned to their capitals that the two principal sponsors of the Charter, the US and the UK, began to have second thoughts, albeit for different reasons. The UK announced that it would not ratify until the US had done so, and the US took no action, and that was the end of the ITO.[35] So instead of a comprehensive trade organization to join the Bretton Woods institutions as a broad-based integrated system for the revival and promotion of world trade and development, the multilateral tariff negotiations that were proceeding in parallel under the title of General Agreement on Tariffs and Trade (GATT) now took centre stage as the main instrument for achieving the multilateral objectives in respect to trade.

In the event GATT, which evolved as a contractual arrangement without any firm institutional base, incorporated the ITO's basic principles of commercial policy (the mfn principle and the principle that tariffs are the only legitimate form of protection) as the basic rules of international trade, and established a programme of multilateral negotiations for the mutual reduction of tariffs. But since agricultural products had been largely excluded from these negotiations, it would be mostly industrial goods that would benefit from the tariff reductions. Consequently, the whole exercise was one that would be of almost exclusive interest to the developed industrial countries. These developments also meant that many of the other important elements in the ITO Charter going beyond the narrow issues of commercial policy found no place in the newly established world economic order, and in particular, that the special concerns and interests of the less developed countries in the area of international trade and development were simply ignored.

The role foreseen for the United Nations

To round off the discussion, we must now consider the role which was foreseen for the United Nations in achieving post-war objectives in the field of international co-operation. The main tasks of this Organization in this field are spelled out most clearly in Article 55 of the its Charter, requiring it 'with a view to the creation of conditions of stability and well-being' to promote 'higher standards of living, full employment and conditions of economic and social progress and development' and in Article 56 where all members 'pledge themselves to take joint and separate action, in co-operation with the Organization for the achievement of the purposes set forth in Article 55.' The Economic and Social Council was assigned the special responsibility of sponsoring and co-ordinating the work in this area.

In line with the original intentions of the drafters of the Charter, the Economic and Social Council focused its attention from the beginning on the question of economic stability and employment, this issue being uppermost in the minds of policy-makers at the time having the experience of the depression of the 1930s still fresh in their minds. Thus at its second session in January 1946 the Council established the Economic and Employment Commission responsible for advising it on 'the prevention of wide fluctuations in economic activity and the promotion of full employment by the co-ordination of national full-employment policies and by international action.' The Commission in turn was directed by the Council to establish a Sub-commission on Employment and Economic Stability to advise it on a detailed programme for the co-ordination of national and international action in this regard.[36]

This was clearly an ambitious programme for international action impinging on traditional prerogatives of national policy, and perhaps it could only have been seriously contemplated in the flush of victory following a gruelling and devastating war and in an atmosphere filled with exaggerated hopes of ushering in a new era of international co-operation. As it turned out, however, these plans for international action in this area did not get very far. Two groups of experts were commissioned, successively, to make recommendations to the Council on international measures for full employment, and their reports, published in 1949 and 1951 respectively, contained bold recommendations for international action on which, however, no agreement among governments could be reached.[37] After this enthusiastic start, interest in the subject quickly waned, and since 1954 full employment has been dropped as a separate item on the agenda of the Council. It is worth mentioning here that the precipitous decline of interest in this subject reflected, among other things, the fact that in the context of the immediate post-war years the preoccupation with unemployment turned out to have been misplaced, the problem then being rather the opposite one of inflation and excess demand.

With the rapid decline and eventual disappearance of interest in this subject, the UN soon turned to the problems of economic development of the less developed countries as the major focus of its work relating to international economic co-operation. And it was the UN in fact that was to be the focus of attention and that was to provide the catalyst for international economic action relating to economic development of the underdeveloped countries. The evolution of the UN's role in this regard will be taken up in the following chapter.

Concluding comments

As commentators never tire of saying, the post-war years, spanning now more than four decades, have witnessed a very impressive performance by the world economy, with remarkably high and sustained rates of growth of world trade and output accompanied by only moderate fluctuations, a performance unequalled in modern history. It would be rash not to suppose that the institutions and mechanisms for international economic co-operation put in place after the Second World War contributed to this impressive performance. Indeed, one could perhaps go so far as to say that it laid the foundations for it. But, as our earlier discussion shows, all countries did not by any means share equally in this expansion, and, indeed, while the developed countries made great strides in the post-war years, the less developed countries mostly faltered, with the gap between the two widening dramatically.

As we have seen, the main institutions created did not at all play the role intended for them, and indeed one of them was still-born. Instead of providing a general framework for the conduct of relations among all countries, as was the original intention, these institutions have instead largely been converted into instruments for the conduct of North-South relations, and so far as relations among the countries of the North are concerned, these have been handled by alternative, more exclusive arrangements. We mentioned a number of these in our discussion of the evolution of the Bretton Woods institutions: bilateral financial arrangements between the US and Europe, the Marshall Plan and the European Recovery Programme, the special arrangements for providing international liquidity to members of the Group of Ten (the General Agreement to Borrow), among others. Important also are such institutions as the OECD (Organization for Economic Co-operation and Development) which grew out of the special arrangements developed for US bilateral co-operation with Europe into a broad-based institution for economic co-operation and co-ordination among the industrial countries of the North. Indeed, we might say that the only non-exclusive (we hesitate to say universal) institution that has played a significant role in the conduct of economic relations among the countries of the North is the GATT, that spin-off from the more ambitious but still-born ITO, which soon came to be known as 'the rich man's club'. And it is probably true that, at bottom, the reason why the ITO never saw the light of day is that in its conception it was too universalist in scope, too democratic in outlook, to serve the needs of the elitist mentality which could not contemplate an institutional setting in which the rich countries might mingle on equal terms with the poor. So what we have seen is the evolution of a framework in which ostensibly universal institutions are created which quickly end up as the instruments by which the North conducts its relations with the South, a sort of ghetto for North-South relations, while for the conduct of relations by the North among themselves, alternative, exclusive clubs are created and flourish.[38]

This is the main lesson we have learnt from our review of the institutional setting of the post-war world economic order, a setting which has evidently served the industrial countries very well. That these countries were able to create and impose a system that served their interests so well *vis-à-vis* the less developed countries clearly reflected the power that they were able to exercise, and it was to be expected that the latter would try to shift the balance, to acquire some of the power, so as to bring about changes in the institutional framework better able to serve their particular needs. It is to this issue that we therefore now turn.

Notes

1. See E. E. Penrose, *Economic Planning for Peace* (Princeton University Press, Princeton 1953), for an account of US planning for post-war international economic co-operation.
2. See William Adams Brown, *The United States and the Restoration of World Trade*: An Analysis and Appraisal of the ITO Charter and the General Agreement on Tariffs and Trade (The Brookings Institution, Washington, D.C., 1950), pp. 47-48.
3. According to Gardner, US policy makers genuinely believed that they would enhance the prospects for multilateralism by exacting specific commitments from the Allies on post-war trade policy. This was an attempt to use bargaining power to achieve aims intended to redound to everyone's advantage, bearing particularly in mind how the US attempt to collect 'war debts' after the First World War had provided a major obstacle to achievement of the multilateral objective. See Richard N. Gardner, *Sterling-Dollar Diplomacy: Anglo-American Collaboration in the Reconstruction of Multilateral Trade* (The Clarendon Press, Oxford, 1956), p. 56.
4. While it is true that Keynesian thinking provided the political and intellectual base for macro-economic policy in the Western industrial countries in the post-war years, this is not to deny that Keynesian economics has never been free from controversy either on political or theoretical grounds. And indeed we have come to see a major backlash against Keynesianism in the 1980s, although in an important sense this backlash is more apparent than real.
5. The story of these Anglo-American negotiations involving the two main authors of the respective plans, Harry Dexter White for the Americans and Lord Keynes for the British, is a fascinating one. See Richard Gardner, *op. cit.*, for a good account of these negotiations.
6. *Ibid.*, p. 110.
7. See Richard N. Gardner, 'The Political Setting' in A. L. Keith Acheson, *et al* (eds), *Bretton Woods Revisited*, University of Toronto Press, Toronto, 1972, p.20. Germany and Japan, the two recently defeated countries, clearly had no role to play, and most of the other European countries were still in too much disarray from the ravages of the War.
8. See Robert W. Oliver, *International Economic Co-operation and the World Bank*, (The Macmillan Press, London, 1975), p.111 ff.
9. See Howard S. Ellis, *The Economics of Freedom: The Progress and Future Aid to Europe* (Harper & Brothers, New York, 1950), for an early account of the European Recovery Programme.
10. See William Diebold, *Trade and Payments in Western Europe: A Study in Economic Co-operation 1947-51* (Harper & Brothers, New York, 1952), for a description and analysis of these payments arrangements.

11. Gardner, *op. cit.*, p. 304.

12. See J. Keith Horsefield (ed.), *The International Monetary Fund 1945-1965: Twenty Years of International Monetary Co-operation*, Vol. 11: Analysis, (International Monetary Fund, Washington, D.C., 1969), p.240.

13. M.M. Scammell, *International Monetary Policy: Bretton Woods and After* (The Macmillan Press, London, 1975), p. 135.

14. See Horsefield, *op. cit*, p. 243.

15. As Scammel has pointed out (*op. cit.*, p. 159), 'Every request by a member for accommodation has been carefully scrutinized and, in later years, made subject to the pursuit of certain policies by the suppliant member - these policies bearing striking identity with official utterances of the American Treasury. ... There was throughout the forties and fifties a strong flavour of American paternalism rather than of international co-operation motivating Fund decisions.'

16. Sidney Dell, 'On Being Grandmotherly: The Evolution of IMF Conditionality', *Essays in International Finance*, No, 144, October 1981 (International Finance Section, Princeton University Press, Princeton), p. 8.

17. See Horsefield, *op. cit.*, p. 524.

18. 'Policies on the Use of Fund Resources', IMF doc. SM/66/14 (Jan. 24, 1966; processed), quoted in Edward S. Mason and Robert E. Asher, *The World Bank Since Bretton Woods* (The Brookings Institution, Washington, D.C., 1973), p. 541.

19. *Ibid.*, p. 541.

20. See Horsefield (ed.), *op. cit.*, p. 401.

21. Harry Johnson, *Economic Policies Towards Less Developed Countries* (The Brookings Institution, Washington D.C., 1967), p. 16.

22. And as we shall see later (Chapter 6), even this private system has been superseded by the growth of international bank credit now widely available to the industrial countries.

23. This was implicit in the decisions to have the headquarters of the Fund located in Washington and to have full-time Executive Directors resident in Washington, decisions which Keynes fought against and much regretted.

24. See Robert W. Oliver, *op. cit.*, especially Chapter V, for a discussion of the early drafts, and Chapter VIII for a discussion of the Bretton Woods negotiations themselves.

25. Mason and Asher, *op. cit.*, pp. 86-87.

26. Alec Cairncross, 'The International Bank for Reconstruction and Development', *Essays in International Finance*, No. 33, March 1959 (International Finance Section, Princeton University Press, Princeton), p. 6.

27. F.T. Moore, *The Failures of the World Bank Missions*, mimeo, The Rand Corporation, Santa Monica, California, June 1958, p. 1.

28. Moore, *op. cit.*, p.8, quoting from a 1954 World Bank report.

29. See Cairncross, *op. cit.*, p. 16.

30. See Cairncross, *op. cit.*, p. 21.
31. This theme underlay the early debates in the UN on the subject of development financing sparked by the recommendations in the report of the UN Expert Group on 'Measures for the Economic Development of Under-Developed Countries'. See the related discussion in Chapter 3 below.
32. See Robert E. Asher, 'Comment: The Leopard's Spot', in John P. Lewis and Ishan Kapur, *The World Bank Group, Multilateral Aid, and the 1970s*, (Lexington Books, Lexington, Mass., 1973), p.25.
33. Asher, *op. cit.*, p. 24.
34. The discussion here and below is based on the excellent compendium and analysis of the Charter to be found in William Adams Brown, *op. cit.*.
35. For a discussion of the post-Havana debates in the UK and the US which led to the death of the ITO, see Richard Gardner, *Sterling-Dollar Diplomacy*, p. 369ff.
36. See Robert E. Asher *et al*, *The United Nations and Economic and Social Co-operation* (The Brookings Institution, Washington D.C., 1957), Chapter V.
37. See UN Department of Economic Affairs, 'National and International Measures for Full Employment' (Report by a Group of Experts Appointed by the Secretary-General, Doc. E/1584 doc.,1949), and 'Measures for International Economic Stability' (Report by a Group of Experts Appointed by the Secretary-General, Doc.E/2156, Nov. 1951).
38. We have seen a repeat of this very same trend with the recent creation of the European Bank for Reconstruction and Development. It is Eastern European that is now to be embraced into the fraternity of the North, but as usual, there is to be no question of the 'universal' institution, the World Bank, being called upon to play the main role of banker. An exclusive instrument has to be created that can follow its own rules and take whatever special actions are required to accomplish its tasks as these are considered necessary, leaving the World Bank to plod along in its usual way in dealing with the Third World.

3. Post-war Decolonization and the Rise of the Development Issue

The realignment of geopolitical forces in the aftermath of the war

When the guns finally fell silent at the close of the Second World War and the former combatants set about the task of putting back together their war-torn economies, the global economic and political scene was very different from what it had been in the years before the guns had started firing, and it was evident that a major realignment of economic and political forces had taken place. With Europe physically devastated and its economy in ruins, with Japan defeated and under US military occupation, and with the Soviet Union ravaged and wholly dislocated from the war effort, the United States emerged in the immediate aftermath of the war as the unrivalled world economic and political power, a position it had hardly had before the war.

When it finally entered the war after the fighting in Europe had been under way for some time and the European combatants had already almost exhausted their mobilization capacity, the US had still not emerged from the economic depression of the 1930s, and thus had vast amounts of idle and under-utilized resources which it was able to mobilize rapidly for the war effort. These resources were mobilized not only to support the American war effort *per se* but, equally important, to support the war effort of America's European allies, effected through lend-lease and similar schemes (see Chapter 2). This support, highly appreciated though it was, resulted nonetheless in the cumulative indebtedness of the European allies to the US at the end of the war, and further reinforced the dominant economic and political position which the US was able to assume in the post-war world.

It was also evident that, notwithstanding the major contribution made in mobilizing resources in support of the war effort, the US was far from economically exhausted by the time the war drew to a close, and indeed a major problem that US policy-makers faced at the end of the war was how to ensure that demobilization did not result in a reversion to the under-utilized resources, idle capacity and mass unemployment that characterized the pre-war years. The fact that US territory bore none of the war, and that its industrial capacity never suffered damage, meant that the US emerged from the war with its vast economic potential intact, and relatively, therefore, greatly strengthened.

The Soviet Union, though war-torn and heavily war-damaged, controlled a vast territory rich in resources and, already highly developed industrially, constituted the only immediate potential threat to US global political and economic hegemony. The fact that the Soviet Union espoused a political and economic ideology radically different from that of the US only served to hasten and intensify the great power rivalry that was destined to emerge between these two giants of the post-war world. Indeed, this inexorable march towards a global geo-political rivalry between these two great powers was already predicted more than a century and a half ago, well before Karl Marx had started work on his *Das Kapital* or published his *Communist Manifesto*, by the uncannily perceptive political scientist and commentator Alexis de Tocqueville, who could not have been more prescient when, in his classic study of the American way of life, he wrote:[1]

> There are at the present time two great nations in the world, which started from different points, but seem to tend towards the same end. I allude to the Russians and the Americans.... Their starting point is different, and their courses are not the same; yet each of them seems marked by the will of Heaven to sway the destinies of half the globe.

Leaving aside North America, Europe and Japan, the rest of the world at the end of the war was a vast backwater or hinterland consisting largely of the far-flung colonial territories of the European powers located in Asia, Africa, the Pacific, South America and the Caribbean. In addition, there were the countries and territories of the Middle East under European suzerainty or outright colonialism, the 'independent' countries of South America largely under US tutelage, and China, long subject to spoliation and unequal treaties perpetrated by the European powers, and then in the throes of civil war. Almost the entire African continent was under European colonial rule, and practically all of Asia apart from China and Thailand.

Background to post-war decolonization

While it should have been evident that the *status quo ante* with respect to the far-flung colonial empires of the European powers was no longer tenable, it is nonetheless true that these powers, though exhausted and much weakened by the war, still entertained the hope, and indeed had very much the intention, of holding on to their colonial territories as a permanent feature of the post-war world. The difficulty of realizing this intention became immediately apparent in respect of those Asian territories that had been overrun by the Japanese and which at the end of the war were no longer under the control of the European colonial powers, particularly Dutch Indonesia and French Indo-China. The war and Japanese occupation had stirred up nationalistic sentiments and political consciousness in these territories, which were no longer willing to see themselves revert to European colonial rule. They were therefore prepared to fight to stave off any such attempt, fortified by the realization that, as the Japanese had shown, the Europeans were by no means invincible. In addition, of course, the weakened position in which the European powers emerged from the war greatly limited their capabilities in this regard. Indeed, in view of the commanding economic, political and military position in which the US found itself in the aftermath of the war, it was only with the support of the US that the European powers could hope to achieve their aims. And that support was far from assured. US reluctance to give such support reflected both geo-political considerations and lingering long-established sentiments unsympathetic to European colonialism, a popular feeling emanating from America's colonial past.

As to geo-political considerations, US ambitions for world leadership would hardly be served if the European powers continued after the war to exercise exclusive control over the human and material resources of their vast colonial empires in Africa and Asia, denying the US access to the rich opportunities for trade, investment and the exploitation of raw materials which they offered. The US therefore had a clear interest in seeing the colonial regimes brought to an end. At the very least, the war created important opportunities for the Americans to forge access to these regions and territories hitherto monopolized by the European colonial powers. Thus, in demanding commitments from its allies regarding post-war economic relations in return for its wartime support, it is not surprising that the US insisted on language (e.g. in the Atlantic Charter) calling for 'access, on equal terms, to the trade and raw materials of the world' (see Chapter 2). Significantly, the Charter also called for the 'self-determination' of subject peoples, a call that was hailed in the US as a 'significant anti-Imperialist manifesto' and which could not but help to fan the flames of anti-colonial nationalism in the subject colonies and territories.[2]

Other factors also contributed to the upsurge of nationalism and to the emergence of political consciousness and demands for change in the colonies. Among these we may mention the disastrous effect on incomes and economic well-being in the colonial territories of the collapse of commodity prices during the depression of the l930s. Most of these territories had been geared up and promoted by their metropolitan masters as producers of raw materials and primary products, and wages, employment and incomes had come to depend on the revenue generated by these exports. The collapse of commodity prices during the long and deep depression of the l930s was catastrophic and had profound repercussions on the social fabric of life in the colonies, leading in many cases to riots and to political confrontation with the colonial authorities. These developments gave rise to growing dissatisfaction with the political status quo and provided a natural breeding ground for political agitation and anti-colonial nationalism.[3]

The events of the war itself probably also made their own contribution in this regard. Thus it is unlikely that the allied war propaganda denouncing aggression and the trampling of peoples' rights to self-determination and freedom did not ring a bell in the colonies, even if the context of this propaganda was not intended to apply there. The language of the Atlantic Charter, to which reference was made above, and which was given wide publicity at the time, served a similar purpose.

Ironically, US enthusiasm for anti-colonial rhetoric began to wane towards the end of the war, perhaps reflecting growing US interest in establishing its own string of sovereign bases in the Asian-Pacific region as well as a desire to keep a lid on Asian and African volatilities, especially in the light of the growing identity of interest of the US with its European colonial allies in the context of the looming confrontation with the communists.

Early collapse of the colonial regimes in Asia

The process of decolonization, however, developed its own momentum soon after the war drew to a close, slowly at first, gradually building up to a great *fortissimo* by the end of the l950s.

Thus the abortive attempt by the Dutch to reimpose by force colonial rule in Indonesia was abandoned in 1948 in the face of stiff resistance from the nationalists, and after perfunctory negotiations, Indonesia was thereafter recognized as an independent state. French efforts to reimpose colonial rule in Indo-China by force of arms were much more prolonged and bloody, but the final outcome at Dien Bien Phu is now a part of history. Here the communists emerged as victors wearing the mantle of the nationalists, and the aftermath of this, leading to the build-up of US involvement in Indo-China and eventually to the Viet Nam War, is too recent and involved to warrant further comment here. We cannot resist noting, however, that US support for the French military effort, considered justified because of the communist dimension to the conflict, was less than wholehearted, and no doubt reflected an American wish to take over the baton and thereby to supplant French interests in the peninsula.

The British also faced a wave of nationalistic sentiment, in the Indian sub-continent, with a long history going back well into the pre-war years. But the British were more astute in recognizing early their inability in the new circumstances to maintain colonial domination over the vast territory and population of a hostile sub-continent. With some grace, therefore, they withdrew without engaging in armed action, though in the process they left behind a sub-continent split along religious lines, with the potential for much communal violence and regional conflict. The independent states of India and Pakistan thus came into being, followed shortly after by independent Burma and Ceylon. Within a few years of the cessation of hostilities, therefore, the European powers had lost most of their Asian colonies with their large populations, and these former colonies now joined the ranks of independent states.

Decolonization in Africa: late start followed by a great crescendo

In Africa the situation in the immediate post-war years was rather different. The colonies were relatively quiet, and the colonial powers could be complacent in thinking that colonial rule would continue undisturbed for many years to come. Of course the African colonies did not remain entirely untouched by the events of the war and pre-war years, including the effects of the collapse of commodity prices in the depression of the 1930s, the boom in demand for colonial produce during the war and its effect on incomes, consumption, education and economic opportunities, and the war propaganda extolling the rights of peoples to freedom and self-determination. These events could not help but raise the level of awareness and expectations in colonized Africa, but at the outset the anti-colonial backlash seemed limited. The cautious and patronizing language in Chapter XI of the UN Charter urging members to 'exercise a sacred trust in the non-selfgoverning territories and to help them advance towards self-government' suggested a leisurely approach to political change in the colonies, and Africa seemed to exemplify the relevance of this approach.

The British, who had the largest and most extensive colonial interests in Africa, began planning early for political change. British plans were two-pronged: to consolidate white rule in those colonies with large white settler populations, with the aim of eventually handing over full political power to these white settlers; and, in those colonies without significant white settler communities, to build up a coterie of native political and administrative cadres on whom appropriate doses of self-government could devolve. The hasty bringing together in 1953 of the two Rhodesias and Nyasaland to form the Central African Federation was a most ambitious and ill-advised attempt to achieve the first objective. Early efforts to promote political change and to encourage local self-government in West Africa, the region where white settlers were most conspicuous by their absence, constituted the most notable example of the latter. In Kenya, on the other hand, the tempo of change could not be so easily controlled, and conflict between the ambitions of the white settlers and the aspirations of the natives led to the eruption of violence in 1952, and to a bloody colonial war, with reverberations throughout Africa and beyond.

Notwithstanding these undercurrents and developments, however, by the mid-1950s very little had changed in the basic colonial landscape of Africa. The colonial powers were still firmly ensconced on the continent, some with plans for devolution towards tentative forms of self-government, but all, it seemed, with every intention of retaining their stake in their African colonies for a long time to come. Yet by the turn of the decade the great bulk of Africa had been decolonized, giving birth to many new nation states. The forces which brought about this avalanche of new African states in this sudden and unexpected eruption of decolonization are varied and complex, and do not lend themselves to brief analysis here.[4] Mention should be made, however, of two events which were of seminal importance in precipitating developments.

One was the Bandung Afro-Asian Solidarity Conference of 1955 which provided an opportunity for African leaders to meet with one another and with leaders from Asian states having a common experience of European colonial rule and facing similar problems affecting national sovereignty, racialism and colonialism. The Conference, which gave a vision of new possibilities for Asian and African peoples in world affairs and led to a ringing call for an end to colonialism in all its forms, fired the imagination and raised aspirations in the colonies, and was a precursor of increasing and more vocal and insistent calls by African leaders for an end to colonialism on the continent.

The other event was the fiasco of the Anglo-French Suez adventure of 1956 when, in the absence of American support, these two colonial powers had to beat a hasty retreat, withdrawing their invasion forces and thereby aborting their attempt to reimpose their rule in Egypt. This forced the realization that in the new circumstances these countries were no longer able to operate as world powers in the underdeveloped world, and this, together with their growing military commitments in Europe necessitated by the East-West conflict and the absence of American support for the maintenance of colonial regimes by force, led to a policy of rapid decolonization. Hence Prime Minister Macmillan's famous 'winds of change' speech which heralded the British decolonization drive in Africa, and French President de Gaulle's dramatic gesture in 1958 offering full independence to France's West African colonies as an alternative to participating in the newly conceived 'French Community' (which only Guinea accepted at the time, though by 1960 all these West African colonies were to achieve full independence).

The build-up of African decolonization seemed dramatic. Between 1956 and 1958 five African colonies achieved independence. There was no activity in 1959, then in 1960 no less than 16 independent states emerged, and by the end of 1962 another seven African states had made their appearance, bringing the total number of new African States in this six-year period to 28. The process of decolonization was in some cases bloody (notably in the case of Algeria), and in others precipitate and hasty, the colonial powers having failed to prepare the ground for the hand-over of power. The case of the Belgian Congo is the outstanding example of the latter, a situation which led to internecine civil war, foreign intervention, and a badly planned and implemented intervention by the United Nations which seriously tarnished the reputation of that world body and served to make Africa the centre of world attention for an extended period. But in most cases the transition was fairly smooth, with the metropolitan powers retaining significant political and economic interests in their former colonies. By the end of 1964, then, Africa had for the most part been largely decolonized, the only significant European colonies remaining on the continent being those of Portugal and the British colony of Southern Rhodesia, then under white-settler rule.

The wave of decolonization had also begun to sweep the Caribbean, an area once regarded as among the most prized of the European colonial possessions and over which major battles were once fought, but which by now was seen largely as an embarrassing appendage, more a burden to be hastily dropped than an asset to be held on to. The British, who were the most heavily engaged of the European powers in this sub-region of the underdeveloped world, quickly set about the task of disengaging themselves, and by the early 1960s, following an abortive attempt at grouping her individual island possessions into a single federated state, began the process of granting independence to the individual colonies in the region. This process was soon to spawn a host of what came to be known as 'mini-states', adding numbers to the rapidly growing group of newly independent ex-colonial states.

The newly independent states make their impact

The impact on the world scene of this explosion of new states was considerable, and this was felt most keenly at the United Nations, where a majority of member states now consisted of former European colonies in Asia, Africa and the Caribbean which had achieved their independence since the founding of that organization. And not surprisingly, this brought about important changes in the character and orientation of the UN. In the General Assembly, these newly independent states now controlled a majority of votes, which gave them a certain importance in the work of the organization. This importance was particularly pronounced because of earlier events which had served to enhance the role of the General Assembly, where each country had one vote, as distinct from the Security Council, which was a closed club dominated by the five permanent members each having a right of veto. Because of the constant deadlock in the Security Council in the early Cold War years when US initiatives always faced a Soviet veto, the US managed to have considerable powers shifted to the General Assembly where it could command a majority of votes. Thus, by the end of the 1950s, these newly independent states found themselves able to command a majority in a General Assembly endowed with considerable powers of initiative. This they used to push through a range of initiatives of particular concern to them, in both the economic and political fields. They also found that their votes were highly sought after by the rivals in the East-West conflict, and this also increased their sense of importance. Moreover, there was also the question of competing for the allegiance of these new states in the ideological battle which so characterized the post-war era, and this also put them very much centre stage.

The entry on the international scene of these ex-colonies as independent states able to hold council and make their voices heard had a marked influence on the parameters within which international economic policy was to be conducted. We saw in the previous chapter how, at the Bretton Woods Conference and in the negotiations leading up to it, the underdeveloped countries had played hardly any role, and that little or no account had been taken of the special problems and needs of these countries in what emerged from the Conference. The San Francisco Conference, which negotiated the United Nations Charter, was hardly any different in this respect. By the time the ITO Charter was being negotiated, however, the war had been over for some time and decolonization had commenced, with the major Asian colonies having already achieved independence or on the verge of doing so. The impact of the emerging new states could therefore already be felt in the ITO negotiations, and, as we have seen, the ITO Charter which emerged from these negotiations included a number of provisions intended specifically to address the special problems of the underdeveloped countries. With the rising trend of decolonization in the 1950s and the increasing influence of the newly independent, underdeveloped ex-colonies in the international arena, it was to be expected that international debate would reflect a growing interest in the economic problems of the underdeveloped countries.

It was in the framework of the United Nations that this interest would be most keenly reflected, as the newly independent underdeveloped countries made their presence felt in the work of that organization and forced the international community to focus its attention on their particular problems. Thus the United Nations soon began to shift, in the economic field, from its original preoccupation with the problems of economic stability and full employment to those of the development of the less developed countries, and by the middle of the 1950s the latter problems had already become the main focus of attention.

The earliest United Nations involvement in the problems of economic development of the underdeveloped countries was in the field of technical assistance. This involvement was largely at US initiative, a spin-off of President Truman's Point Four Programme. Thus, from tentative beginnings on an *ad hoc* basis, the rendering of technical assistance to underdeveloped countries was soon to become a major operational activity of the UN, beginning with the inauguration in 1950 of the Expanded Programme of Technical Assistance (EPTA), to be followed by what was to become a much larger and more institutionalized involvement of the UN in this field. But this was largely low-key, non-controversial activity, apparently serving the interests and needs of all involved, and did not require any particular drive by the underdeveloped countries to get it going. Instead, the newly independent states were to use their new-found influence and power in the UN to seek to achieve much more ambitious and controversial aims in terms of international measures required to improve their economic development prospects, aims which would inevitably bring them into head-on confrontation with the industrial countries well ensconced in their privileged economic position.

The question of development finance

The issue on which the most sustained effort was to be expended and the fiercest battles fought during this initial phase in the evolution of the North-South dialogue concerned the question of development financing. The newly independent states saw this as an issue on which they had a strong case on moral and economic grounds, and pushed hard to have the UN approve and get established a development financing facility to meet their particular needs. Ideas about what sort of institution might be required had their roots in a report of a group of experts appointed by the Secretary-General of the United Nations to consider and make recommendations on 'Measures for the Economic Development of Under-Developed Countries'. The report, published in 1951,[5] included a proposal for an International Development Authority to make capital available to underdeveloped countries on a grant basis. It considered the World Bank, which was still finding its feet, much too cautious in its lending policy, and noted that the Bank did not in any event finance 'non-self-liquidating' projects (i.e. social overhead capital such as schools, hospitals, etc.) where the needs of the underdeveloped countries were greatest.

This idea of the expert group caught the imagination of the underdeveloped countries and a major campaign was mounted in the General Assembly to gain acceptance of the need for a grant agency under UN auspices. The United States, which would be expected to put up most of the finance, led the opposition, but this did not prevent the campaign from gathering momentum, and at its fifth session in 1950 the General Assembly recommended that the Economic and Social Council consider 'practical methods . . . for achieving the adequate expansion and steadier flow of foreign capital, both private and public, and pay special attention to the financing of non-self-liquidating projects which are basic to economic development.'

The pressure for action in this area mounted and in time led to the proposal for a Special United Nations Fund for Economic Development (SUNFED) put forward in 1953 in a report by a Committee appointed by the Secretary-General to make recommendations on the issue. While modest in scope (a fund of US$250 million was envisaged), it would differ greatly from existing multilateral financial institutions in that control would be shared equally between the 'major contributors' and 'other members', and finance would be available largely as grant or on 'soft' terms. Its main purpose would be to help the underdeveloped countries finance economic and social infrastructure such as roads, power stations, schools, hospitals, housing, etc.

This proposal was extensively debated in the Council and the General Assembly for five or six years. It had wide support among underdeveloped countries and also attracted the support of a number of industrial countries. It was vigorously opposed, however, by the United States, and in lesser measure by the United Kingdom.

By 1956 a number of industrial countries had signalled their willingness to contribute to SUNFED, including the Netherlands, Denmark, Norway and France, the last fixing its contribution at the princely sum of US$15 million, a figure corresponding to its share in the UN budget. By then most of the debate was about the timing of the establishment of the Fund, and draft resolutions were introduced calling for the preparation of draft statutes for SUNFED. The resolution finally adopted at the 11th Session of the General Assembly (GA), while carrying forward the momentum, stopped short of calling for the actual drafting of the statutes, in deference to continuing strong US opposition and its warning that it could not participate in the drafting of the statutes. Instead, the resolution asked the *Ad Hoc* Committee on SUNFED to 'set forth the different forms of legal framework on which [a Special Fund] might be set up and statutes drafted'.

The report of the *Ad Hoc* Committee led to mounting pressures for the General Assembly to take the necessary steps for the establishment of SUNFED. The US responded to these pressures by, first, announcing that it continued to oppose the immediate establishment of SUNFED, would vote against the resolution calling for its immediate establishment, and would refuse as well to participate in the work of any preparatory commission which might be appointed to draft the regulation of such a fund, and second, by proposing the establishment of a Special Projects Fund to aid in the financing of surveys of natural resources, industrial research, training and public administration as an integral part of existing UN technical assistance programmes. This proposal, modest and limited in scope though it was in comparison with the original aims of SUNFED, was eventually accepted as the only realistic goal attainable at the time. Thus was established, as a consolation prize as it were, the United Nations Special Fund, which was to become the main channel for UN technical assistance activities in support of the economic development of underdeveloped countries. It came into being in 1959 with a limited budget of US$26 million for the first year. In order not to close the door on the idea of SUNFED, and as a sop to those who had been so active in promoting that idea, the GA resolution establishing the Special Fund provided that 'as and when the resources prospectively available are considered . . . to be sufficient to enter into the field of capital development, . . . the Assembly shall review the scope and future activities of the Special Fund and take such action as it may deem appropriate.'[6]

As was to be expected, this time was never to come, especially since the pressure for the provision of capital development funds on soft terms through a United Nations agency was soon deflected by the United States proposal at the Bank and Fund meetings in September 1959 to establish the International Development Association (IDA) as a soft-loan window of the World Bank. The IDA, whose purposes are

> To promote economic development, increase productivity and thus raise standards of living in less-developed areas of the world . . . by providing finance to meet their important developmental requirements on terms which are more flexible and bear less heavily on the balance of payments than does a conventional loan, thereby furthering the development objectives of the International Bank for Reconstruction and Development and supplementing its activities,

was brought into being in September 1960. The IDA is managed by the Bank and run as part of its regular business. Unlike the Special Fund, but as in the Bank, voting in the IDA is proportionate to subscription. The decision-making power on the use of IDA resources therefore rests with the main contributors. During the first five years the IDA was provided with financial resources amounting to approximately US$160 million annually.

The intense campaign mounted by the underdeveloped countries during the 1950s to bring about the establishment of a development fund under United Nations auspices in which they would have an important if not controlling voice is an important example of their early determination to bring their new-found strength to bear on the design of international economic institutions. The story of this campaign also provides an early example of the frustrations they would face in these efforts, particularly where these involve issues relating to development finance. Thus, notwithstanding the intense pressure upon them, the US was able to stonewall and hold out while talks continued, and eventually to deflect the pressure by introducing substitute proposals which partially filled some of the felt needs but which left intact its iron grip on international development finance through its tight control of the Washington-based institutions.

Promoting private investment and the birth of the IFC

The story of the coming into being of the International Finance Corporation (IFC) in the mid-1950s, as an affiliate of the World Bank concerned with the task of promoting private investment in developing countries, provides a revealing footnote to the tug-of-war that was going on between the under-developed countries on the one hand and the developed countries (particularly the US) on the other as to the role that the United Nations was to play in fashioning international institutions to deal with the problem of development financing. It was widely recognized at the time, by both groups of countries, that private investment (both domestic and foreign) had an important role to play and needed to be encouraged as part of overall efforts to promote the economic development of the underdeveloped countries. The idea of creating such an institution originated in the World Bank itself, and received public support from an influential US advisory group in a report to the US President.[7] The idea quickly caught the attention of the participants in the UN debates, and the World Bank was requested by the Economic and Social Council to prepare a report on the contribution that such an institution could make.

The Bank's report concluded that such an institution could fill an important gap in the existing machinery for economic development. It stressed the importance of private investment, particularly equity capital, in the develop-ment field, and indicated the ways in which an international finance corpora-tion could help to promote such investments. There was wide support among underdeveloped countries for the creation of the new institution, but the US Administration, curiously, was for a time cool to the idea and the matter was temporarily shelved, with a call for further consultations. Official US policy soon changed, however, and in 1954 the General Assembly requested the World Bank, in a resolution initiated by the US, to prepare draft statutes for the proposed institution for discussion by the Bank's members and to report back to the Council on its work.

From then on matters proceeded speedily, and in April 1955 the President of the Bank informed the Council that the Executive Directors of the Bank had approved the proposed articles of agreement of the IFC, and that all was set for the Corporation to come forthwith into being, with an authorized capital of US$100 million to be subscribed by member governments of the Bank in amounts proportionate to their subscriptions to the capital of the Bank. The issue was therefore taken entirely out of the United Nations and placed squarely in the hands of the World Bank, where weighted voting ensured a predominant voice for the United States and a small group of leading industrial countries in the decision-making process. As it turned out, therefore, there was no opportunity for the Council or the General Assembly to discuss or influence in any way the statutes of the Corporation, of which they were only informed. Despite the rather awkward situation created by this peremptory action by the Bank (a situation commented on wryly by the representative of the Netherlands in the GA), the Assembly adopted a resolution in which it expressed its appreciation to the Bank for its efforts and looked forward to the successful operations of the Corporation. But the US had made its point. The UN, where the underdeveloped countries had such influence, was not to be allowed to dabble in the fashioning of the development financing institutions.

Proposals for action on commodity prices and the terms of trade

Another area where underdeveloped countries made concerted efforts to promote beneficial changes in the international economic order through United Nations action concerned the problem of primary commodity prices. These countries were wholly dependent on primary commodities for their export earnings, and were all too well aware of the vulnerability of these products to sharp fluctuations in export prices and to prolonged periods of depressed market conditions, the traumatic experience of the 1930s still being fresh in the memory. They therefore attached high priority to obtaining assurances of greater stability in primary commodity trade and pressed for international action in this regard, with emphasis on the price objectives of intergovernmental commodity agreements. Pressure for action in the commodity field was so strong that an expert group appointed to recommend measures for international economic stability found their terms of reference modified to include the preparation of recommendations '. . . concerning the appropriate national and international measures required to mitigate the vulnerability of the economies of underdeveloped countries to fluctuations in international markets, including measures to adjust, establish, and maintain appropriate relations between prices of raw materials on the one hand, and essential manufactured goods on the other.'[8]

The terms of reference here reflect much more ambitious aims than the limited objectives established for the commodity control agreements provided for in the Havana Charter for an ITO, which were intended to respond to situations of 'burdensome surpluses' in international commodity markets, rather than to 'establish, and maintain appropriate relations between prices' in international trade.

The experts responded with enthusiasm to this modification in their terms of reference, and a major portion of their report was devoted to proposals for international commodity arrangements 'as a means of keeping short-run movements of primary product prices, both upward and downward, within reasonable bounds, and of helping to stabilize the international flow of currencies.'[9]

The commodity problem was given a new twist at the 7th Session of the GA in 1952, when it was boldly linked to the related question of financing economic development in a resolution presented by the developing countries. The resolution, which was finally adopted by a roll-call vote which pitted the underdeveloped countries with their growing majority in the GA against the industrial countries, was far-reaching in scope and broke new ground in its sheer audacity. It started out by recognizing 'that the problem of financing the economic development of countries in the process of development is fundamental to the maintenance of the peace of mankind,' and among other things, called for the 'correction of maladjustments resulting from cyclical fluctuations in the prices of individual primary commodities and from secular movements in their value as a group in terms of manufactured goods,' and for the establishment of international commodity agreements for the purpose of '[e]nsuring the stability of the prices of the said commodities in keeping with an adequate, just and equitable relationship between these prices and those of capital goods and other manufactured articles.' It also requested the Secretary-General to prepare a study on the 'financial repercussions which changes in the terms of trade between primary commodities and capital goods and other manufactured articles produce on the national incomes of countries in the process of development,' and to appoint a group of experts to suggest practical measures to give effect to the recommendations contained in the resolution.

The resolution was vigorously opposed by the industrial countries, led by the United States. They argued that there were no objective criteria for determining an 'adequate, just and equitable' relationship between prices of primary commodities and those of manufactured goods, and hence that the decision of the market had to be accepted. Furthermore, they argued, such a system would make the economic structure more rigid and less adaptable to change, and would not be conducive to increased productivity. While these are certainly strong objections on technical grounds, they do not reveal the strongest objection of all, which concerns the income transfers from industrial to underdeveloped countries which would occur under the umbrella of the scheme. To see the significance of this it is only necessary to note that these same industrial countries, in dealing with their own primary agricultural producers, were at the very same time pursuing policies designed to achieve 'adequate, just and equitable' price relationships, and were presumably not bothered in this by all the technical arguments on which their objections to the main demands in the resolution were based.

At its 17th session in April 1954, the Council considered the report of the Committee of Experts appointed to propose practical measures to give effect to the sense of the resolution.[10] While emphasizing the importance of the terms of trade and of greater stability of price relations for the economic development of underdeveloped countries, the experts shied away from any attempt to deal head-on with the issue of fair or equitable prices. Instead they focused on the issue of reducing short-term fluctuations around long-term price trends, and, considering single commodity agreements to be of only limited value in meeting the needs of underdeveloped countries, recommended that the possibilities of negotiating a number of commodity agreements simultaneously or a single agreement covering a number of commodities should be examined. The experts also proposed compensatory financing measures which would enable countries experiencing a deterioration in their terms of trade to maintain their importing capacity, for example through the IMF. Finally, the experts proposed that an intergovernmental trade stabilization commission should be established to deal with the issue on an on-going basis.

The experts' report led to a decision by the Council, opposed by the US, the UK and the other industrial countries, to establish a Permanent Advisory Commission on International Commodity Trade to examine and make recommendations on measures designed to avoid excessive price fluctuations, 'including measures aiming at the maintenance of a just and equitable relationship between the prices of primary commodities and the prices of manufactured goods in international trade.' The Commission was duly constituted, though the US, which was one of the 18 elected members, indicated that it would not take part in the Commission's work. The Commission held a number of sessions starting in 1955, focusing its attention largely on reviewing commodity trends, for which purpose it issued periodic commodity bulletins and reports and promoted studies on fluctuations in commodity trade. In 1958 the Commission's terms of reference were amended to delete reference to 'just and equitable' price relationships in order to encourage US participation in its work. This was duly achieved, though by then the Commission had become little more than a talking shop for the general discussion of commodity problems.

In the meantime, efforts were also under way to negotiate international commodity agreements, though of the commodities involved (olive oil, lead and zinc, wheat and sugar), only one (sugar) was of wide interest to underdeveloped countries as an export commodity.

All in all, notwithstanding the considerable number of studies undertaken on the subject and the extensive debate generated, very little was achieved by these UN initiatives in the commodity field, and the essential problems of the commodity-dependent underdeveloped countries remained basically unchanged.

The main issues of the 1950s: some noteworthy features

We conclude here with a summary of some of the noteworthy features characterizing the evolution of North-South relations during the 1950s, as suggested by our discussion of the actions proposed, debated and taken within the framework of the United Nations during this period. Basically, the focus was on three issues: technical assistance, development finance, and commodity prices.

Provision of technical assistance was among the first measures to be stressed and actively promoted in the United Nations as a means of helping to promote the economic development of underdeveloped countries. On this issue there was never any basic controversy between the industrial and the underdeveloped countries, both sides seeing it as a useful and mutually beneficial means of achieving desired objectives: for the underdeveloped countries, the acquisition of technical skills and technology essential for economic development; for the developed countries the opening up of the underdeveloped countries as receptacles for their technologies, equipment, manufactures, investment and economic and business philosophy, at minor cost. These objectives were particularly important for the United States, which had been largely excluded from the European colonial territories in Africa, Asia and the Middle East, and which therefore attached high importance to devising mechanisms for penetrating these former colonies now emerging as independent states. It is therefore not surprising that it was the United States that took the lead in promoting the concept of technical assistance, first in the context of the American Point Four Programme proposed by President Truman, and later in promoting UN technical assistance activities.

The other two issues, however, were the subject of conflicting pressures and sharp differences of opinion between the different groups of countries, and generated so much intellectual and emotional appeal in the atmosphere of the period that they quite dominated the UN debates on North-South issues during those years, though in fact little was to be achieved.

In respect of development finance, the proposals and debates of the 1950s have two aspects which need to be distinguished. One concerns the question of whether such finance was to be made available to underdeveloped countries in sufficient volume, in the form of grants or as 'soft' loans, to make a significant contribution to their economic development. The other aspect concerned the related question of the institutional arrangements for administering and controlling such finance. The countries, which pushed for UN action on this issue, chose the UN as the appropriate forum in which to pursue their case, for two reasons: first, because with the voting structure in the GA based on the principle of one country one vote, they could expect to muster a majority in support of their demands, and hopefully thereby force a favourable outcome; second, because the voting principle in the GA represented the kind of model which they wanted to see applied to the new institution. The idea was for an institution radically different from the World Bank. The Bank's loans were based on hard commercial principles, and its management was completely dominated by the United States and other industrial countries. The arguments used by the proponents of the new institution to justify their demands ranged all the way from the claim that financing provided by such an institution would redound to the advantage of the industrial countries (by promoting world economic development in which all would prosper) to the assertion that the industrial countries had an obligation to provide such financing in compensation for all the exploitation that the underdeveloped countries had suffered at their hands under colonialism.

For the industrial countries, on the other hand, and particularly for the United States (which led the opposition to these demands, sometimes almost single-handedly in the face of lack of determination and varying degrees of support from other industrial countries), these two aspects were sharply distinguished. Even if they were to concede the principle of a multilateral institution for development finance in the form of grants and soft loans, it would have to be under the firm control of the main contributors. The UN, where the underdeveloped countries could exercise great influence because of their voting power in the GA, was therefore not the place to take action on a development financing institution. Hence the stonewalling by the US, and the eventual deflection of the pressure for UN action by a two-pronged approach which met essential US interests: the creation of a UN-based technical assistance agency in the form of a Special Fund; and the creation of a World Bank-based development finance institution (the IDA) to perform the soft loan function.

Pressure for action on the commodities front faced similar conflictual interests. In respect of commodities, two kinds of actions were demanded: measures to reduce fluctuations in commodity prices, and measures to stabilize the terms of trade between commodities and manufactured goods. There was fairly wide acceptance of the need for the first type of measure, though in practice there was not the will to do much. But on the second there was never any chance that the demands would be taken seriously, especially since, apart from other considerations, this would in effect involve capital transfers without the possibility of the contributors being able to exercise detailed control over the use of the funds. Again it was left to the US to provide the main opposition to these demands (supported in large measure by the UK).

The second feature to which we wish to draw attention here is the rather fluid state of the coalition of forces in the confrontation between the industrial and the underdeveloped countries during the UN debates on these leading issues during the 1950s. While the confrontation was clearly between these two groups, there was often little or no cohesion among the groups in reacting to the issues. On the side of the industrial countries, the US often found itself almost alone in opposing the demands of the underdeveloped countries. This was especially so in relation to the demands for the creation of SUNFED, when many of the other industrial countries expressed themselves as favourably inclined to the idea, and in many cases backed this up with concrete offers to contribute to such a fund. On the side of the underdeveloped countries there was also a noticeable lack of cohesion on important issues and at critical points in the debate.

This lack of cohesion among the industrial countries in responding to the demands of the underdeveloped countries was a peculiarly interesting feature of the early post-war years. It reflected the peculiarities of this period in a number of respects. First, the position of the US at this time as the world's dominant financial and economic power meant that it would in any event be carrying the bulk of any burden resulting from meeting the demands of underdeveloped countries and would therefore have the decisive voice.

Second, the European countries were still in (or only just emerging from) a position of financial and economic dependence on the United States, and therefore still saw themselves as underdogs, making it as yet difficult for them to empathize wholly with the US point of view on these matters. The strained relations between the European countries and the US-dominated IMF during the 1950s, discussed in Chapter 2, is an indication of the mood of the period. Third, as ex-colonial powers, some European countries probably felt a certain responsibility for promoting economic development and welfare in the newly independent underdeveloped countries, and were therefore probably more sympathetic to their demands, especially so if these demands were to be met in a multilateral setting where others would share the burden.

While it is true that the flurry of activity initiated by the underdeveloped countries during the 1950s, to bring about desired changes in international policy measures, led to few if any concrete results, there is no denying that the process of decolonization and the advent onto the international scene of a host of newly independent nation states radically changed the matrix of international relations, introducing new elements which had to be taken into account. But, while new voices were being heard, they were not as yet sufficiently strong nor coherent to command any great attention, and hence no concessions needed to be made. Indeed, with the other industrial countries still in the process of recovering from the ravages of war (and many of them from the emotional shock caused by the loss of their colonial empires), it was practically left to the US alone to fend off the advances, and this it did without too much effort. The scene was being set, however, for more determined advances, to which we shall turn in the next chapter.

Notes

1. See Alexis de Tocqueville, *Democracy in America*, (specially edited and abridged for the modern reader by Richard D. Heffner, A Mentor Book, New American Library, New York, 1956), p. 142.
2. Sumner Welles, one of the chief US negotiators of the Charter, was moved to exclaim after the Charter was released: 'The age of imperialism is ended. The right of all peoples to their freedom must be recognized. . . . The principles of the Atlantic Charter must be guaranteed to the world as a whole - in all oceans and in all continents.' (See Richard N. Gardner, *Sterling-Dollar Diplomacy*, Clarendon Press, Oxford, 1956, p. 49).

3. See R. F. Holland, *European Decolonization 1918-1981: An Introductory Survey*, (Macmillan, London, 1985), Part 1, especially pp. 11-15.

4. But see Holland, *op. cit.*, for some interesting thoughts on this.

5. 'Measures for the Economic Development of Under-Developed Countries', Report by a Group of Experts appointed by the Secretary-General of the United Nations (May 1951).

6. Resolution 1219 (XII) adopted by the GA in December 1957.

7. The US International Development Advisory Board, *Partners in Progress: A Report to the President* (March 1951), p. 84. Quoted in Robert E. Asher, *et. al.*, p. 215.

8. Council resolution 341 (XII); see *Yearbook of the United Nations*, 1951, p. 367.

9. United Nations, *Measures for International Economic Stability*, Report of a Group of Experts, 1951: II.A.2, p. 25.

10. UN Department of Economic Affairs, 'Commodity Trade and Economic Development', Report Submitted by a Committee appointed by the Secretary-General, Doc. E/2519 (Nov., 1953).

4. Confrontation and Dialogue: The 1960s

As we saw in the previous chapter, the demands of the underdeveloped countries during the 1950s were focused on a few selected issues or areas of action where *ad hoc* concessions were sought on the grounds that these would help to promote their economic development. The institutional framework established after the Second World War to provide the basis for post-war international economic co-operation (in the design of which these countries played little or no role) was taken for granted and hardly questioned, and there was no real attempt to demand basic changes in the system to accommodate the developing countries' special needs. The developed countries, on the other hand, represented largely by the voice of the United States, were content to play for time, allowing the underdeveloped countries scope to voice their demands, and *in extremis* even to pass resolutions, but conceding nothing of substance in return (except in the limited area of technical assistance where there was, as noted in Chapter 3 above, a certain congruence of interests).

A number of developments during the late 1950s and early 1960s contributed to a changed climate which nurtured a growing trend towards confrontation and dialogue between the North and the South. In this climate the South were able to put forward and press their demands for international policy changes in a sufficiently coherent and forceful manner to oblige the North to engage in serious dialogue and to make some grudging concessions.

Responding to the Soviet challenge

Cold War developments played an important role in this. The latter part of the 1950s saw a number of Soviet advances and initiatives which led to spreading doubts in the West (particularly in the US) about their ability to meet Soviet ideological, economic, political and military challenges. Soviet achievements in military and space technology were important triggers to the alarm bells of the West, and the successful launching of the Soviet spacecraft 'Sputnik' in 1957 struck deeply at the West's complacency about its own military and technological supremacy. The inauguration of manned Soviet space flights shortly afterwards, well ahead of the US, raised the world-wide prestige of Soviet science and technology, and led to a good deal of soul-searching in the United States about the relative merits of the Soviet and American education systems, the teaching of mathematics in schools and institutions of higher learning, the relative numbers of engineers and scientists being trained and the methods of training them, and so on. This was also the age of the 'missile gap', that discovery by which the aspiring US presidential candidate John F. Kennedy was able to argue that the incumbent US Administration had sat idly by while the Soviets were allowed to steal a march on the US in a vital area of military technology.

This era saw the Soviets challenge the West by flaunting the alleged superiority of their economic system as a means of achieving rapid economic development. These challenges were characteristic of Khrushchev's flamboyant and brassy style, and were well reflected in his famous epithet to the capitalist West: 'we shall bury you', a remark which, in the sense in which he meant it, was for some time taken quite seriously in the West.[1]

And perhaps more importantly from our present point of view, this was also an era which saw a great many Soviet initiatives for establishing and intensifying trade, economic and political relations with the underdeveloped countries, particularly with Asian and African states newly freed from colonial rule. The aim of these policies was to undermine Western influence in these countries and to gain political allies in the ideological and political confrontation with the West. This was to be achieved by, among other things, brandishing in these countries the ostensible superiority of the Soviet model of rapid industrialization and economic growth, and linking such claims with actual Soviet aid and technical assistance in the establishment of modern industries. Khrushchev's outright challenge to the West for open competition between the two systems only served to make these policies more poignant. And it could be expected that the underdeveloped countries' actual or incipient disenchantment with their former colonial masters could be capitalized on to make these policies more effective.

The Soviet offer in 1956 to finance and build the Aswan High Dam in Egypt after the World Bank, under US pressure (purely on political grounds), declined to fund the project, was a dramatic illustration of this new Soviet approach to relations with the South. This ambitious project, critically important for Egypt's development, was subsequently financed and built by the Soviet Union, creating a tangible symbol of Soviet technical capacity and of communist support for economic liberation and development in the face of Western opposition. Other high-visibility Soviet aid projects were also undertaken during this period, including steel mills in India and Indonesia, and although total Soviet aid to underdeveloped countries was considerably below the level of Western aid, the concentration of Soviet credits in a few strategically important countries and on ambitious projects lent considerable lustre to its aid programme. It is reckoned that by 1964 the Soviet Union was extending credits to some 30 underdeveloped countries, though the bulk of these credits went to a small group of about eight countries.[2] A feature of Soviet credits that was especially welcome to the less developed countries perennially short of foreign exchange, was that repayments could be made in local currencies or in the form of traditional exports. On a broader level, the impact of these Soviet initiatives could be seen in a reorientation of the policy stance in underdeveloped countries, characterized by an acceleration in the pace of nationalization and by a growing emphasis on industrialization, planning, public ownership and other measures meant to strengthen the economic independence of the new states.

The effect of this flurry of Soviet activity extending and cementing relations with the South was to create anxiety in the West concerning Soviet potential for capturing the minds, and bringing within its orbit the economies and political allegiances, of the underdeveloped countries of Asia, Africa and Latin America, with their vast populations and natural resources. In the US the alarm bells were clearly audible, with a chorus of concern being expressed about the implications of Soviet aid programmes. The statement by US Under-Secretary of State Douglas Dillon that 'the Soviet economic offensive is a means for carrying the struggle against us in its economic aspects to the most vulnerable sector of the free world,' which appeared in a 1960 US State Department publication entitled *Communist Policy in the Less Developed Areas*, gives full expression to these concerns.[3] Another effect of these Soviet activities was to provide the justification for an enhanced American aid effort in the underdeveloped countries, apparently under the assumption that Soviet competition had to be met head on.[4] And on a wider international level, they helped to set the stage for an emerging dialogue between the North and the South, by helping to build a self-assertive consciousness among the under-developed countries, and by putting pressure on the West to try to meet some of these countries' aspirations.

The dilution of the US leadership role

The recovery of the European countries from the devastation of the war was fairly complete by the middle of the 1950s, and by the end of that decade these countries were to join the ranks of the prosperous, financially strong, self-assured industrial countries. This meant that the US was to lose the unique position it had held since the end of the war as the unquestioned leader and spokesman for the Western industrial countries, on whose last word everything depended, and was now forced to share leadership with the European countries, who by then had joined together into an economic bloc and could begin to speak with a common voice. The result was that the industrial 'North' would in future no longer be represented, as before, by a dominant leading voice, but rather by a coalition of voices having common general interests but with enough important nuances and differences of emphasis becoming manifest to shift the centre of gravity of the position of the North as a whole in relation to North-South issues. In the previous chapter we saw manifestations of these differences reflected in the debates on proposals for UN action. But in all cases the US was the final arbiter of what was acceptable, and the other countries had limited influence on the outcome. With the changing balance of economic and financial power among the Western industrial countries that began to become evident by the end of the 1950s, however, this situation was to change perceptibly, and was to help to provide the climate and set the stage for the initiation of a more serious attempt at North-South dialogue than had been seen hitherto.

Growing consciousness and increased assertiveness in the South

The other important development which helped to make possible and give meaning to the emerging dialogue was the sudden growth in the number of newly independent underdeveloped countries in the early 1960s, to which reference has already been made in the previous chapter. The entry of these new countries onto the international scene was accompanied by a wave of consciousness in the underdeveloped world regarding, on the one hand, their lack of economic power and economic opportunities, and, on the other, of the potential political power which now lay in their hands as sovereign states and of the use to which that power could be put to achieve economic ends. The common colonial experience of the newly liberated Asian and African states provided a uniting strand which served to embolden these countries in seeking ways to press demands for a proper place in the international economic order. What started as the Afro-Asian bloc, largely anti-colonial in origin, was soon to lead to the more cosmopolitan Non-Aligned Movement, embracing a wider political platform, and eventually to a wider coalition or grouping of developing countries whose objectives were more closely focused on economic issues.

The scientific and technological advances in the Soviet Union, as reflected in the spectacular achievements of its military and space industries, the combative attitude of the Soviet leadership in challenging the West to open economic competition and in extolling the virtues of their system for promoting forced industrialization and rapid economic development, and the intrepid efforts of the Soviets to promote closer economic and political links with the underdeveloped countries and to encourage them to experiment with the new system, all served to engender in these countries the vision of an alternative to continued dependence on a world system defined and dominated by their former colonial masters. They also helped to instil a determination to be more assertive in formulating demands for changes in the system. It was thus the existence of this alternative Soviet model, and the manner in which it was flaunted in the ideological and political battle of the Cold War that, in combination with the growth in the number of underdeveloped countries, was largely responsible for bringing about this increased assertiveness on the part of these countries. It was also the existence of this alternative, and the perceived need on the part of the West to prevent the underdeveloped countries from choosing it and thus falling into the Soviet orbit, that precipitated incipient competition between the two blocs for the favours of these countries and that contributed to a growing willingness on the part of the industrial North to engage in a dialogue with the South.

The Kennedy Administration and US policy towards the underdeveloped countries

Another development that helped to make the climate more propitious for dialogue was the election to the US Presidency in 1960 of the liberal Democrat John F. Kennedy to replace the hard-nosed Republican Administration of President Eisenhower. Kennedy brought with him to the White House inspiring rhetoric, the profession of lofty ideals, and a more humane attitude to questions concerning relations with the newly independent states and the economically deprived masses of the underdeveloped world. This rhetoric, and these ideals, ignited a spark in the American public, generating an atmosphere predisposed to assisting the South in overcoming poverty and promoting economic development. The Kennedy rhetoric struck a particularly vibrant chord in the younger members of the educated middle classes, the response finding expression in the eagerness with which they responded to his call for volunteers to join the Peace Corps, that phenomenon of the 1960s where thousands of young American graduates from well-to-do families and the best universities set out, in a wave of idealism and a spirit of adventure, to work in conditions of relative poverty in the underdeveloped countries, helping to impart technical knowledge, to build bridges between peoples, and to promote the economic development of these countries.

In the US back-yard, Latin America, this rhetoric was to find expression in the 'Alliance for Progress', which was to provide the conceptual framework for the conduct of US economic assistance policy in that region. The policy was proclaimed by the new President in his inaugural address when he said: 'To our sister republics south of the border we offer a special pledge - to convert our good words into good deeds - in a new alliance for progress - to assist free men and free governments in casting off the chains of poverty.'[5] This pledge was to lead to the Declaration of Punta del Este, in which the United States undertook to provide 'a major part of the minimum of US$20 billion, principally in public funds, which Latin America will require over the next ten years from all external sources in order to supplement its own efforts'; and for their part, 'the countries of Latin America agree to devote a steadily increasing share of their own resources to economic and social development, and to make the reforms necessary to assure that all share fully in the fruits of the Alliance for Progress.'[6] The Declaration was accompanied by a detailed Charter with separate titles listing, for example, the objectives (with specific targets for economic growth, income distribution, health, education, housing, etc.), the framework for the preparation of national development plans and programmes, immediate and short-term action and measures to be taken, and the conditions under which external assistance would be provided in support of national development programmes.

It was in this framework that US economic assistance programmes to the region would seek to support such liberal ideals as land reform, democratic government, improvements in the basic social services such as health, education and housing, and, more generally, greater opportunities for economic and social improvement and for political participation of the great masses of disenfranchised poor, whose condition clamoured for change. But ideals apart, *realpolitik* was the driving force behind US action, and Cuba's growing allegiance to the communist bloc, and the increasing appeal of the Cuban revolution to the Latin American masses, provided the political underpinning for this policy. As Levinson and Onis observe, 'The spirit in which the U.S. Congress agreed to the creation of the Alliance was less one of compassion for Latin America's needy millions than fear of a spread of Castroism.'[7] The political logic behind the Alliance for Progress was therefore that it was the most effective way to combat the revolutionary appeal of the communists, on the assumption that this could best be achieved by eradicating the conditions considered the breeding ground of this appeal. It may be added, however, that the more idealistic elements of this approach did not survive long into the implementation phase, which soon saw a return to business as usual in supporting the traditional military oligarchies as the best bastion against communism and radical change.[8] Nevertheless, the rhetoric implicit in this approach reflected an important strand in the thinking of the US Government of the day, and was indicative of a certain disposition to take a wider view of US national self-interest when contemplating action relating to the under-developed countries.

Prelude to dialogue

It had become evident by the end of the 1950s that the post-war economic expansion which had then been underway for some 15 years, which saw the full economic recovery of Western Europe and vigorous growth in the economies of the industrial countries at high levels of employment, was not accompanied by a correspondingly favorable performance of the economies of the less developed countries, who were consequently being left further behind. A number of studies carried out under UN auspices confirmed this sad fact. Between 1950 and 1960 the share of the less developed countries in world trade fell from one-third to almost one-fifth. Furthermore, the expansion of their export earnings decelerated significantly during the decade, falling from 8.4 per cent per annum during the early 1950s to only 5 per cent per annum by the end of the decade. This deceleration reflected, among other things, worsening terms of trade for the primary commodity exports of the developing countries, an issue that had been much discussed and debated in the 1950s. With this deceleration in the growth of export earnings the balance-of-payments squeeze became more acute, and desirable growth targets more difficult to attain. The plight of the less developed countries was therefore coming to seem quite desperate, especially in comparison with the very successful economic perfor-mance of the developed industrial countries.

The problem of the underdeveloped countries caught the imagination of the incoming US President, and the rhetoric behind the Alliance for Progress produced an echo in the wider UN setting when President Kennedy, speaking at the 16th session of the GA, proposed that the 1960s should be officially designated the 'United Nations Development Decade'. He suggested that by so doing the efforts of the United Nations in promoting economic growth could by expanded and co-ordinated. Something of the flavour of what the US President had in mind was brought out by the US representative in the subsequent debate on the proposal. It was the view of the US that 'the proclamation of the United Nations Development Decade would give fresh impetus to national and international efforts to accelerate the development of the less developed countries and would help to strengthen the role and enhance the authority of the United Nations and its related agencies.' He drew attention to the importance of the international financing agencies, and suggested that '[a] detailed plan for the Development Decade would have to be drawn up; an inventory of all available resources should be made, goals should be set and the progress made towards them should be constantly measured.'[9] The President's proposal fell on fertile soil, and after the necessary debate and negotiation over language, a resolution designating the 1960s the 'United Nations Development Decade' was duly adopted, replete with specific growth targets and detailed objectives and measures at national and international levels. The parallel with the Alliance for Progress stopped here, however, since there was no corresponding commitment from the US to underwrite the costs of meeting the targets set for the Decade.[10]

An interesting feature of international initiatives during these years was the high importance attached to economic planning as a *sine qua non* for dealing with the problems of economic development. It may seem strange today, in an age where privatization, deregulation, and a hands-off approach by government to the economy have become articles of faith, to recall that in putting forward ideas in the early 1960s for the Alliance for Progress and the UN Development Decade, no less a country than the United States could call for the formulation of national development plans and programmes as essential elements for the success of these undertakings. But such was the nature of things, and the Secretary-General's report containing 'proposals for action' for implementing the objectives of the Development Decade gave high priority to helping developing countries 'to work out sound development plans and carry them through, both by mobilizing national resources and by securing supplementary external aid'. A three-stage area of action was envisaged: '(i) help in obtaining information for planning, in the establishment of planning machinery and in the choice of methods of planning; (ii) help in the formulation of the development plan; and (iii) assistance in implementing the plan.'[11]

The UN Conference on Trade and Development

It was in the area of trade that the underdeveloped countries decided to focus their efforts in bringing to bear their increasing numerical strength and vigour to push for changes in the international economic system. This no doubt reflected the growing recognition that their effective participation in the expansion of world trade was essential to enable them to transform and develop their economies. The evidence cited earlier of the extent to which these countries had failed to participate in the expansion of trade during the 1950s, evidence which was then being widely commented on, underlined the seriousness of the problem they faced in this regard.

It was against this background that at the 16th session of the General Assembly, in 1961, a group of Latin American states submitted a draft resolution requesting the Secretary-General to consult governments on 'the need for holding international meetings and conferences in order to find an effective solution to the problems affecting the trade of the developing and underdeveloped countries. . . .' A similar resolution submitted by a group of African states went further in requesting the Secretary-General to prepare, after consulting governments and with the assistance of a preparatory committee, 'a provisional agenda for an international conference on world trade problems, including those relating to the primary commodity trade market. . . .'[12]

In July 1962, a Conference on the Problems of Developing Countries was held in Cairo, attended by representatives of 35 developing countries in Africa, Asia, Latin America and Europe. This conference has a particular importance in the evolution of the North-South dialogue since it was the first attempt to concert the thinking and co-ordinate the positions of governments from all the major geographical regions of the developing world on the important international economic issues of the day. The 'Cairo Declaration of Developing Countries', adopted at the conference, identified a number of issues and urged action in a number of areas that were to figure prominently in the subsequent debates and confrontations, but of immediate interest is the fact that it came out strongly in favour of the early convening of a conference, within the United Nations framework, 'to consider international trade, primary commodity trade and economic relations between the developed and the developing countries'.

The idea of convening a United Nations economic and trade conference had often been mooted by the Soviet Union during the 1950s, but had always met a cool reception from the Western industrial countries, led by the US. Their lack of enthusiasm for this idea reflected their reluctance to have the UN, over which even in the 1950s they had less than full control, become involved in a discussion and review of the basic institutions for economic and trade co-operation put in place and fully controlled by them. The idea was therefore never seriously pursued. When, however, the underdeveloped countries, with their expanding numbers, rising voices, increasing political dynamism, and growing influence took up the call in the 1960s, it was not so easily brushed aside. Thus, while the major western industrial countries continued to oppose the idea, they were unable to prevent the momentum from building up, and eventually found themselves reluctantly conceding to the call for a conference on trade and development, when the matter was finally brought to a vote in the GA in December 1962.

A Preparatory Committee was established to prepare the agenda and make other necessary arrangements for the Conference. Raul Prebisch, the dynamic, outspoken and intellectually resourceful head of the UN's Economic Commission for Latin America (ECLA), with strong, well-known views on the development issue, was appointed Secretary-General of the Conference with responsibility for guiding the whole preparatory process and the Conference itself. Not surprisingly, Prebisch was to dominate the preparatory process and set the tone of the Conference. He was to be particularly influential in setting the Conference agenda and in organizing the preparatory work of the less developed countries, sensitizing them in the process to his own particular view of the North-South issue and guiding them to supporting his approach. His own report to the Conference, entitled 'Towards a New Trade Policy for Development', was something of a personal testament, reflecting the evolution of his thinking on the development issue over the previous 15 years, largely from a Latin American perspective. This document, well argued, comprehensive, intellectually appealing and philosophically coherent, in both its diagnosis and its prescriptions, served to define the principal demands of the developing countries and to set the tone and largely determine the proceedings of the Conference. Perhaps owing to Prebisch's dynamic leadership, this Conference largely determined the framework and set the parameters for North-South confrontation and dialogue in the years ahead. Much of our subsequent discussion will therefore be concerned with this Conference and its outcome.

The Conference itself - the United Nations Conference on Trade and Development (UNCTAD) - was held in Geneva from 23 March to 16 June 1964. It was attended by some 2,000 delegates from 119 countries, and, according to Gardner, 'was the largest and most comprehensive intergovernmental conference ever held.'[13]

The Prebisch thesis and the agenda for the Conference

The point of departure for the Prebisch thesis is an alleged gap between the export earnings of developing countries (assumed to be effectively determined by world market conditions) and their import demand, corresponding to a given target rate of growth of GDP (the rate used was the 5 per cent target set for the UN Development Decade). The argument focuses on the excessive dependence of developing countries on primary products for their export earnings and on the predominance of manufactures in their imports, and on an alleged secular tendency for the terms of trade to move against primary products and in favour of manufactured goods. These structural characteristics and tendencies lead to a persistent trend towards external imbalance in developing countries, manifested in a 'trade gap' which acts as an effective break or limit on the rate of growth of GDP. It is to overcome this 'gap', and thereby to remove the limit, that the 'new trade policy for development' is proposed.

The above is a skeletal summary of the main thesis. Prebisch adds not only flesh, but full regal attire. He includes an analysis of the underlying statistical data on the terms of trade, and an elaborate, economically sophisticated and heuristically appealing explanation of the underlying structural characteristics and tendencies which lead to their worsening. This is not the place for a detailed critique and analysis of the Prebisch thesis, the basic elements of which pre-date his report to the Conference.[14] Over the years it has been the subject of a good deal of criticism, both on statistical and on theoretical grounds.[15] There is no denying, however, that his views on this subject have always made a deep impression and demanded attention, both from his critics and his adherents. What is important for our present purposes is that his diagnosis of the problem provided the basis on which prescriptions for international action were formulated for consideration by the Conference.

The problem as posed requires the identification of mechanisms for bridging the trade gap implicit in the difference between the level of imports corresponding to the desired growth target and the level of imports that could be financed from the (slower) growth of export earnings. In principle there are three possible approaches to bridging this gap: expanding exports at a rate above that previously considered possible; suppressing imports relative to income growth; and the infusion of external capital. The suppression of imports involves import substitution which Prebisch considered had already gone too far (based on his Latin American experience) and, in any event, to be inefficient and counter-productive. He did not see it as a viable option. The effective choice was therefore between export expansion and capital inflows, or, in the language of the day, between trade and aid.

Since for obvious reasons trade is clearly the more effective and reliable of the two for bridging the gap and assuring a satisfactory rate of economic growth over the long term, much of the subsequent analysis was concerned with the means for achieving the required expansion of exports. And since, furthermore, in the framework of the analysis it is world market conditions that provide the effective constraint to export expansion, the search for solutions necessarily involved the question of how to make these conditions more responsive to the export needs of the developing countries.

For purposes of analysis a sharp distinction was made between primary products, subject to slow growth in international demand but on which the developing countries were heavily dependent for their export earnings,[16] and manufactures, which faced much brighter export prospects, but in which developing countries had scarcely begun to make a mark as exporters. In both cases the solutions proposed called for international action, or, more specifically, for action by the developed industrial countries, and were therefore highly suitable subjects for discussion at the Conference.

For primary products the solution proposed involved the more extensive use of international commodity agreements designed not only to reduce price and market instability but also to assure fair terms of market access and equitable prices to exporting countries. A scheme for compensatory financing was also proposed to compensate less developed countries for losses incurred as a result of worsening terms of trade. These losses, it was argued (speciously), represented an income transfer from the less developed to the developed countries,[17] creating a moral obligation on the part of the developed countries to transfer back the income thus accruing to them. Furthermore, it was well known that developed countries made widespread use of domestic price support policies in favour of their own primary producers. There should be no problem of principle, therefore, in applying such policies at the international level, especially since these internal price support policies restricted access to the markets of the developed countries, and were thus harmful to competing exports of less developed countries.

Recognizing the need for some degree of protection to facilitate the establishment of new industries in less developed countries, the report proposed a system of preferences for the industrial exports of these countries, both in their own regional markets (within the framework of regional integration groupings), and in the markets of the industrialized countries. In the latter case, to which more importance was attached, the proposal was put forward as a logical extension of the infant-industry argument for protection, and envisaged free entry for exports of manufactures of the less developed countries into the markets of the developed countries for a period of 10 years, thus providing temporary protection against competition from other developed countries. No reciprocal concession would be expected of the less developed countries in return. This was clearly the boldest and most far-reaching proposal to emerge from the report, and was to be the subject of intense debate and controversy during the Conference.

The report also deals with a number of other matters, such as the growing debt burden of developing countries, the need for changes in the GATT rules to adapt them to the requirements of the new trade policies recommended elsewhere in the report, the cost of maritime transport and insurance and the impact of shipping conference rates, the scope for expansion of trade between the socialist countries and the rest of the world, particularly the developing countries, and a discussion of the responsibilities of the developing countries themselves (which occupies two pages in a 64-page report). These issues, however, do not form part of the main thrust of the report.

Some background considerations

Before commenting on the Conference itself and its outcome, it will be useful first to draw attention to some of the special circumstances which helped to define the climate in which the Conference was held. The first point to stress is that the Conference was convened against the clear wishes of the major western industrial countries. From the moment the issue was broached, these countries, particularly the largest and most important among them, used all the diplomatic, negotiating, debating and persuasive skills at their disposal to block attempts to convene such a conference. When the call had been made earlier by the Soviet Union and its allies, this was easy enough to achieve. When, however, the call was taken up by the growing number of less developed countries with their increasingly militant demands for beneficial changes in the international economic system, the pressure mounted, and the industrial countries, after much procrastination, eventually agreed to the conference.

Their agreement was, therefore, something of a last-ditch effort to ease the pressure, and it was as if they were dragged kicking and screaming to the conference table. Thus, it was to limit the damage that they decided to attend and participate in a conference that they did not wish to see take place and that they were persuaded could not possibly produce any result of benefit to them.

Indeed, they were convinced that any concrete result could only be to their disadvantage.

The second aspect which deserves special mention here, and one which was to have a enormous bearing on the whole course of the Conference, concerns the remarkable extent to which the less developed countries were able to form a united front in putting forward and defending their demands. This was something quite new in the annals of United Nations diplomacy and indeed in post-war international relations. Before, there had always been loose coalitions of countries with broadly common interests supporting common positions on particular issues, but this was usually *ad hoc* and subject to shifting alignments depending on the particularities of each issue. The situation that now presented itself was of a solid bloc of countries (no less than 75) which had caucused beforehand, concerted their individual positions, and finally put forward common positions which the entire group would then support and defend. A foretaste of what was to come was the 'Joint Declaration of the Developing Countries' made at the 18th session of the General Assembly in November 1963, in which the developing countries as a group set forth their views of what they expected from the forthcoming conference, views which largely paralleled the thinking of Prebisch. This was the prelude to a process of close consultations and internal debate leading to joint positions on the part of the developing countries as a whole that was to characterize the preparations for the Conference and the Conference itself, and that was to reflect an extraordinary degree of group discipline in agreeing to, and defending, group positions. The unity and discipline maintained was especially remarkable considering the great diversity of the developing countries in terms of levels of development, export interests, racial and geographic affinities and special contacts and arrangements with the various metropolitan powers. This process gave birth to what has come to be called the Group of 77, the developing countries caucusing and economic pressure group through which the North-South dialogue would henceforth be conducted.

The emergence of this close-knit, disciplined, mutually supportive developing countries' pressure group was a phenomenon which at the time came as something of a surprise, and it is of interest to comment on the underlying factors that made this possible. As already mentioned, the developing countries, in growing numbers, had come to realize that they were not sharing anywhere near adequately in world economic expansion, and were convinced (by the writings of Prebisch, among others) that the international economic system established by the industrial countries, in which the industrial countries prospered, did not serve the interests of the developing countries, and needed to be changed. Whatever the differences in the situations facing individual developing countries, therefore (and these were clearly quite significant), they all faced a common problem and had a common interest in bringing about change. If they could define a programme for change that they could all support, differences could be buried, and a joint stand taken. Of course, there is also the question of the merits of a programme commanding such support, but this is a question to which we return later. For the moment what is important is that a basis is provided for an international political pressure group, made all the more potent by its numerical strength, by the fact that a large number of its member countries had only recently emerged from colonial rule and were especially resentful of their degraded economic status, which they considered largely attributable to the very system then under attack, and by the ideological dimensions of the East-West conflict which appeared to offer alternatives and which at the same time served to increase the bargaining power of the developing countries as the two blocs competed for their attention and allegiance.

We may note that the Western industrial countries were not at all prepared for the sudden emergence of this solid developing countries' bloc with whom they had to deal. They themselves were still operating on the same casual basis as before, sharing common interests but retaining their individual viewpoints on the particularities of each issue. And their preparations for the Conference were nowhere near as thorough as those of the developing countries, perhaps partly because they were hardly willing participants. The fact that the US no longer held the overriding position of leadership among the industrial countries, and that the European countries, now economically strong and financially powerful, could play a more independent and assertive role in international economic forums, also meant that there was considerable scope for divergences in viewpoints and differences in position to emerge among the industrial countries.

The third issue concerns the general approach to the purpose and agenda of the conference. The background to the call for the conference was the developing countries' dissatisfaction with the existing international economic system and the institutions that underpinned it. It was therefore the underlying problem which gave rise to this dissatisfaction that they sought to tackle by means of an international conference. While there was perhaps no clear notion of how this was to be achieved, it would necessarily involve an attack on existing institutions, with demands for their reorganization, conversion, replacement, whatever was necessary to achieve a system more responsive to the needs of the developing countries and more amenable to their interests. The IMF, the World Bank and the GATT were the three key institutions that would necessarily be the main targets for change. As the call for a conference mounted, however, the emphasis shifted away from the need for fundamental changes in the system and towards greater stress on *ad hoc* policy measures for the benefit of developing countries. This was implicit in the shift from a call for a conference on 'trade' to one on 'trade and development'.

From the point of view of the Western industrial countries, of course, what they most feared was any attempt to tamper with the institutions themselves, institutions which they had established and which they considered to serve their global economic interests very well. It was because of their fear of any such attempt that they had always been so quick to react negatively to any call for an international conference on world trade. At the same time, in response to the political realities and the growing demands of the increasing number of less developed countries, there had recently been some attempt to make minor adjustments to the policies of these institutions to cater to the particular needs of those countries. In the late 1950s the IMF began to study a scheme for the compensatory financing of deficits arising from export short-falls, a scheme intended specifically to meet the balance-of-payments problems of less developed countries dependent on the vagaries of the primary commodity markets for their export earnings. At about the same time the GATT also began to take an interest in the problems of the less developed countries, and commissioned a report from a group of exports, the 'Haberler Report', which revealed the failure of these countries' exports to grow as rapidly as those of the developed countries, due in part to tariffs and other barriers erected by developed countries against imports from less developed countries.[18] This report led to detailed studies identifying barriers to trade and recommendations for action, and resulted in the 1961 Declaration on Promotion of the Trade of Less Developed Countries, and subsequently in the 1963 Programme of Action, both of which, it is generally agreed, accomplished little of substance.[19] In the Bank, the main innovation was the establishment of IDA, discussed in the previous chapter.

The softening in the industrial countries' opposition to the call for a conference was clearly linked to the shift in emphasis in its purpose noted above. Once it was clear that the focus would not be on the actual institutions but on amorphous issues of 'trade and development', a more light-hearted approach to the idea of a conference was possible. This was made clear by the

US representative in the statement in which the US finally agreed to the convening of the conference. Stressing that the conference should be focused on the trade problems of developing countries and should not try to cover the whole field of world trade, he thought the latest text presented 'a wise and careful approach', and could support the proposal 'with a fair degree of optimism because of the manner in which the draft resolution set forth the character of the conference and laid down the manner for its preparations'.[20]

It is not entirely clear what brought about this shift in focus, but it may be noted that Prebisch, in his own report to the conference, which provided the framework for the agenda, came down heavily (if not exclusively) in favour of the 'trade problems of the developing countries' approach, and made no real attempt to deal with the wider issues of world trade and development. Thus we find that the analysis in the report was carried out solely from the developing countries' perspective, with the prescriptions for international action each linked to the particular trade problems of these countries as identified in the analysis. More important, however, is the fact that the actions proposed or envisaged nearly all involved the idea of *ad hoc* concessions by the industrial countries, with the result that the question of whether fundamental changes in the basic institutions and framework of the international economic system may be appropriate (and necessary) to provide space for the developing countries was never really explored. It was therefore as if the developing countries were expected to come to the conference, cap in hand, begging for chunks from the table (knowing full well that in the circumstances they were more likely to get crumbs), rather than demanding the right to sit at the table. An item on institutional machinery was, of course, included as the last item on the agenda (almost as an afterthought), and, as it turned out, was the central issue at the conference.

Little of substance is achieved

The conference itself was long and wordy, and attracted a good deal of attention, but it is fair to say that at the end of the day it achieved little of immediate practical benefit in relation to the specific items on the agenda on which concessions on matters of substance were sought. The remarkable unity and solidarity achieved by the developing countries, even on issues where their interests substantially diverged (e.g. preferences), assured them of voting majorities in support of their demands. It soon became apparent, however, that using their automatic voting majorities to pass resolutions, over the opposition of the developed countries, calling on these same countries to give concessions they were unwilling to grant, would accomplish little, and efforts then shifted to attempts to negotiate language the other side could accept.

The industrial countries, in contrast to the developing countries, were ill-prepared and divided among themselves, differing markedly in their responses to the demands of the developing countries and in the sympathy they appeared to show for their problems, and hence had no common response to make. This did not make it any easier to negotiate mutually acceptable language, and for the most part what finally emerged did not go much beyond a general statement of the issues and of the possible lines of action.

On commodities little was achieved, not even an agreed general statement of the issues. On preferences there were important differences in the responses of the industrial countries, but only the United States flatly refused to consider the idea. The other industrial countries were sympathetic to the idea, but differed on whether preferences should be generalized - made available to all developing countries (the British view) - or selective - limited to a few countries, such as the overseas affiliates of the EEC (the French view) - and on whether it was a necessary precondition for all developed countries to participate in granting the preferences. In the end the matter was left unresolved and referred to a special machinery to be set up to consider it further. In fact only in the traditional area of financial assistance was a significant measure of general agreement reached, reaffirming the 1 per cent target for development assistance established for the United Nations Development Decade, making recommendations for improving the terms and conditions of financing, and calling for a study (by the World Bank) on the need for 'supplementary financial measures' to assist developing countries when declines in export earnings or deteriorating terms of trade threatened to disrupt implementation of their development programmes.

Apart from the specific issues on which concessions of immediate practical benefit were sought, there were two areas of the conference's work to which the developing countries attached great importance and which were to occupy a good deal of the time and energies of the conference. One concerned the somewhat theoretical question of enunciating general rules and principles governing international trade relations, and the other the all-important and very practical question of institutional machinery.

Proposals for a declaration of principles for international economic co-operation were mooted in the UN at least as early as 1957, initiated originally by the Soviet Union. These proposals were received without enthusiasm by the leading Western countries, and when, during the 15th session of the General

Assembly in 1960, the Soviet Union submitted its 'Draft Declaration of Principles of Economic Co-operation', containing elements of considerable appeal to developing countries, the UK put forward, with the support of a mixed group of seven developed and developing countries, an alternative draft resolution entitled 'Partnership for Economic and Social Development' (later amended to read 'Concerted Action for Economic Development of Economically Less Developed Countries'), which took the steam out of the Soviet proposal. The latter was then withdrawn.[21] But the idea of proclaiming general principles caught the imagination of the developing countries and lingered.

During the conference the group of developing countries drafted and proposed for adoption 15 general and 13 special principles to govern international trade relations and trade policies conducive to development. The topics dealt with covered a range of issues, including fundamental principles (relating, for example, to the sovereign equality of nations, decolonization, and the right of nations to trade with whom they want and to dispose of their natural resources); general pronouncements (recognizing, for example, the need for faster economic growth, a narrowing of the income gap, etc.); and principles governing action in specific areas. The last dealt largely with areas which were the subject of negotiations in the wider conference, and for the most part took the form of demands addressed to the developed countries ('developed countries should . . . grant concessions', etc.). Overall, these latter principles may be seen as a manifesto encapsulating the developing countries' demands and aspirations as they crystallized at the time of the conference. It is also of interest to note that the developing countries, in proposing draft principles, were not indifferent to the particular concerns of the Soviet bloc (perhaps in recognition of their broaching the subject of principles), and included as one of the principles that there should be no discrimination in trade based on socioeconomic differences between nations. This appeared prominently as Principle Number 2, following the hallowed principle concerning the sovereign equality of nations.

During the latter stages of the conference a good deal of effort was made to negotiate changes in the draft to make it more acceptable to the Western developed countries. But notwithstanding the many changes that were incorporated in the text to accommodate the concerns of these countries, the text as finally adopted did not enjoy the support of many of the developed countries. Thus the United States voted against nine of the 15 general principles, abstained in a further two, and stood alone in voting against the principle of sovereign equality of states! (But it voted in favour of the principle that regional groupings should not harm outsiders, a principle on which the EEC countries abstained.)[22] All in all, the voting revealed the general lack of support among the industrial countries for the principles (and programme of action) that the developing countries were seeking to promote. It is therefore doubtful whether the importance attached to the question of principles was justified, although it might be said that the debate and the voting did serve the purpose of isolating the US from the main body of industrial countries on a number of important issues.

There could be no doubt, however, as to the importance of the question of institutional machinery, an issue that was tagged on as the last item of the agenda. In a sense, this may be said to have been the only real issue for negotiation at the conference, the other issues not really involving negotiations at all but rather the one-sided presentation of requests for the granting of concessions which it was wholly in the gift of the other side to grant or refuse. Admittedly, we should not push the point too far, since, depending on how the presentation is made, how it is linked to surrounding circumstances and to the implications of non-compliance, it might be made to seem in the interest of the other side to comply with the request. In fact this is often the very stuff of international politics and the cementing of alliances, as witnessed by the 'generous' US bankrolling of the European Recovery Programme. Indeed this was the sense in which the British 'negotiated' with the US on lend-lease and the post-war stabilization loan. But in the context of the 1960s, and notwithstanding the dynamics of the Cold War and the battle for ideological allies, there was hardly the basis for such 'generous' outpouring in favour of the less developed countries. And as the conference approached and evolved and it became more and more obvious that there was not much that the Soviets had to offer as an alternative, particularly in the critical area of trade, which now occupied centre stage, there was even less reason for such outpouring - indeed, it began to appear that competition among the Western industrial countries for favours in the less developed countries would, if anything, be the only factor capable of evincing some positive responses. It may safely be concluded, therefore, that the requests were pretty one-sided and did not partake of the flavour of negotiations.

The institutional issue takes centre stage

On the institutional issue, however, the situation was different, and here there was real scope for negotiation and for the extraction of concessions at the bargaining table. The panoply of economic institutions established by the industrial countries after the war provided the main basis for worldwide international economic co-operation. These institutions remained under the tight control of these countries, and the developing countries, whose partici- pation in the international economy (and hence economic prospects) depended on the policies of these institutions, found themselves subjected to a policy framework that was simply imposed on them and on which they could exert little or no influence. It was therefore of the greatest importance to them to try either to gain access to the levers of power in these institutions or to attempt to supplant them with others in which they could exercise influence and participate in controlling. The question was therefore one that went to the heart of the matter.

Since it was obvious that the Bretton Woods institutions were a closed shop from whose corridors of power outsiders were effectively barred, the GATT became the main target in the drive for institutional change. It was a suitable target for a number of reasons. First, it had no firm legal or institutional basis, having come into existence *de facto*, by the back door as it were, to perform some of the functions foreseen for the aborted ITO, but without any charter or other legislative sanction. In fact, its only legal basis was the fiction of being an 'Interim Committee' of a non-existent United Nations body. Second, there was a widespread feeling among the less developed countries that the GATT had focused its energies on improving the trade prospects of the industrial countries, and had largely ignored their own trade problems. The fact that the GATT trade negotiations had always centered on industrial goods, exported largely by the developed countries, and that agricultural products and other primary commodities, in which the less developed countries had their main export interest, were largely ignored in these negotiations, gave substance to this feeling, which was in any event confirmed in the report of the expert group belatedly appointed by GATT (in 1958) to examine the issue.[23] In specific cases the less developed countries had even been flagrantly deprived of benefits legally due to them under the GATT. This was the case, for example, in the Long-Term Arrangement on Cotton Textiles which, while not sanctioned by any provision of the GATT, was negotiated within its framework, and under which exporting developing countries agreed 'voluntarily' to limit their exports to those developed countries that demanded such action on the grounds that their domestic markets were being disrupted by excessive imports.[24] And in addition to everything else, the fact that the ITO was still-born, and that many of the functions foreseen for it remained to be performed, had left a major institutional vacuum which, it seemed, could conveniently swallow the precariously established, much-criticized GATT, dubbed by the poor 'the rich man's club'.

Apart from the intrinsic importance of the subject matter, the issue of institutional machinery took on special significance from the fact that it was the only item on the agenda where use of the developing countries' voting majority to push through resolutions could have real meaning, rather than being just expressions of pious wishes, emotional appeals or rabid exhortations, all easily ignored. Neither side in the confrontation that was to follow could therefore afford to treat lightly the need to evaluate and assess the costs and benefits of the positions they would take. It is therefore no exaggeration to say that here the real battle of the conference was to be fought.

The Soviet Union in a pre-conference document had presented a detailed proposal for an International Trade Organization, and the developing countries in their various regional pre-conference declarations had all indicated in rather general terms a wish for some such new institution. It was clear to all, however, that an ITO along the lines of the Havana Charter would necessitate a new international treaty requiring, for its coming into effect, explicit approval by the major western countries, an eventuality that could hardly be taken for granted given their known opposition to the idea of a new world trade body. For the developing countries, therefore, the practical approach was the creation of a new institution under the UN umbrella, the birth of which could be brought about by the necessary votes in the General Assembly, and the ambit of whose membership and authority would encompass the entire UN membership. This was the approach followed by the developing countries in playing their trump card, an approach already suggested by Prebisch in his report to the Conference (though it may be said that, in outlining his ideas, Prebisch went into too much detail, and prematurely conceded more than the developing countries needed to have conceded during the negotiations).

The developed countries soon recognized the logic of the situation they faced, and from then on the question was how to cut their losses at the bargaining table by limiting the authority, functions and independence of the new body. Equally important was the question of control.

The eventual negotiation of an agreed text on the nature and functions of the new body was facilitated by the fact that the developing countries as a group finally accepted and supported the main ideas put forward by Prebisch in his report to the conference, envisaging a continuing organization within the framework of the United Nations based on periodic UNCTAD conferences, a standing committee or council, and an independent secretariat with the authority and capacity to submit proposals to governments. Bolder ideas envisaging the incorporation of GATT in the new body were thus no longer being pushed. Negotiations with the developed countries focused on such issues as the extent of independence of the new secretariat from the main UN Secretariat in New York (an issue of importance to them since they felt comfortable with the extent of their own control of the main Secretariat), whether the new body would be an organ of the General Assembly or of the Economic and Social Council (the developed countries preferring the latter since they had greater control of the Council than the GA), and the manner in which reference would be made to the long-term aim of eventually establishing an ITO. On the question of the functions of the new body careful drafting was also needed to balance the wish of the Western countries to protect the jurisdiction of GATT and to preserve the Council's primacy in the economic and social field against the desire of the developing countries and the Soviet bloc to endow the new institution with wide and overall responsibilities in the field of trade and development. The wording on functions finally agreed - 'to promote international trade, especially with a view to accelerating economic development, particularly trade between countries at different stages of development, between developing countries and between countries with different systems of economic and social organization, taking into account the functions performed by existing international organizations' - reflects the delicate balance reached. But on these and related matters the negotiations proceeded fairly smoothly.

What was to cause great difficulty, however, on which the fate of the conference was to hang, was the question of representation and voting in the decision-making organs of the new body. On this there appeared hardly any scope for compromise, with the developing countries insisting on application of the GA principle of the equality of states in voting rights, and the Western countries equally insistent that they could not accept a system where, by majority vote of an international body, they might be asked to adopt changes in their trade policies to which they were opposed. They advanced various formulae involving weighted voting and blocking votes, all rejected by the developing countries, zealous to preserve the cherished principle of one-country-one-vote. In the end the developing countries' viewpoint prevailed, though the heat was somewhat taken out of the issue by a proposal to introduce a procedure of conciliation intended to postpone (or avoid the need for) resort to voting.[25]

The implications of the Conference in the longer term

In the history of the evolution of North-South dialogue the 1964 conference was of seminal importance. From the point of view of the less developed countries, while it did not achieve much of immediate benefit in terms of practical measures or other concessions (and, as indicated above, it would have been fanciful to suppose that it would), it was nonetheless of capital importance in demonstrating their ability to galvanize their political energies and to organize and conduct themselves as a disciplined and cohesive political group in opposition to the developed countries.

By using this political punch and group solidarity to ram through the creation of a major new international body to which the Western industrial countries were openly opposed, they had provided a springboard which could be used to launch a series of attacks on the existing order of things and, in time, bring about the kinds of changes in the international economic order that they sought. The conference was also important in drawing public attention to the seriousness of the trade and development problems that developing countries faced, and to the way in which these problems were linked to, and aggravated by, the policies of the developed countries. It was hoped that this heightening of consciousness would help provide a climate of opinion in developed countries in which the desired changes could more easily be undertaken. The conference was also useful in exposing significant differences among the developed countries in their attitudes towards the issues, differences which could be exploited by the developing countries in the subsequent pursuit of their efforts.

From the longer-term perspective of promoting development, however, a more sombre note was struck by the manner in which the agenda for the conference was approached and the issues put before it. As we mentioned earlier, the approach was basically that of identifying the various ways in which the existing international order acted to frustrate or limit the trade and development potential of the less developed countries, and to propose in each case appropriate remedial measures. This led to a set of proposals which took the form, essentially, of demands on the developed countries to grant concessions, change policies, and so on. Now it is true that the purpose of the conference was to consider international policy measures required to facilitate and help promote trade and development. It was a mistake, however, to think that these policies could be considered in isolation, as if one could assume that development would automatically follow if the proposed international policies were adopted. The need for related domestic policy initiatives was obvious.[26] Equally obvious was the fact that these would not necessarily be forthcoming, especially in those cases where they might require disturbing the privileges of ruling elites in countries dominated by military-oligarchic regimes, a situation not uncommon in Latin America during the 1960s. The outpouring of official and academic literature on the Alliance for Progress (see p. 72) was devoted in considerable measure to highlighting the need for just such policies, for example land reform, improved and more equitable tax systems, greater emphasis on education and social services in government expenditure (at the expense particularly of the military), to mention some obvious examples.

The implication of this approach was that, by devoting attention so exclusively to the international aspects beyond the control of the individual developing country, and by assigning such primordial importance to those aspects, it tended to divert attention from, and to belittle the importance of, the need for appropriate domestic policy measures. The result is a sort of ideology of fatalism, where the responsibility for failure can always be shifted elsewhere. While it may be doubted whether and to what extent the analytical argumentation and the rhetoric of the conference actually influenced the course of domestic policy in individual developing countries, there is little doubt that in some quarters it induced a sense of complacency, which served to postpone the hard choices that needed to be made. It may well be, therefore, that by popularizing a theory of dependency as a prop in a bargaining process, a psychology of dependency was nourished and sustained which served to inhibit the realization of full development potential. From a long-term developmental point of view, this was undoubtedly one of the more unfortunate aspects of this approach.

On a more practical level, Prebisch's approach to the agenda and the issues certainly simplified the problem of lining up the support of developing countries behind the proposed programme of measures, since these all involved concessions that the other side was being asked to make, at no cost to the developing countries. It also played an important role in bringing about the unity and solidarity of the developing countries displayed at the conference. Since the approach implied zero cost to developing countries (not always true in practice, for example in the case of preferences - see below), all benefits deriving from concessions granted are net benefits. Thus, provided there is something in the package for each developing country, they will each have an incentive to support the package as a whole, irrespective of the proportions in which the benefits are shared.

For the Western industrial countries, the conference was something of an eye-opener and a bit nerve-racking, and, while it left them somewhat shaken, they could be reasonably satisfied that the basic task of damage control had, all things considered, been accomplished. Concerning the demands made on them for taking practical measures in the various areas in which concessions were sought, they could note with satisfaction that nothing of substance had been conceded. But the debates had revealed such disarray and divisions between them in their attitudes and responses to the various demands that they might well fear that weaknesses thus exposed could be exploited by the other side. Much would therefore depend on how things developed in the framework of the continuing machinery that they had been forced to concede.

The outcome on the issue of institutional machinery could also be viewed with some relief. It was here that they were most vulnerable and under the most sustained and intense attack, and it was here also that most was to be gained or lost in the longer term. But they were able to protect existing institutions, particularly the GATT, at least for the time being, from imposed reform or from being effectively replaced, and the new machinery was so circumscribed in its functions and still so amorphous and inchoate, that they could have good reason to hope that, in time, it might be neutralized and made benign (from their point of view). But much would depend on the dynamics of how matters developed and on how things were handled in the immediate years ahead.

In one aspect the conference had an important bearing on the future conduct of business by the developed countries. They realized the disadvantageous position they were in, facing a united and solid bloc of developing countries making demands on them and prepared to use their numerical strength, with its assured voting majority, to try to impose their demands and to extract concessions. This appeared to call for greater co-ordination and a more united front on the part of the developed countries, and this they set about creating, using their Organization for Economic Co-operation and Development (OECD) as the centre for such activities.

The new institutional machinery gets to work

The institutional framework agreed included a periodic plenary conference to be convened every three years, a permanent standing body to be known as the Trade and Development Board, and four subsidiary committees dealing respectively with matters relating to commodities, manufactures, invisibles and financing related to trade and shipping. The Board and the Committee on

Commodities were to have 55 members and the other committees 45 members, all elected for three years under a complex formula that was designed to ensure both equitable geographic distribution and continuous representation of the principal trading states. The whole machinery, to which the acronym UNCTAD came to be applied, was to be supported by a separate secretariat to be financed within the general United Nations budget, and would be headed by a Secretary-General appointed by the Secretary-General of the UN with the approval of the General Assembly. Raul Prebisch, the animator of the 1964 Geneva conference and the architect of this new institutional machinery, was appointed its first Secretary-General. Given the whole background to the creation of this new institution, and given also Prebisch's strong advocacy of and unwavering commitment to the views he espoused, it was to be expected that the secretariat would pursue vigorously the broad lines of the programme presented to the conference and fully endorsed by the developing countries.

The momentum was maintained and the new institution got off to a business-like start in pursuing the various substantive issues raised at the conference. The issue that seemed most likely, in the light of the debates at the conference, to lead to early concrete action was preferences. While the proposal, as put forward, was audacious, the idea of preferences was not really a radical one, since at the time preferences already existed, including the remnants of the British Commonwealth system and, more importantly, the recently instituted preferential arrangement between the EEC and its former (largely French) colonial territories which had been incorporated into a special protocol to the EEC Treaty. The idea of preferences was therefore not entirely repugnant to most of the industrial countries, and, as indicated above, the US was the only major country at the conference that flatly opposed the idea.

In the subsequent consideration of the issue the US attitude was to change. They did not wish to appear unnecessarily obstructionist in the face of the wide consensus that was developing to move forward on the issue. Equally important for the US was the need to be able to influence the course of the debate, especially in view of the growing danger of the widening and consolidation of the EEC-based preferential arrangement, which the US did not at all regard with favour. A particularly undesirable feature of the EEC scheme from the US point of view was that it involved 'reverse preferences', by which the EEC countries benefited from preferences in the markets of their African associates, leaving the US at a competitive disadvantage in these markets. Also, since the Latin American countries were (and would remain) excluded from the EEC scheme, the US was under some pressure to extend similar preferences to its

Latin American neighbours. Significantly, the change in the American position was announced by the US President himself at a conference of inter-American heads of state with the words: 'We are ready to explore with other industrialized countries - and with our own people - the possibility of temporary preferential tariff advantages for all developing countries in the markets of all the industrialized countries.[27] The US thus came down firmly on the side of those who advocated a generalized system of preferences, as opposed to the EEC-led view favouring a selective approach.

With broad agreement on the goal of implementing a system of preferences now reached, it remained only to work out and agree the details. These raised a host of complex and at times difficult issues (related, for example, to the question of 'equivalent advantages' to the African associated states for the loss of their exclusive preferences in the EEC market, the phasing out of reverse preferences, product coverage, the definition of 'developing countries' for the purposes of the scheme, the question of whether it was necessary for all developed countries to apply a uniform scheme, among others). This is not the place to go into these issues in detail.[28] Suffice it to say that enough progress was made in resolving them that by the second plenary of the conference, which took place in New Delhi in 1968, it was possible to reach general agreement on the outlines of a scheme and to set up the necessary machinery to work out the details and to put it into effect.

The scheme, finally agreed in the autumn of 1970, became known as the Generalized Scheme of Preferences (GSP), and was the first and indeed only UNCTAD initiative in the field of trade to achieve concrete results. It provided a remarkable example of what could be achieved with the right combination of political pressure, goodwill, understanding, and choice of issue, and it is interesting to speculate on the elements that made progress on this issue possible.

The essential feature of the scheme, which sought to achieve a degree of uniformity in the concessions offered by individual developed countries, was that these countries would reduce duties on imports from developing countries on most industrial goods, and in respect of the major industrial countries, including the EEC, the US and the UK, duty-free entry was envisaged. Provision was also made for safeguards, to allow these countries to retain some degree of control over the trade which might be generated by the new tariff preferences. Rules of origin were also agreed, so as to be able to determine which products could properly be said to have originated in a developing country and thus be eligible for preferences. In the climate of co-operation and goodwill which prevailed in the negotiations at the time, the Soviet Union and her East European allies also offered to make contributions to the aims of the GSP. This would take the form, for example, of preferential treatment for developing countries' products in procurement policies and the inclusion of special provisions into their economic plans to help expand imports from these countries.

While the scheme represented a major policy innovation and a significant effort by the industrial countries to respond positively to the intense pressures from the less developed countries for meaningful trade concessions, it was also clear that the scheme would have only a limited impact. Thus, given the product coverage, the range of countries that might be meaningful beneficiaries under the scheme was limited to perhaps a dozen or so in Asia and Latin America that were or seemed poised to become significant exporters of manufactures. For the large majority of developing countries, particularly those on the African continent, the earliest stages of industrialization had scarcely begun, and there was no hope of becoming significant exporters of manufactures in the near future and thus being able to benefit from the scheme. Indeed, the only industrial products many of these countries could perhaps hope to be able to export in the near future were processed agricultural products based on the processing of their own agricultural raw materials, and such products were largely excluded. It was evident, therefore, that the scheme would have a very uneven impact. (We return to the question of assessing the impact of the scheme later.)

In the area of commodities, follow-up action during the 1960s in the continuing machinery of UNCTAD did not achieve any major results. Major importance was attached to the negotiation of international commodity agreements as a means of sustaining and stabilizing commodity prices, but, apart from the renegotiation of previously existing agreements (including on tin and sugar within UNCTAD, and coffee and wheat elsewhere), no new international commodity agreements were negotiated, though an abortive attempt was made to negotiate one on cocoa, a commodity of particular export interest to a large number of developing countries. This attempt failed largely on the inability to agree a floor price acceptable to producers, an indication that the industrial countries' attitude to 'remunerative prices' for the primary commodity exports of developing countries continued to be as negative as ever.

In response to renewed pressure for some concrete results, the New Delhi session of the Conference adopted a programme of international action on commodity market stabilization, setting target dates for studies, consultations and negotiations on 19 commodities. But there was little enthusiasm for this programme among the major industrial countries, in particular the US and the UK, and little was accomplished.

On one question of principle, some progress was achieved. This concerned the financing of buffer stocks used as a price stabilization mechanism in international commodity agreements (ICAs). The cost of financing such stocks (for example, in the tin agreement) was at the time borne entirely by the producers, all of which were developing countries, and this imposed on them a heavy burden which they sought to share with the industrial countries, the main consumers. An agreement in principle to share such costs in appropriate cases (assuming, in the event, that the relevant ICA had been negotiated and was in operation) was reached in the UNCTAD Committee on Commodities in 1968.

It was in respect of agricultural products that access to the markets of the developed countries was most restricted, and that developing countries could probably have gained most, in the short term at any rate, from reductions in trade barriers. This was an issue, however, that went to the most sensitive nerve centre of domestic agricultural policies in the developed countries, and it is not surprising that, notwithstanding the various alternative formulations and options that were put forward in support of their demands, the developing countries made no headway in breaking down barriers to entry. In fact, this was a problem that went well beyond the ability of the developing countries, with scarcely any bargaining power, to crack, and would subsequently embroil the leading industrial countries in bitter and protracted trade conflicts among themselves within the more formal framework of GATT. Not even in respect of the less sensitive issue of non-competing agricultural products could any meaningful progress be made. The issue here was that a number of European countries imposed high duties on certain primary commodity imports from developing countries, in particular coffee and cocoa, which deprived the developing countries' exporters of markets and revenue, but which was a source of considerable revenue to the governments of the developed countries concerned and which, for budgetary reasons, they were loath to relinquish. Demands for concessions on this issue were sympathetically received, but in practice little or nothing was done.

Apart from the trade issues, external financing was the major topic on which attention was focused in the immediate aftermath of the 1964 Conference. The 1 per cent target fixed for the Development Decade and reaffirmed at the 1964 Conference became the subject of scrutiny and debate aimed at clarifying its scope and meaning. The points in dispute included the question of setting a specific date for achieving the target, the question of whether a sub-target should be set for government aid (or 'official development assistance', in contrast to private investment which many felt was motivated by normal business considerations and should not really be included in the aid target at all), and various technical problems of definition. While the leading industrial countries, particularly the US and the UK, were reluctant to be pinned down more precisely on aid targets, there was a much greater willingness on the part of the medium and smaller industrial countries. As a result, the General Assembly, in setting out a strategy for the Second Development Decade (which the 1970s were declared to be), set a date by which the 1 per cent target was to be achieved (1975 at the latest) and fixed a sub-target of 0.7 per cent of GNP for official development assistance (ODA). While these new targets were accepted only with reservations by some donors, others (including Australia, Canada, Denmark, the Netherlands, Norway and Sweden) soon introduced legislation or took administrative steps aimed at achieving them.

Scrutiny of aid flows from developed countries was carried out both by UNCTAD and by the Development Assistance Committee (DAC) of the OECD. This revealed a deteriorating performance by the traditional major donors (especially the US, the UK and France) since the early 1960s. As a result, despite the improved performance of a number of the smaller and medium-sized developed countries, the overall performance for the DAC member countries as a group was on the decline, and the 0.7 per cent target for ODA seemed to be getting further from realization.[29] Both in UNCTAD and in the DAC, efforts were also made to improve the terms and conditions of aid, and these efforts led to a number of guidelines and recommendations which, it was hoped, would contribute to this end.

On the question of supplementary financing, the World Bank carried out the study requested by the 1964 Conference and came up with a detailed proposal for a possible scheme to protect the developing countries from disruption of their development plans caused by unexpected shortfalls in their export earnings. The proposed scheme was rather complex, estimated to cost at the time some US\$300-400 million per annum. It was put before the New Delhi Conference in 1968 and extensively discussed, both there and subsequently in the permanent UNCTAD machinery, but it never came to anything, partly because of its complexity, and partly because the developed countries were unwilling to foot the bill.

In the field of finance, UNCTAD also made a major effort during the follow-up to the 1964 Conference to intrude on the policies of the IMF, an institution zealously guarded by the US in association with the other leading industrial countries. At the time, negotiations on international monetary reform were being conducted exclusively by the Group of Ten (see Chapter 2), outside the formal framework of the IMF, and it was the intention of this Group to work out a system for the creation and distribution of new reserves limited to a small group of developed countries. These countries were strongly opposed to the discussion of monetary issues in UNCTAD. However, as a result of a recommendation of the 1964 Conference (made without the support of the developed countries), a Group of Experts on International Monetary Issues was appointed by UNCTAD. The Group, in its report, noted that the developing countries had a legitimate need for additional liquidity, and argued that they should be represented in the discussions leading to new liquidity arrangements. They also thought that a link should be established between the creation of international liquidity and the provision of development finance, a suggestion which would assure a growing flow of development finance *pari passu* with the growth in the demand for world liquidity. Thanks largely to the report of this Expert Group, and to the determination with which the developing countries pushed the issue, it was possible for these countries to intervene in the decision-making process on the creation of new liquidity (supported, oddly enough, by the management of the IMF, which had previously been excluded from the discussions and which now saw the opportunity of coming back into the picture in the framework of a widening of the discussion beyond the closed Group of Ten). The new liquidity thus created (the SDR or Special Drawing Rights) was in the event distributed widely among all IMF members, though of course the bulk of it went to the large industrial countries with their large quotas in the Fund. The idea of the link with development finance was pursued vigorously for a number of years, but met the strong opposition of the major developed countries which, apart from anything else, did not wish to see a system of development finance evolve that would escape their budgetary, legislative and immediate political control.

Policies and developments elsewhere

The momentum built up by the demands of the developing countries for greater benefits from the operations of the international economic system, which led to the 1964 Conference and its aftermath, also had an impact on the operations and policies of existing institutions. This was perhaps most noticeable in the case of the GATT, under heaviest attack from this momentum, and was reflected in a number of changes focusing on the problems of the less developed countries and intended to improve GATT's image in their eyes. We have already mentioned the report of the Expert Group appointed to look into this matter, and of the initiation of an action programme in the GATT based on recommendations contained in that report. This was eventually to lead in 1965 to the adding of a whole new Chapter to the General Agreement (Part IV) dealing specifically with the problems of developing countries, and entitled, conveniently enough, 'Trade and Development'. It sets out a number of objectives and principles recognizing, for the first time, the need for special and more favorable treatment for the less developed countries in the light of their economic status and development needs, principles which went along the lines of those demanded by the developing countries in the context of UNCTAD. These included recognition of the need for a rapid and sustained expansion of the export earnings of the less developed countries, the right of less developed countries to use special measures to promote their trade and development, and the principle that the developed countries 'do not expect reciprocity for commitments made by them in trade negotiations to reduce or remove tariffs and other barriers to the trade of less-developed contracting parties'. In addition, developed countries committed themselves to taking various measures designed to help remove barriers to, and to help promote, developing country exports, including giving 'high priority' to the reduction and elimination of relevant trade barriers. There was even a commitment on prices, carefully worded, whereby developed countries, whose governments 'directly or indirectly' determine the resale price of products produced in less developed countries shall 'make every effort . . . to maintain trade margins at equitable levels'. It was clear, however, that these commitments were of a rather vague and general nature, and that only time would tell whether they would make any meaningful difference to trade policy and provide any material benefit to the trade of developing countries.

The IMF also had taken steps, cautious and limited though they were, to respond to some of the special needs of the less developed countries. This was in the framework of the new policy announced in 1963 relating to the compensatory financing of export fluctuations.[30] Under this new policy, the IMF declared itself willing to adjust the quotas of some members exporting primary products, particularly those with relatively small quotas, to make them more adequate in the light of fluctuations in their export receipts, and at the same time introduced a system of drawings designed to compensate for a temporary shortfall in export receipts. While the new policy applied to all members, whether developed or less developed, in practice it would be of benefit mostly to less developed countries who faced the special problems of small quotas and heavy dependence on primary commodity exports. Also, in response to criticism at the 1964 Conference that the new policy was too limited, the Fund (in 1966) took steps to liberalize its policy somewhat, increasing the amount of drawings that could be outstanding under the new policy from 25 per cent to 50 per cent of a member's quota, and, in effect, removing compensatory credits from the regular quotas of the IMF.[31]

In the General Assembly, the developing countries pursued their efforts, in the face of continuing strong opposition from the developed countries, for the establishment of a United Nations Capital Development Fund. The matter was brought to a head at the Assembly's 21st session in 1966 when the developing countries presented and voted through, against the solid opposition of the developed countries, a resolution by which such a Fund was to be brought into operation 'as an organ of the General Assembly', and setting out provisions governing the functioning of the Fund. Significantly, the resolution provided that the administrative expenses of the Fund would be borne by the regular budget of the United Nations (while the financing of its operational activities would be met from voluntary contributions). This resolution was to be something of a watershed in indicating the limits to which the developing countries could usefully and effectively go in using their voting majority in the GA to bring about desired change. What the developed countries most objected to in the resolution was the provision that the administrative expenses of the Fund were to be met from the UN regular budget, and in this the Western countries made common cause with the Soviet bloc. The developing countries were evidently transposing the strategy used at the UNCTAD Conference in dealing with the question of institutional machinery to the new situation relating to the Capital Development Fund. But the situation was not the same, since in the latter case only voluntary contributions could make the Fund operational, and, as was to be expected, there was a total boycott of the Fund by the developed countries. Without such contributions the Fund was still-born, and the United Nations Development Programme (UNDP), as the Special Fund was now called, was asked to administer the token contributions, largely in non-convertible local currencies, made by the developing countries themselves. The question of the administrative expenses being met from the UN budget therefore became academic.

The other important development to emerge from these pressures in the 1960s was the establishment by the General Assembly, also at its 21st session in 1966, of the United Nations Industrial Development Organization (UNIDO) as an organ of the GA with responsibility to assist in promoting and accelerating the industrialization of developing countries. While there was some initial reluctance by developed countries to support the creation of this new institution, their resistance to the idea was never very strong. UNIDO therefore came into being without any great controversy. It is important to note, though, that UNIDO's role is restricted to technical assistance, and does not include the all-important function of financing, without which, of course, industrialization can hardly be expected to make much progress.

We should also mention here that in Latin America and in Asia regional development banks were established. These were largely patterned after the World Bank, with substantial capital subscriptions from the US and other Western industrial countries who largely determine the banks' policies. These banks differ from the World Bank largely in the fact that their lending operations are regionally based, and that the (regional) developing country members are somewhat more active participants in the capital subscriptions and in policy-making than is the case at the World Bank.

Some concluding observations

What exactly was achieved by this flurry of activity in North-South relations during the 1960s? From the point of view of the developing countries, for whom the question is most poignant, the achievement was rather one of promise than of concrete results. The major accomplishment, from their standpoint, was the demonstration of their ability to force the North into serious dialogue and negotiation, and the consequential creation of new institutional machinery which, they could hope, might provide a launching pad for bringing about the kinds of changes they desired. This was the promise - of being able to use, at the same time, both their new-found bargaining strength and the newly created institution to forge ahead with the task of achieving the concrete changes desired. In terms of concrete measures, the only clear result achieved was in respect of preferences, where the basic outlines of the approach demanded by the developing countries was adopted. For the rest, while much went on in terms of debate, proposals and counter-proposals, arguments and counter-arguments, and the emergence of agreed texts reflecting compromises and concessions, very little of substance was attained.

Despite the limited results, the fact that serious debate, discussion and negotiation was proceeding on the range of issues raised was significant. It reflected a willingness on the part of the developed countries to listen seriously to the demands of the other side, and to seek to find areas where concessions could be made and measures taken that would go some way towards satisfying these demands and thereby relieving the pressure for change, while at the same time ceding as little as possible detrimental to their own vested interests.

One significant aspect of developments in the latter part of the 1960s was the fact that the USSR was no longer as active a competitor with the West in the promotion of trade and aid links with the underdeveloped countries as had been the case in the latter part of the 1950s. In fact, ever since the fall of Khrushchev, Soviet trade and finance links with the South had become much more business-like and cost/benefit-conscious, much less dominated by political considerations, and this led to a toning down of the brassy and ostentatious style that had prevailed earlier. The result was that the threat, to the West, which Soviet economic policies in the underdeveloped countries had earlier seemed to pose now appeared much more benign, thus relieving somewhat the pressure to accommodate these countries' wishes and aspirations. The 1964 UNCTAD Conference had also revealed how little the Soviets had to offer in solving the problems as formulated and discussed, and this served further to marginalize their influence as economic competitors in the underdeveloped countries and to leave an open field to the West. Soviet political and military power was still an important factor, however, which gave the underdeveloped countries some room to manoeuvre, particularly in the exercise of sovereignty over the control and disposition of their natural resources. This factor was to be of some importance in the next phase in the development of North-South relations, to which we turn in the next chapter.

Notes

1.   It is perhaps a little difficult for us now, from the vantage point of history 30 years on, and in the light of the recent collapse of the communist regimes in Eastern Europe and the economic disarray in the former Soviet Union, to appreciate the seriousness with which the contemporaries of the late 1950s and early 1960s viewed the economic threat posed by the single-mindedness with which the communist regimes were apparently able to pursue industrialization and other development objectives. There was at the time quite a large industry of scholarly

writings devoted to comparing Western and Soviet economic performance, and the scholarly camps were about equally divided as to whether Khrushchev's boast about the Soviet Union's overtaking the West economically was in the process of being realized. In any event, the academic debate had a profound effect on political thinking and on the popular mind, and led to much discussion about the implications and the need for appropriate counter-measures. For a careful summary of the state of the debate at the end of the 1950s, see James R. Schlesinger, *The Political Economy of National Security: A Study of the Economic Aspects of the Contemporary Power Struggle* (Atlantic Books, London, 1960) especially Chapter 7.

2.   See Elizabeth Kridl Valkenier, *The Soviet Union and the Third World* (Praeger Publishers, New York, 1983) p. 8.

3.   Quoted in Valkenier, *op.cit.*, p. 9.

4.   See Schlesinger, *op.cit.*, p. 240 *et seq*, for a critique of the official State Department position on this subject. Schlesinger takes the view that there was no need to respond to Soviet policy in kind, since for various reasons he did not consider the Soviet threat as real.

5.   Quoted in Siman G. Hanson, *Five Years of the Alliance for Progress: An Appraisal* (The Inter-American Affairs Press, Washington, 1967), p. 1.

6.   Jerome Levinson and Juan de Onis, *The Alliance That Lost Its Way: A Critical Report of the Alliance for Progress, A Twentieth Century Fund Study* (Quadrangle Books, Chicago, 1970), p. 351.

7.   Levinson and Onis, *op.cit.*, p. 15.

8.   According to Levinson and Onis 'If [the Alliance] has succeeded in preventing any new Castros from coming to power in the hemisphere, it has done so by military means, failing conspicuously to advance the cause of the democratic left. The United States has intervened openly in the Dominican Republic and less obviously in Brazil and Guatemala to assist not the democratic left but the military and civilian forces of conservatism.' (*op.cit.*, p. 13).

9.   See *Yearbook of the United Nations*, 1961, p. 229.

10.   For a comparative analysis of the aims and objectives of the Alliance for Progress and the United Nations Development Decade see William F. McLoughlin, *Universalism and Regionalism: A Study of the Development Decade of the United Nations and the Alliance for Progress of the OAS as Universal and Methods for Promoting Economic and Social Development*, University Microfilms Inc. Ann Arbor, Michigan, 1967.

11.   See *Yearbook of the United Nations*, 1962. p. 233.

12.   See Diego Cordovez, 'The Making of UNCTAD', *Journal of World Trade Law*, Vol. 1, No. 3, May-June 1967, p. 256

13.   Richard N. Gardner, 'The United Nations Conference on Trade and Development' in Richard N. Gardner and Max F. Millikan, *The Global Partnership* (Praeger Publishers, New York, 1968), p. 99.

14. See for example the 1950 ECLA report, 'The Economic Development of Latin America and its Principal Problems', United Nations, Sales No. 50.II.G-2, New York, 1950.

15. See for example, C.P. Kindleberger, *The Terms of Trade: A European Case Study;* or GATT, *Trends in International Trade, A Report by a Panel of Experts,* (Geneva, 1958). See also Harry G. Johnson, *Economic Policies Toward less Developed Countries,* p. 26ff and Appendix A.

16. The slow growth in international demand for primary products was explained in terms of such factors as the influence of technical progress in providing synthetic substitutes for natural products and in reducing the raw material content of manufactures, the influence of the relatively lower income-elasticity of demand for primary products as compared with manufactures, and the influence of technical progress in the agriculture of the developed countries in increasing domestic supplies. With thirty years of additional historical experience now behind us, the importance of these factors in slowing the growth of demand for primary products has become increasingly evident. Indeed, the impact of technical progress in this regard is being felt at an accelerating (and, from the point of view of exporters of primary products, an alarming) rate.

17. We were to hear the same argument again, but being used by the other side this time, when the oil producers were able to jack up their prices in the 1970s.

18. See GATT, *op.cit.*.

19. See Harry Johnson, *Economic Policy Towards Less Developed Countries* (The Brookings Institution, Washington D.C., 1967), p. 19.

20. See Cordovez, *op.cit.*, p. 261.

21. See *Yearbook of the United Nations,* 1960, p. 219.

22. See Harry Johnson, *op.cit.*, p. 37 and Appendix B for an analysis of the voting of the developed countries on the 'Principles Governing International Trade' adopted at the Conference.

23. See above.

24. This Arrangement, which was to last for five years and was supposed to be a 'temporary' measure intended to facilitate adaptation to market conditions, has been renewed and its product coverage extended in successive renegotiations, and is still with us now, 30 years on. It was a telling example of the problems facing less developed countries able to find an export niche for themselves in the markets of the developed countries. It is significant that the limitations were to apply only to exports from less developed countries, a reflection of the inability of these countries to retaliate.

25. See Branislav Gosovic, *UNCTAD: Conflict and Compromise* (A.W.Sijthoff, Leiden, 1972), pp. 35ff, for an account of the negotiations on institutional machinery. For a more detailed documentary history of these negotiations, see Cordovez, *op.cit.*. We might remark here that the Soviets appear to have remained on the side-lines during the North-South confrontation on the voting issue, perhaps not wholly unsympathetic to the Western consensus.

26. It is interesting to compare Prebisch's approach here with that of the Group of Experts whose report 'Measures for Economic Development of Under-Developed Countries', published in 1951, was one of the earliest attempts by the international community to formulate policies for the economic development of these countries. This report, prepared under the intellectual leadership of W. Arthur Lewis and T.W. Schultz, devoted the great bulk of its contents to 'national measures' which the underdeveloped countries themselves should take, in sharp contrast to Prebisch, who dealt almost exclusively with 'international measures'. See p. 55 for a reference to the earlier UN report.

27. Quoted in Richard N. Gardner, *The United Nations Conference on Trade and Development*, p. 110.

28. The reader is referred to Gosovic, *op.cit.*, Chapter III, and Gardner, *op.cit.*, p. 109 ff. for a fuller discussion of these issues.

29. For DAC member countries as a whole, official flows represented 0.4 per cent of GNP in 1968, compared with 0.6 per cent in 1963. (See Gosovic, *op.cit.*, p. 120). These results are based on official figures reported by the donor countries themselves, and no doubt were constructed with a view to putting their performance in as favourable a light as possible.

30. See above.

31. See Edward M. Bernstein, 'The International Monetary Fund', in Gardner and Millikan, *op.cit.*, p. 143.

5. The Decade of the Oil Weapon, of False Hopes and Missed Opportunities

If the 1960s were the decade where confrontation and dialogue between North and South first achieved prominence on the international agenda, the 1970s were to see this phenomenon centre stage, for a while the very focus of international attention and debate. During these years North-South confrontation and dialogue was to reach a high pitch of intensity and were to achieve something of a catharsis, after which they would subside and again fade into the background. This turn of events was precipitated by a number of developments that were to disturb the complacency of the North and seriously shake their confidence in their ability to master and control the international economic environment, and were to give the appearance for a while of greatly strengthening the hand of the South in their struggle for an enhanced role in the international economy.

These momentous developments took place on three fronts: exchange rates, with the abandonment of the Bretton Woods system of fixed exchange rates in August 1971; oil, with the quadrupling of the price of petroleum in late 1973, consequent upon the seizure of control over oil pricing decisions by the developing countries oil exporters' cartel, the Organization of Petroleum-Exporting Countries (OPEC); and raw materials, with the widespread and quite unprecedented increases in commodity prices across a broad front, which occurred during the first half of the 1970s. Also helping to set the stage was the tendency in the leading industrial countries towards uncontrolled inflation, which accompanied these developments. These were the events that provided the backdrop against which North-South relations during the 1970s would be conducted. It will be important, therefore, to say something about these events.

The end of the Bretton Woods system

While economists were still busy writing learned treatises on why the dollar shortage would be a persistent feature of the post-war world, the reality had slowly started to change: the 'dollar shortage' was noticeably being transformed into a dollar glut. Even in the late 1950s it was becoming evident that the US balance of payments was tending towards deficit, and that the dollar was no longer in short supply. By the early 1960s the situation had become sufficiently alarming for the Kennedy Administration to introduce the interest equalization tax as a means of reducing the outflow of dollars on capital accounts. As the 1960s wore on, and the problem persisted, other *ad hoc* measures were introduced, including increased tying of US foreign aid, growing insistence that US Government agencies purchase their supplies from US sources, the imposition of controls on foreign investments of US firms and financial institutions, and exhorting US military allies to buy more military equipment in the United States to offset the impact of US military expenditures in their countries.

It was during the years of the Viet Nam War, however, that the situation really began to get out of control. Unwilling to raise taxes or to cut back on domestic ('Great Society') expenditures to meet the costs of the war, the Administration resorted to loose fiscal policies, which resulted in an acceleration in the rate of inflation, and, more importantly from the present point of view, to large and growing deficits in the balance of payments. It was these deficits that were to lead to the dollar glut, to the suspension of gold convertibility, and hence to the eventual demise of the Bretton Woods exchange rate system. To understand how these different aspects all linked up to bring about the fall of a system on which the whole post-war international economy had been built, it will be useful to say a few words here about the role of the dollar in it.

To a certain extent, the US played the role of banker and lender of last resort, somewhat similar to that of a central bank in a nation state. Thus the US dollar was (and indeed is) widely used internationally as a means of payment, as a store of value (i.e. as international reserve), and, in varying degrees, as a standard of value (prices in international trade are often quoted in US dollars). It thus fulfils the main functions of money at the international level. This special role of the US currency in the Bretton Woods system was underpinned and made widely acceptable by the undertaking of the US Government to stand ready to exchange, on demand, US dollars for gold at a fixed rate (approximately US$34 per ounce of gold). The system had advantages both for the world at large and for the US in particular. For the world at large the advantage was primarily the convenience of having a currency to hand with the necessary attributes to serve as international money, without having to go about the task of creating one. And as long as the system functioned, dollar assets combined the qualities of providing interest income with the assurance that they could be readily exchanged into gold at a fixed rate (that is to say, they were 'as good as gold').

For the US there were first the profits of seigniorage to be earned from the use of its currency as international money, a not inconsiderable cash benefit. More important, perhaps, was the freedom it allowed the US to be able to finance its balance-of-payments deficits by the simple expedient of printing dollars, without having to worry about the availability of international reserves or other adjustments problems. But this advantage was a two-edged sword, which required a good deal of self-discipline on the part of the US authorities to prevent it cutting the other way. If the US balance-of-payments deficit got out of hand, the dollar glut would build up, and confidence in the continuing ability of the US to honour its pledge to redeem dollars for gold would begin to fall, leading in turn to a rise in the demand for gold and, since this demand could hardly be met in view of the profligate increase in the supply of dollars, to the eventual collapse of the system. This, of course, is exactly what happened.

Demands for the conversion of dollars into gold had been building up throughout the 1960s as the weakened position of the dollar became increasingly evident, and by 1971, US gold holdings had declined to US$10 billion (from US$25 billion in 1950), while foreign holdings of dollars stood at US$50 billion (having climbed from US$3 billion in 1950). It was thus obvious that the US would be quite unable to meet the demands for redemption, and that the dollar was effectively inconvertible into gold. It was the realization of this fact that led to President Nixon's dramatic announcement, on 15 August 1971, that gold sales had been suspended, a watershed in the post-war international economy.

The announcement of the suspension of gold sales brought home the reality that the Bretton Woods system of fixed exchange rates was now dead, and that the world economy was entering uncharted waters, with no markers or guideposts to help the wary keep clear of hazards and to lead the way to the promised land of stability and growth. The collapse of the Bretton Woods system left two major gaps in the international policy framework. First, the absence of an appropriate co-operative arrangement for fixing the exchange rates between the major currencies, thus avoiding that bane of the pre-war period, beggar-thy-neighbour type policies of competitive devaluations. And second, the question of what would replace gold in the role it had played in providing an anchor to the international monetary system.

A series of *ad hoc* agreements and arrangements among the major industrial countries, starting with the Smithsonian Agreement of December 1971, tried to deal with the first problem, and have been more or less successful in preventing international monetary arrangements from degenerating into the worst forms of competitive devaluation and other undesirable consequences of uncoordinated exchange rate policies.[1] On the second problem nothing was done, and the consequence was the tendency for runaway inflation to take hold in the industrial North in response to the various disturbances and shocks that these countries were soon to face. The fixed exchange rate system having broken down, the exchange rate itself now became a front-line variable able to take the impact of adjustments in domestic fiscal and monetary policies, which could now operate free from the exchange rate constraint. The international monetary system had, as it were, been cut loose from its anchor, and left free to drift in response to the waves and cross-currents of national policies, or indeed to take off into uncontrolled flight. The menace of uncontrolled world inflation now seemed a real possibility, and indeed for a time was becoming self-fulfilling, as a general flight from money into commodities developed, exacerbating the boom in commodity prices that was to be one of the hall-marks of this period. It was this aspect of the breakdown of the Bretton Woods system - the absence of a rule-based system for money growth world-wide - that left the biggest hole in the international policy framework, and that was the most alarming threat to the stability so highly prized and sought after by the industrial North. The escalation in the price of gold, which took place following the collapse of the system, rising from less than US$40 per ounce in 1971 to exceed the wholly fantastic level of US$800 per ounce during 1980, was the most vivid symbol of the flight from money and of the total lack of confidence in existing arrangements.

Meanwhile, the developments of August 1971 had put the final nail in the coffin of the IMF as an institution whose main task was to promote and support a stable exchange and payments system. We saw earlier how, soon after it was founded, the IMF was debarred from playing any role in one of the principal tasks for which it was designed, the restoration of balance-of-payments equilibrium in Western Europe. Not long after, it was again bypassed, and became superfluous for another of the principal roles intended for it: that of provider of short-term liquidity to the main industrial countries to assist them in adjusting to temporary disequilibria in their balances of payments.[2] Since the early 1960s, therefore, supervision and management of the fixed parity system remained the only significant function that the IMF had still to perform in relation to the exchange and payments problems of the industrial countries. And with the demise of that system, it now became totally irrelevant so far as these problems were concerned. Even the SDR scheme, which could have given some new role to the IMF in this context, had, by the time it became operational in 1970-72, also become irrelevant in this regard. This was a curious fate for an institution into whose design so much careful thought had been put and on which such high hopes had been placed. But, as we shall see, the IMF was to find new life, and a justification for its continued existence, in other spheres.

OPEC and the oil shock

The four-fold increase in the price of oil imposed by the newly-assertive Organization of Petroleum Exporting Countries between August and December 1973 was a dramatic event of the first importance. It shook the world economy to its very foundations and, almost overnight, changed radically the world political and economic landscape. It became the major preoccupation of governments and policy-makers all round the world. For the industrial North, after decades of controlled stability and docile and compliant behaviour from its traditional sources of raw materials in the underdeveloped world, this event was out of character and thus especially shocking, and made a deep impact. The reaction it produced is reflected well in the words of a contemporary West German writer:

> Since the 16th of October 1973, the day the 'oil crisis' started, world economic and political conditions changed rapidly. Traditional concepts such as 'poor' and 'rich' countries took on a different meaning than they had before that day. The date marks . . . the start of a new era. The format of worldwide distribution of political influence and wealth, which had undergone only gradual change since World War Two, was revolutionized from one day to the next by the secular 'oil crisis' occurrence.[3]

With the hindsight of history we can now see how exaggerated this reaction was. But in the heat of the moment reactions are formed that dominate thinking and determine policy.

Oil: the North-South dimension

In the history of North-South relations, oil has always held a very special place. It is the quintessential raw-material sector where the dominance of the North over the South has over the years been most complete. In 1970, 63 per cent of world exports of crude petroleum originated in the underdeveloped world, but production was under the complete control of the multinational companies based in the developed world. The only benefits the host countries derived from the production and export of their petroleum were taxes accruing to the governments in the form of per barrel payments made by the companies. In fact, the entire industry in the exporting countries was under the control of seven major western oil companies (five American and two British), popularly known as 'the seven sisters', who between them dominated the international oil industry in all its phases, from the production of crude petroleum to transport, refining, retailing and marketing, world-wide. To give the flavour of the extent of this dominance and control we can perhaps best quote from Anthony Sampson on the subject:

> For decades the Companies (with a capital C) seemed possessed of a special mystique, both to the producing and consuming countries. Their supranational expertise was beyond the ability of national governments. Their incomes were greater than those of most countries where they operated, their fleets of tankers had more tonnage than any navy, they owned and administered whole cities in the desert. In dealing with oil they were virtually self-sufficient, . . . controlling all the functions of their business and selling oil from one subsidiary to another.[4]

Throughout the post-war period up to 1970, the companies were able to keep per barrel payments to the governments of the oil-exporting countries at a constant or declining level.[5] Given that world inflation advanced at a steady pace throughout this period, holding per barrel payments constant in dollar terms implies a substantial reduction in real terms. In fact, during the 1960s the inflation rate in the main industrial countries (the appropriate index of world inflation) averaged 3.0 per cent per annum, meaning that in real terms per barrel payments declined by 27 per cent during the 1960s alone. These were the kind of deteriorating terms of trade that often faced developing country exporters of primary products, about which so much was heard in the earlier discussion. Of course, everybody recognizes that petroleum is a special case, and no one could claim that petroleum prices were determined by the free play of market forces, and hence that prices, and the resulting terms of trade, must be accepted as acts of God, as was argued by the industrial countries in the general debate on the terms of trade.

With the oil majors in control and able to keep per barrel payments from rising, the oil exporters had only one avenue available for increasing their oil revenues, and that was by increasing production. The companies were thus able to stand by and see the exporting countries competing with each other for the favour of increased production off-takes. This suited the companies and, even more, their home base industrial countries, very well, since it assured a plentiful supply of cheap oil to drive the economies of these countries and to underwrite their growing prosperity. It is not surprising, therefore, that the demand for oil in these countries was increasing at a spectacular rate, almost as if it were free. Thus, between 1950 and 1970, imports of petroleum into the main industrial countries (of North America, Western Europe and Japan) increased from 2.6 to 20.3 mbd (million barrels per day), growing at an average rate of 11 per cent per annum. There was even an acceleration during the 1960s, with the rate in that period averaging 12 per cent per annum. The result was a dramatic increase in the share of petroleum and natural gas in total energy consumption over these years, from less than 50 per cent in 1950 to more than 70 per cent in 1970. Projections at the time foresaw similar spectacular increases in consumption in the decades ahead.[6]

Since production costs in the oil-rich regions of the developing world were very low,[7] it was to be expected that the consuming countries would want to treat petroleum almost as if it were a free good. And since they controlled production decisions, they could ensure that it was so treated. From the point of view of the exporting countries, however, this was hardly a satisfactory situation. For them, petroleum was a wasting asset, a precious resource of high value from which maximum revenue and national benefit should be derived.

OPEC enters the picture

Founded in 1960 by a number of leading developing-country oil producers, the chief initial objective of OPEC was to counter the downward pressure on prices through a unified approach to dealing with the companies. While not much of importance was achieved on prices during the 1960s, OPEC as an institution did provide a forum which facilitated comparison of producer/company arrangements in different countries, and in this way helped considerably to improve the bargaining position of the producers. Equally importantly, it provided a forum in which producers could learn more about the industry, thereby helping to disperse the mystique which was such an important factor in the companies' hold on the industry. Such knowledge would clearly be of inestimable importance in any future show-down with the companies.

A confluence of circumstances led to the dramatic events of 1973. The galloping demand for oil brought about by the low prices was finally beginning to run ahead of production plans, and, by the end of the 1960s, a tight supply situation was becoming evident. With the enhanced confidence deriving from the years of consultation and mutual exchange of information and ideas in OPEC now beginning to bear fruit, and with the more favourable market situation then developing, producing countries were presently to find themselves in an improved bargaining position *vis-à-vis* the companies, and were soon exploiting it. Starting about 1968, the producers, through OPEC, began a serious bid to get a better deal from the companies for their oil resources. In this the new revolutionary government of Libya, which came to power following the overthrow of the monarchy, was the trailblazer, confronting the companies, demanding higher payments, threatening to cut back production, actually ordering cutbacks in production, and emerging victorious with much higher oil revenues. The other producers took notice, and soon were negotiating with the companies through OPEC. These negotiations led to the Teheran Agreement of 1971 which marked an important step towards achieving some of the goals long sought by the producers. Thus not only were prices adjusted upwards, but provision was made for a built-in escalator to take account of inflation. Subsequently, in 1972, the Agreement was adapted to take account of currency variation (prices were denominated in dollars, and this was the period of floating exchange rates and dollar devaluation).

Not content with gaining concessions on prices, producers moved quickly to the next pressing issue, which was the question of control over their oil resources. Again with Libya acting as trailblazer, the companies were obliged to concede substantial levels of participation to the producing countries in the ownership of the oil produced. This concession was to have an important bearing on subsequent developments, since the ability of the producers to dispose of their 'participation' oil provided the means by which they could test the market, and thereby strengthened their hands in their price negotiations with the companies.[8] These tests confirmed much of the talk then current concerning tight supply and an impending energy crisis.

When the Arab-Israeli war started in October 1973, therefore, the oil producers were already in a much stronger position than they had been a few years before, having in the meantime demanded and obtained a wide range of concessions that had fairly revolutionized their relations with the companies and the industry. The politically motivated decision by Arab producers to reduce production progressively by 5 per cent per month and to ban shipments to the US provided a real test of the market, and quickly revealed its state and the power of the producers to dictate price through production controls. The era of the OPEC-dominated oil market thus began, with the four-fold increase in price registered by the end of the year as the opening shot.

The impact of this rise in prices was sudden and dramatic. The world had become so dependent on cheap oil that by the end of the 1960s oil was by far the most important commodity in world trade, accounting for one-half of total world tonnage (though for only 10 per cent of value). Economic structures and life-styles had been adapted and fashioned to reflect the availability of cheap oil, and now were wholly dependent on this product, almost like a narcotic. The realization that a new era had dawned where unlimited supplies of cheap oil could no longer be taken for granted brought forth the image of withdrawal symptoms, as the process of adapting to the new situation got under way.

For the major industrial countries, which had become most dependent on imported oil, and which were largely responsible for advancing the whole process to the point where the oil producers were now able to wield such power, the problem was not so much the need to adjust (for them, adjustment to change is a normal part of the growth process), but the magnitude of the adjustment required in one step, and the realization that they had now lost control of production and pricing decisions affecting a vital raw material. For the oil-importing developing countries, the rush of events in the oil sector carried mixed signals. On the one hand, they had also become dependent on oil in response to the same forces working in the industrial countries, and, moreover, were much less able to adjust to sudden change. On the other hand, they saw the actions of the oil producers in wresting control from the industrial North of their vital raw material resource, and in pursuing a determination to deploy this resource in their national interests, as a dazzling affirmation of the potential for change in a system of economic relations they had always considered deeply unjust. It also gave them ideas about how the actions of the oil producers could be generalized to other raw material sectors where developing countries were the major exporters.

In the short term, the most immediate problem posed by the oil price rise was a financial one of balance of payments. At the 1973 level of exports, the higher prices effective in 1974 would bring the OPEC countries revenue of some US$125 billion, compared with revenue of US$27 billion in 1973, an increase in revenue of some US$100 billion. Since it would clearly be impossible for the oil producers to expand their imports rapidly enough to make a serious dent in this increased revenue in the immediate future, the bulk of it would necessarily have to take the form of a payments surplus for the oil producers, the other side of which would be a payments deficit for the rest of the world, and mechanisms would have to be found to finance this deficit. To give an idea of the order of magnitude involved, it may be noted that total world exports in 1973 amounted to US$570 billion, meaning that the expected US$100 billion surplus in 1974 that would need to be financed amounted to more than one-sixth of the 1973 value of world trade. It would obviously require a series of major international financing operations, and extensive adjustments on all sides (both in the surplus and deficit countries), to effect this massive wealth transfer. The story of how these operations were carried out, and how these adjustments were made, is a fascinating one which unfortunately cannot be told here, though we return later to some of their consequences since, as often happens, it is the short term adjustment process that determines the long-term outcome.

The commodity price boom and the bogey of raw materials shortage

The OPEC price rise was not the only harbinger of the commodity price boom and the raw materials crisis of the 1970s. Indeed, a full year before OPEC started to do its business, primary commodity prices began shooting up on a wide front. Food products were particularly affected, and, starting in 1972, a number recorded some spectacular price increases. Grains, sugar, cocoa, and vegetable oils, accounting between them for a major share of total world food trade, were among those with the most dramatic price increases. Between 1972 and 1974, the price of wheat increased three-fold, maize two-fold, rice and sugar four-fold, and the vegetable oils three- to four-fold. These figures refer to annual average prices, thus masking the much more spectacular increases that would be seen using daily, weekly or even monthly averages. Industrial raw materials, both agricultural and mineral, also experienced massive price increases during this period, even if, on average, not on as large a scale as for the major food products. Indeed, it reached the stage where the problem was not just one of prices but of physical shortages as well, with the United States in the summer of 1973 imposing an embargo on the export of a large number of agricultural products and scrap metal.

There has been a lot of debate and discussion on the causes of this extraordinary explosion of commodity prices in the first half of the 1970s. The explanations are often *ad hoc*, attributing the cause to a number of independent events that just happened to coincide: for example, a series of bad harvests and unusually rapid economic expansion in the leading industrial countries.[9]

Inflation in the main industrial countries was probably both a cause and an effect of this boom in commodity prices. It was an effect to the extent that price increases resulting, say, from bad harvests were fed through the price system, and a cause to the extent that inflationary expectations (resulting, say, from the uncertainties created by the breakdown of the fixed exchange rate system) may have caused a flight from money into commodities. Whatever the final word is on cause and effect in this price boom (and it is clear that the final word is yet to be said on the subject), there is no doubt that this massive, broad-based and unprecedented rise in commodity prices contributed to a psychosis of scarcity that was to affect thinking profoundly on the raw materials issue. The OPEC price action, superimposed on the price developments taking place independently in the other commodity markets, served to increase the tension and to place in clearer relief the raw materials problem that the world appeared to face.

It was at about this time that the writings of the Club of Rome began to make the headlines. Based on studies conducted by a group of scholars at the Massachusetts Institute of Technology, using the computer-based technique of systems dynamics, the authors, in their widely publicized and much discussed report, appropriately enough entitled *The Limits to Growth*,[10] argued that owing to the operation of a number of constraints depicted in their mathematical model of the world economic system, continued world economic growth could not be sustained much beyond the end of the century. Important among these operating constraints were the non-renewable natural resources whose depletion was implied by the mathematical model. While the analysis in *The Limits to Growth* was severely criticized by economists for being too simplistic and mechanical in its approach, and for ignoring elementary principles of economic analysis leading to unreliable and unlikely results, the report nevertheless caught the attention of the public and achieved a good deal of notoriety. Its preoccupations and predictions fitted well the atmosphere of crisis engendered by the unexpected explosion of raw materials prices, the physical shortages being experienced in some sectors, and, finally, by the oil price shock and the realization that oil could no longer be assumed to be in unlimited supply. It therefore provided grit to the purveyors of doom on the raw materials front, and helped to add drama and scientific respectability to the prevailing atmosphere of crisis.

Learning from OPEC

It was not surprising that other producers of primary products began to wonder if they too could emulate the OPEC example and engineer a coup by which they could radically increase the benefits they were deriving from their raw material resources. It would be the developing country producers who would be most attracted by the thought of pursuing this possibility, though developing countries were by no means the sole, or even the predominant, producers of primary products.[11] They just happened to depend overwhelmingly on these products for their export earnings.

Even before the oil producers had begun to flex their muscles, the copper producers, using OPEC as a model, had founded, in 1967, an exporters' association, *Conseil Intergouvernemental des Pays Exportateurs de Cuivre* (CIPEC), with aims and objectives very similar to those of OPEC. The founding members were Chile, Zambia, Peru and Zaire, accounting between them for 40 per cent of world copper production and 70 per cent of world exports. As in the case of OPEC, CIPEC provided a framework where producer countries could exchange information and learn more about each other's industries, all of which were dominated by foreign companies. Following OPEC's example, there was also a movement towards increased government participation in the industry, sometimes smoothly, as in the case of Zambia, or with recriminations, as in the case of Chile. But for various reasons relating to the structure of the industry, the potential entry of new producers, possibilities of substitution between copper and other materials, and so on, it was unlikely that CIPEC would be able to carry out a coup anywhere approaching that of OPEC.

Bauxite producers also made an early bid to emulate OPEC. Four less developed countries (Jamaica, Guyana, Suriname and Guinea) between them accounted for 40 per cent of world bauxite production, and Jamaica was for many years the world's largest producer. As in the case of petroleum and copper, the industry in the developing countries was controlled in all its aspects by foreign companies, and operated with minimal linkages to the local economy. In fact, the only benefits accruing to the local economies from the extraction of the raw material from their territories were the taxes and royalty payments to governments and the wage payments to the minuscule local labour force required by this highly mechanized extractive industry.

Largely at the initiative of the Caribbean producers, particularly Jamaica and Guyana, the International Bauxite Association (IBA) was founded in

March 1974, soon after the oil shock. The founding members were, in addition to the four countries mentioned above, Sierra Leone, Yugoslavia, and, notably, Australia. Australia, a developed country, was also heavily dependent on raw materials and other primary products for its export earnings. Its inclusion in the membership of the new bauxite exporters' group was significant therefore in indicating the possibility of some realignment of traditional forces in the wake of the emerging raw materials crisis. As in the case of both OPEC and CIPEC, the main objectives of the IBA included the sharing of information so as to put the governments in a better position to bargain with the companies. This would lead to co-ordinated demands for better tax and price terms and for more local processing, and eventually to greater local participation in the ownership and control of the industry.

In the short term, and in the heady atmosphere of the time, producers, particularly in the Caribbean, were able to achieve some major successes in increasing the tax take from the companies, in enhancing local processing, and in forcing greater local participation in and control of the industry. It was the Jamaican Government which set the pace, forcing the companies to accept a formula which linked revenue to the price of the finished product (aluminium), and which resulted in a spectacular eight-fold increase in government revenue from bauxite from US$25 million in 1973 to some US$200 million in 1974. The companies were also forced to make other concessions, including granting participation to the Jamaican Government in the operations of the industry and reversion to the government of bauxite land held by the companies. Other bauxite producers were able to make moves along similar lines. It may be added, however, that the companies did not take this battering lightly, and, bauxite not being petroleum, were able eventually to extract their pound of flesh. This took the form of running down their investments in the offending countries and gradually shifting their production elsewhere, a process facilitated by the downturn in the aluminium industry that was soon under way. The severe cut-backs in production and revenues that they would face would be a salutory lesson to those countries for having dared to confront the companies.

Other raw materials in which exporters' associations were formed include iron ore, uranium and phosphate, among the minerals, and bananas and natural rubber among the agricultural commodities. We need only note here that while these groups have played a role in facilitating exchange of information among producers and in helping producers understand industries often dominated by foreign companies, and in some cases have contributed to carrying forward the process of increasing local participation in the operation of these industries, they have not succeeded in making any dramatic impact on prices. We may also note here that in the case of iron ore, two developed countries, Australia and Sweden, became members of the exporters' association.

Demands for a new international economic order

Taking advantage of the shock produced by developments on the oil front, and of the resulting sense of uncertainty and confusion which reigned in the camp of the industrial countries, the developing countries launched a major drive for a restructuring of international economic relations. The forum was again the United Nations General Assembly, and the time was early 1974, when the effect of the oil crisis was at its height. The opening shot came from the President of Algeria who, acting in his capacity of President-in-Office of the Non-Aligned Movement, called for a Special Session of the General Assembly to consider the problems of raw materials and development. The developing countries quickly went about the task of making the necessary preparations, and by the time the sixth Special Session of the GA was convened in April 1974 (barely two months after it was requested), were able to present for the consideration of the Assembly a draft Declaration on the Establishment of a New International Economic Order and a Programme of Action for its implementation. These were comprehensive and far-reaching documents which, in effect, called for a thorough restructuring of international economic relations and for a major shift in the distribution of economic power and benefits favourable to the developing countries.

The atmosphere of crisis brought on by the rise in commodity prices, by the physical shortages and the accompanying concerns about access to supplies, and by the action of OPEC in raising oil prices and in enforcing embargoes, had suggested to the developing countries that control of raw materials markets could be used as a means to bring about a major realignment of world economic power, something they had been pushing for in their earlier dialogue with the North but had been unable to make credible as a concrete demand. The other developments mentioned previously—the collapse of the Bretton Woods system of fixed exchange rates, galloping inflation in the industrial countries, accompanied by recession and record unemployment (explored further in Chapter 6) - also contributed to the feeling of system breakdown, where the industrial countries seemed to have lost control and were no longer the masters of events. The call by the developing countries, with their new-found strength, for the establishment of a new international economic order (NIEO), seemed to have a ring of authenticity about it, and struck a vibrant chord in many ears.

The industrial countries reacted to the dramatic events in the oil sector in some initial confusion and disarray. Oil was the very underbelly of their economies, and the leading industrial countries had taken great pains over the years to fortify their hold over supplies in the outlying territories, some of which had been carved up into independent countries with this specific purpose in mind. In the circumstances of the 1970s, however, with the Cold War and the East-West military confrontation then at its height, the use of naked military power to secure supplies and to re-impose the *status quo ante* was out of the question, and was probably never seriously considered. The strategy used by the British against Premier Mossadeq of Iran in the confrontation in 1953 over the nationalization of the Anglo-Iranian Oil Company (attempting to bring Iran to its knees by organizing a boycott of Iranian oil on the world market) was, for obvious reasons, also not available in the present circumstances.

At the US initiative, efforts were made to organize the major oil-consuming industrial countries into a forum where they could co-ordinate policy and develop a strategy to deal with the energy problem. These efforts were made difficult, however, by the considerable divergence of interests among the industrial countries. The European countries and Japan, wholly dependent on imported oil for their needs, were much less eager than the US to take a confrontational stance, and in many cases had been quietly arranging bilateral deals to ensure their oil supplies. France was particularly active in this regard, affirming the right of each nation to deal with the oil situation bilaterally, and generally taking an apparently more conciliatory approach towards OPEC and developing countries' concerns. It proposed that the developing countries be included in consultations which should take place within the framework of the United Nations, and called on the UN Secretary-General to convene a world energy conference to determine principles of co-operation between energy producers and consumers. This French initiative was to lead to the Conference on International Economic Co-operation (CIEC) which would meet in Paris over an extended period during the mid-1970s. In the meantime, the more conciliatory approach of the French reflected a wider spectrum of European thinking, hence the US tended to be isolated in its efforts to harness the other industrial countries behind its non-conciliatory, confrontational approach to dealing with OPEC and the new emerging demands of the developing countries.

The South maintains a common front

It appeared to come as a surprise to many, including policy-makers in the North, that the South would use the oil crisis as an issue around which to unite and as the stepping stone for confronting the North with a common platform for a major restructuring of international economic relations. After all, the oil developing importing countries would be as seriously embarrassed by the oil price increase as would the developed importing countries (if not more so). There was thus a clear divergence of interests between the oil exporting and oil importing developing countries. Why then did they stand united and choose to support a common platform in presenting their demands to the North, rather than engage in mutual recriminations, as might have been indicated?

For the oil exporters, making common cause with the rest of the developing world was clearly important for achieving much-needed protective group solidarity and for deflecting the focus of the North from the oil issue, on which the exporters might be placed on the defensive. It was for this reason that, in responding to the call of the North for a conference on energy, they insisted on linking oil and other raw materials in any negotiations. Their immediate or short-term interest in maintaining a united stand with other developing countries in the confrontation with the North is not difficult to discern.

For the oil importing countries, the idea was to ride on the backs of the oil exporters, as it were, capitalizing on their new found strength and importance to achieve basic long-term objectives. On these long-term objectives there was a coincidence of interests between the oil exporters and the oil importers on which they could fruitfully unite. And while the oil importers would derive no immediate short-term benefit from uniting with the exporters, nothing was to be gained from mutual recrimination. Indeed, they could only lose, for example, the goodwill of the exporters, and any financial contributions to which this may give rise, and only the North had anything to gain from the open spectacle of disarray and dissension among the countries of the South. Hence the curious phenomenon, much remarked on at the time, of the continued unity and cohesion of the South despite their divergent interests on the oil front.

The basic elements of the NIEO demands

With some amendments, reflecting compromises, the draft Declaration and Programme of Action on the NIEO prepared by the developing countries was adopted without dissent by the sixth Special Session of the GA. This did not mean, however, that there was universal agreement on the substance of these documents, as was made clear in statements by individual industrial countries, particularly the US, after the resolutions were adopted. But it is nonetheless the case that these documents, which now had the status of universally accepted UN resolutions, contained bold and far-reaching ideas and demands, going well beyond the rather timid 'general and special principles' adopted by majority vote at the first UNCTAD conference. And, as Meagher has remarked, 'If little of substance was new in the developing country demands, the tone in which they voiced them represented a dramatic change from that of earlier years.'[12] The reluctance of the industrial countries to register their votes against these NIEO demands, and their willingness to sit still and allow them to take the form of uncontested UN General Assembly resolutions, was a symbol of the extent to which these countries were for a while uncertain about the situation they faced and how best to proceed, following the oil crisis and related events of this period.

The set of demands for the NIEO was presented in a package of three documents: the Declaration and the Programme of Action, adopted at the sixth Special Session of the GA, and a Charter of Economic Rights and Duties of States. Work on the Charter started as a result of a resolution adopted at the third UNCTAD conference in Santiago in 1972; the draft document would be debated at the 29th session of the GA in the autumn of 1974. The relationship between the three documents was as follows: the Declaration contained a list of general principles which should guide the new international order; the Programme of Action translated these principles into concrete actions and measures; and the Charter was to provide a legal framework to give effect to the NIEO. Basically, all three documents cover the same issues from different points of view. While the first two documents were adopted without dissent at the sixth Special Session of the GA in April 1974, the Charter was adopted only at the 29th regular session in the autumn of 1974, by which time the developed countries had somewhat regained their composure from the oil shock and were able to register their opposition to the proposals contained therein. The Charter was therefore adopted by vote, with the industrial countries voting against or abstaining; it therefore has a somewhat different status from the two other NIEO documents.

It will not be necessary to review these documents here. The NIEO has spawned a large literature of a descriptive, analytic, critical and supportive nature, and a good deal of useful material has long been widely available.[13] Our comments here can therefore be quite selective.

From the point of view of the developing countries, of course, the reason for demanding the NIEO is that the old order, built by the rich, is unjust, unduly favouring the rich to the detriment of the poor. In the words of the Algerian President in his address to the sixth Special Session of the GA, 'Inasmuch as [the old order] is maintained and consolidated and therefore thrives by virtue of a process which continually impoverishes the poor and enriches the rich, this economic order constitutes the major obstacle standing in the way of any hope of development and progress for all the countries of the Third World.'[14] Put in these blunt terms, the issue becomes one of confrontation and not of co-operation, since the rich are being asked to agree to change an economic order which assures their continuous enrichment, for one which presumably will be less efficacious from this point of view.[15] In the circumstances, only by convincing the North that they do not have the option of continuing with business as usual, and of the dire consequences of non-cooperation with the South in their efforts to change the economic order, could the South hope to get the co-operation of the North in this regard.

Broadly speaking, the demands made in the NIEO were of three kinds: those asserting general rules and principles which should guide international economic relations; those calling for international action on specific issues or for changes in international institutions or the creation of new institutions and mechanisms; and those calling plainly and simply for the developed countries to take specific actions or measures at the national level favourable to the developing countries. These three categories may not always be that distinct, and there are demands that are sometimes so vague and addressed to no one in particular that they do not fall into any of these categories. This seems nonetheless a useful way of organizing the discussion.

The idea of new rules and principles to govern international economic relations was in a sense at the very centre of the demands for a new international economic order. But it is quite clear that, in themselves, rules and principles are only words on paper, and are only meaningful to the extent that they actually provide a guide to action and behaviour. Thus, whether adopted unanimously or by vote, only the future could tell whether the new rules and principles would make any difference to the actual conduct of international relations in the years ahead. Hence the issues here were not really considered to be of burning importance.

In fact, among the broad range of issues that fell into this category the only ones that were the subject of keen debate and controversy were those involving the related issues of permanent sovereignty over natural resources, the control of transnational corporations, nationalization, jurisdiction over foreign invest-ment disputes and compensation. These were issues of very practical day-to-day concern to both developed and developing countries, and the latter were by no means passive bystanders awaiting the agreement of the former to move ahead in implementing the new principles. In fact, for some time they had been taking matters into their own hands, and had been increasingly asserting the right of national control over key sectors of their economies, such as mining, banking and public utilities, where foreign companies had traditionally held sway. The Egyptian take-over of the Suez Canal in 1956 was perhaps the first major successful example of this trend, and the latest action by OPEC was only the pinnacle of a trend that had been underway for some time. By calling for the adoption of new rules and principles in this area, the developing countries were therefore seeking international codification and approval of what they were doing anyway. It was because of the immediate practical importance of the issues raised that they were the subject of such heated debate. The importance of this issue is highlighted by Meagher when he remarks, 'Most agree that consensus on these points [relating to private foreign investment] would have made possible an overall consensus on the Charter.'[16]

The demands in the third category could also be handled without too much difficulty. These took the form largely of exhortations and pleadings, and were not likely to give rise to commitments of a legal or contractual nature. Concessions granted, and commitments made, are easily diluted or ignored; witness, for example, the aid commitments made in the early 1960s, honoured more in the breach than in the observances. In many cases, in fact, the demands were put in such vague terms that even monitoring could not be meaningfully undertaken. These demands could therefore be treated somewhat lightly, and were thus not at the core of the NIEO.

It was the demands falling in the second category that would be the principal subjects of debate and the main issues around which confrontation and dialogue would take place. These were indeed expected to give rise to, or to affect, commitments of a legal or contractual nature. Agreement in principle on these demands would lead to the necessary follow-up action preceding implementation. It was here therefore that the main operational aspects of the NIEO, in terms of the capacity of the international community to implement measures and actions, would lie.

The major issues on which international action was called for covered three subject areas: raw materials, money and finance, and preferences. Not surprisingly in the circumstances, it was in the area of raw materials that the most complex and far-reaching proposals appeared.[17] In the area of money and finance, the demands were also quite comprehensive, if not as far-reaching.[18] Preferences are a subject with which we are already familiar from the previous chapter; the call here was for the implementation, improvement and enlargement of the scheme already agreed in principle. In addition, there were proposals for international codes of conduct on the transfer of technology, and on transnational corporations, intended to protect the interests and meet the needs of developing countries.

Implementing the NIEO

With the NIEO now adopted and having the status of General Assembly resolutions, there remained only the question of its implementation. As implied by the discussion above, this concerned largely the issues falling under the second of our categories. The main forums where the negotiations on implementation were to take place were the seventh Special Session of the GA in September 1975, the Conference on International Economic Co-operation (CIEC), which took place intermittently in Paris between 1975 and 1977, and the fourth UNCTAD conference which took place in Nairobi in May 1976.

The seventh Special Session, originally intended to be devoted to the wider problems of development and international economic co-operation, provided the occasion for a follow-up on the NIEO negotiations, and marked an important turning point in the evolution of the North-South confrontation during these years. At this meeting Henry Kissinger, the US Secretary of State, delivered a major speech which reflected a significant shift in the US position towards a more conciliatory approach, more in tune with European thinking. This set a more positive tone for the deliberations which focused on the developing countries' demands for an NIEO. The debates revealed that the basic differences between the two groups remained unbridged, but also indicated a willingness on the part of the developed countries to display a more sympathetic attitude towards these demands. And while no definite agreement on any of the specific issues could be reached at the Special Session, they were disposed of in such a way as to raise hopes that meaningful concessions would be made in meeting these demands. The whole conundrum of issues falling under raw materials (price indexation, terms of trade, commodity agreements and buffer stocks), as well as the problem of debt and the question of a code of conduct on the transfer of technology, were shifted to the forthcoming UNCTAD conference. Regarding a number of issues relating to the international monetary system and the financial institutions, the developed countries either agreed in principle to go some way in meeting the demands or to give consideration to doing so. It was thus agreed that the IMF's Compensatory Financing Facility would be expanded and liberalized, that the Fund's Buffer Stock Facility would be liberalized and that a study would be undertaken of possible amendments to IMF rules to permit the provision of assistance to international buffer stocks, and that the process of decision-making in the financial institutions was to be fair and responsive 'in accordance with existing and evolving rules'. Consideration was also to be given to an SDR-aid link, and to the establishment of an IMF Trust Fund for assistance to developing countries. Expressions of willingness to make best efforts to meet some of the demands requiring action by developed countries at national level, for example involving market access, aid, and so on, were also made.

All in all, the seventh Special Session ended in a rather up-beat and optimistic mood in terms of meeting NIEO objectives. Below the surface, however, very little of a concrete nature had been achieved, and it is fair to say that the optimism was based more on vague promises and on a willingness to introduce relatively minor reforms than on any commitment to fundamental restructuring of economic relations.

It is interesting to note that while the developing countries maintained their unity and negotiated as a group, the developed countries showed much greater signs of disunity. The main thrust of the developing countries' demands, visible in the whole range of issues raised - price indexation, integrated commodity programmes, regulation and control of transnational corporations, code of conduct on transfer of technology, compensatory financing - was based on the ideal of comprehensive, interventionist measures to regulate and direct the market mechanism. In this framework, the United States, West Germany and Japan were at the free market end of the spectrum, and the most hostile to the NIEO demands; most of the European countries accepted limited forms of intervention and occupied the middle ground; while the Scandinavians, Australia, New Zealand and, to some extent, Canada were the countries most sympathetic to the interventionist goals.[19]

The CIEC was a rather special event. As we mentioned earlier, it originated from a French initiative to convene a conference on energy involving a small number of countries representing the oil producing and consuming states, the latter including both developed and developing countries. The oil exporters objected to the focus on energy and insisted on an agenda covering the broader issues of raw materials and development. It was eventually decided that the conference would cover four topics: energy, raw materials, development, and finance, and each would be assigned to a separate commission. Twenty-seven countries were invited, nineteen developing and eight developed. The conference met on and off during 1975 and 1976, but failed to achieve any spectacular results. This was reflected in the communique issued by the final ministerial meeting in June 1977. The developed countries failed to achieve any agreement on energy, the issue of most interest to them (for example, with respect to pricing, continuing consultations, etc.), and failed to make any meaningful concessions on issues of interest to the developing countries. The conference therefore petered out, and can scarcely be said to have been a useful exercise.

UNCTAD IV: the climax of the confrontation

The fourth UNCTAD conference, held in Nairobi in May 1976, will probably go down in history as the high water mark of this process of confrontation and dialogue that we have been discussing, a process which started to gather force in the 1950s, gained considerable momentum in the 1960s, and in the 1970s reached such intensity and caused such commotion that for a while it seemed that something would give, that some of the basic demands of the developing countries for changes in the world economic order would be met. That the conference would be important stemmed from the fact that, in the atmosphere of goodwill prevalent at the seventh Special Session, it had been designated as the forum for resolving the issues raised in meeting some of the basic demands of the developing countries. It was natural, therefore, that it would generate high hopes and great expectations, that some efforts would be made to meet these hopes and expectations, and that it would be the scene of some drama.

As we mentioned earlier, the main issues referred to UNCTAD for follow-up action were those relating to raw material prices and commodity arrangements, debt, and transfer of technology. The main focus of attention, however, was to be on the raw materials and commodities issue. This was perhaps to be expected. The whole crisis of the 1970s had originated from developments affecting a major raw material, petroleum, and from the beginning the raw materials issue had been at the centre of the debates and discussions. This was also an area where developing countries saw definite scope for internationally sanctioned interventionist policies which could be of benefit to them. They had been groping and pushing for such policies since the 1950s, and now saw the way clear for a more determined presentation of their demands.

The UNCTAD secretariat, under the leadership of its new Secretary-General, Sri Lankan economist Gamani Corea, had taken quite seriously the ideas on the commodities issue contained in the NIEO demands, and had been elaborating and discussing with governments detailed proposals on the subject. By the time of the Nairobi conference, therefore, the secretariat was able to present for consideration a comprehensive, detailed and far-reaching set of proposals for international action in the field of commodities. The proposals carried the ambitious title of 'Integrated Programme for Commodities', and had, as one of their principal objectives, 'The establishment and maintenance of commodity prices at levels which, in real terms, are equitable to consumers and remunerative to producers, taking full account of the world rate of inflation.'[20] The heart of the programme was the operation of international buffer stocks to stabilize (and maintain) commodity prices, and to finance these commodity stocks it was proposed that a special commodities fund be established, referred to as a common fund. Seventeen commodities, accounting for about 75 per cent of developing countries' primary commodity exports (excluding petroleum), were identified for inclusion, of which 10 were considered suitable for stocking. For the programme to become operational, international agreements on the individual commodities covered would have to be separately negotiated. Prepared in consultation with the developing countries, and having their full support, the proposals quickly became the centre-piece of the conference.

They were received without enthusiasm by the industrial countries, particularly those, such as the US, West Germany and Japan, which espoused most strongly the principle of the supremacy of market forces. To them, the proposals were anathema, going against the very grain of their thinking. To try to go some way in meeting the concerns of developing countries dependent on commodities for their export earnings, the US had proposed, at the seventh Special Session of the GA, what Kissinger, who introduced the proposal, referred to as a 'development security facility'. Essentially, this proposal would amount to a substantially liberalized and extended version of the IMF's compensatory financing facility, linked to the IMF Trust Fund then under discussion. For these developed countries, compensatory financing was an acceptable method of dealing with the problems caused by fluctuations in export earnings, since it did not involve interference with commodity markets. But while the developing countries recognized an important role for compensatory financing, and indeed made provision for such financing in the integrated commodity programme, this did not deal with the range of issues for which they sought solutions. The idea of an 'international resources bank', also proposed by Kissinger at the Nairobi conference, should also be mentioned here. The idea was not well received by the developing countries, and came to nothing.

The specific proposal in the integrated programme most disturbing to industrial countries was for the establishment of a common fund to finance commodity stocks. They would be asked to make financial contributions to this fund the purpose of which they considered inimical to their interests and philosophically unsound. They therefore strongly opposed the idea of the common fund. For the rest, they would have no great objection to going along with the proposals since, in the absence of the common fund, they become far-fetched and hypothetical, raising more questions than they answered, and unlikely to lead anywhere. In essence, therefore, the negotiations were really over the question of whether support for the common fund could be achieved. At the same time, the commodities programme had become such a burning issue, had attracted such wide attention, and was being viewed by so many as a litmus test of the North's willingness to make some gesture towards meeting the demands of the South, that there was some considerable pressure to find a solution. An agreement was reached at the very last moment, and only after political intervention at a high level. The conference therefore ended with the adoption by consensus of a resolution which endorsed virtually the entire commodities programme proposed, and called for its implementation according to a tight time schedule, though not without some important nuances in the wording, particularly in relation to the common fund, which left exit doors open and minimized commitments. As far as it went, the developing countries therefore appeared to have achieved an important victory in securing the agreement of the North for moving ahead on one of the important planks in their platform. As we shall see, however, securing agreement in principle is one thing, achieving progress in implementation is quite another.

On the debt issue, the developing countries themselves were somewhat divided between those who wished to seek relief from their rising debt burden and those, such as Brazil and Mexico, who thought that requests for such relief might prejudice their standing in international capital markets to which they continued to have ready access. The developing countries therefore proposed that debt relief on official bilateral debt be accorded to those developing countries 'seeking such relief'. It was also proposed that commercial debt of 'interested' developing countries be consolidated and rescheduled, and that UNCTAD convene a debt conference to agree the details of a debt relief programme. The consensus resolution finally adopted at the conference fell far short of these goals, recognizing only the need for considering individual requests for debt relief, with 'appropriate existing forums' (meaning, of course, the Washington-based financial institutions) being invited to 'provide guidance in future operations relating to debt problems as a basis for dealing flexibly with individual cases.'[21] In fact, far from providing a framework for dealing with debt in a preventive and anticipatory way, the resolution that emerged gave more than a hint of the repressive and asphyxiating manner in which the debt problem would eventually be dealt with when it finally erupted as a major issue. But more on this later.

On the transfer of technology the main question concerned developing countries' access to technology on suitable terms. This question had been under debate at least since the first UNCTAD conference, and at the third conference in Santiago in 1972 a fairly comprehensive resolution on the subject was adopted calling for an intensification of UNCTAD's programme in the area and for developed countries to facilitate an accelerated transfer of technology to developing countries on favourable terms. Technology is a driving force in the development process, and in the nature of things developing countries are necessarily on the receiving end in its diffusion. Technology also has some peculiar features of a public goods nature that make it rather special. Once developed, there is a public interest in ensuring that technology is used for the public good and not just for the benefit of private interests. This is why national laws which recognize certain proprietary rights in new technology (in the interest of promoting the development of new technology) also imposes obligations on the holder of these rights regarding its use, diffusion, and so on. Developing countries felt that existing international rules, including the Paris Convention, did not serve their needs and should be revised. Appropriate changes in technology policy were therefore called for in the context of proposals for the NIEO. These changes, which were intended to improve the terms and conditions under which technology was made available to developing countries, would be incorporated into a compulsory code of conduct on the transfer of technology. The proposal for the negotiation of such a code was therefore at the centre of the discussion. Agreement was reached that work should proceed on the development of a code, but there was no agreement on the critical question of whether such a code would be binding.

The follow-up on implementing NIEO demands

We now raise the question of what concretely was achieved by these demands to restructure international economic relations, as reflected in the NIEO? Bearing in mind the three-way categorization of these demands made above, we may note that in respect of two of these (those relating to changes in international rules and principles and to national actions and policies of developed countries) the question does not admit of a straightforward answer. It would take extensive, qualitative, judgemental analysis to determine whether and to what extent the demands made in these areas actually affected relevant behaviour. On the basis of our own subjective impressions we suggest that the answer would be 'very little or not at all', but this is not a subject that is worth pursuing further here.[22] Only in respect to the third category, calling for international action in specific areas, does it seem useful to pose and try to answer the question.

We can identify at least four areas where demands for international action achieved enough consensus for implementation to be pursued. These relate to the commodities programme, preferences, the code of conduct on the transfer of technology, and various issues in the general area of money and finance. We shall now turn to the question of what exactly was achieved in these areas in terms of implementation, and say something as well about the significance of these achievements.

In the money and finance field the North was clearly prepared to make some concessions, not much to do with restructuring, of course, but in the nature of reforms and adaptation. Perhaps the most concrete result achieved was the liberalization in 1975 of the IMF's compensatory finance facility along the lines suggested by Kissinger (see p.121), and the implementation of the Trust Fund the following year. The liberalization involved an increase in drawings to 75 per cent of quotas and a modification of the method for computing compensable shortfalls. In 1976, 48 countries drew on the IMF facility. On average, their export earnings were 13 per cent lower in the shortfall year than in the preceding year, and the 1975 liberalization permitted drawings of SDR 2.35 billion, whereas only SDR 0.48 billion could have been drawn under the pre-1975 rules.[23] The Trust Fund, which was decided on at the Kingston meeting of the IMF in January 1976, provided for the profits from the sale of one-sixth of the IMF's gold holdings to be used to make loans on concessionary terms to the poorest developing countries - those with per capita incomes below SDR 300 in 1973. During the two-year period 1976-78 SDR 841 million were disbursed to 43 low-income developing countries, and during 1979 an additional SDR 350 million to 27 such countries. Disbursements from the Trust Fund thus averaged some SDR 20 million per country during 1976-78 and SDR 13 million in 1979. The loans were additional to normal drawings, carried low interest rates, had relatively long repayment periods, and involved minimal conditionality. They were therefore an important source of finance to the recipient countries, though, as has been pointed out elsewhere, the rich developed countries have gained far more from the revaluation of gold than have the poor countries from the operation of the Trust Fund.[24]

The fiasco of the Integrated Commodities Programme

Following the agreement in principle reached in Nairobi in April 1976 to proceed with implementation of the Integrated Commodities Programme, the momentum generated by the issue was maintained, and no time was lost in getting the necessary work under way. A hectic series of meetings and negotiations was organized, according to the two-pronged approach of the programme, calling for the negotiation of individual commodity agreements and a common fund. For the individual commodities, preparatory meetings were convened. It was clearly the intention that these preparatory meetings would lead to the negotiation of commodity agreements, and provision was made for such negotiations. For the common fund, preparatory meetings were also called for, their task being to prepare for a negotiating conference on a common fund which was to be convened not later than March 1977. The whole process of implementing the integrated programme was to be concluded by the end of 1978. Bearing in mind that 17 commodities were listed for inclusion in the programme, it will be apparent that implementation would be a highly charged affair.

While the pace of activities was intense, accomplishments were meagre. The conference on the common fund was duly convened in March 1977, but little progress was made in reaching agreement. It was resumed in November 1977 with similar results. The main difficulty of course was the deep disagreement between developed and developing countries as to the nature and purpose of the fund. The developed countries, which never really accepted the concept of a common fund, even when, to satisfy the political pressures of the moment, they lent their support to the resolution calling for it, were now insisting that the common fund should be financed by contributions from individual ICAs that cared to associate themselves with it, and that there was thus no need for direct government contributions. This was something quite different from the original concept, which was to have a fund with independent financial means which, by virtue of the financial resources at its disposal, could help to bring ICAs into being and could therefore play a catalytic role in controlling and stabilizing commodity markets. It was not until the third session of the negotiating conference in March 1979, almost 18 months after the previous session, that agreement was reached on the main elements of the common fund. This was to be a greatly scaled down and diluted version of the original concept. While the original proposals had envisaged a fund capitalized at US$6 billion, the eventual agreement called for capital contributions of merely US$470 million. Of this, US$400 million was to be available for the financing of commodity stocks and US$70 million for financing other measures through the so-called second window (soft loans for commodity development, productivity improvements, marketing, etc.). While the developed countries would contribute somewhat more than half of the capital, they would not command a majority of votes.

Since agreement was reached on this scaled-down version of the common fund in March 1979, there has been a distinct slackening of interest in the fund on all sides. Although all the technical work, regarding the drafting of the articles of agreement, and so on, had long been completed, little or nothing was done for many years to make the fund operational. Indeed it was not until 1988 that the formal conditions were met for the common fund to come into being (i.e. ratification by the required number of countries accounting for the required share of the capital stock). While the common fund has been technically operational now for some time, it is still largely dormant, and there is little prospect of it ever being involved in the financing of buffer stocks.[25]

Progress on individual commodities was equally disappointing. Of the 18 commodities included in the integrated programme, four (coffee, cocoa, sugar and tin) were already covered by agreements. Of the remaining fourteen, all except two (bauxite and bananas) had by 1979 been the subject of preparatory meetings under the integrated programme, and for many a large number of such meetings had been held. In respect to only three commodities did the preparatory process lead to the negotiation of ICAs (natural rubber, jute and tropical timber), and only in the case of natural rubber did the ICA involve market stabilization objectives of the type that the common fund was intended to support.

Progress on the common fund was always meant to bear close relation to progress on the negotiation of individual ICAs. But in view of the catalytic role that the common fund was expected to play in facilitating the negotiation of

ICAs, the time-table had called for the early completion of work on the common fund. That this was not achieved contributed to the slow progress of work on the negotiation of ICAs. On the other hand, this slow progress could be used (and was used) to question the need for a common fund. Slow progress on both fronts thus became mutually interactive and self-reinforcing, with the result that before long both ground to a virtual halt. In fact, by the early 1980s, interest in the integrated commodity programme had waned, and the excitement had completely disappeared. Nothing was left but faint memories of the often acrimonious confrontation and dialogue of the 1970s, a rump common fund that no one wanted nor knew what to do with, dying interest in ICAs, and a worsening of the problems of instability and price declines facing the developing primary commodity exporters. This was clearly an initiative that had failed, that had raised high hopes and given rise to a lot of implementation activity but that had finally been abandoned, having accomplished nothing of value (except perhaps for having created a few jobs in the international bureaucracy). What went wrong?

The commodities programme has been criticized on a host of grounds. The criticism is on three levels: that the objectives sought are not appropriate or valid; that the means proposed for achieving the objectives are by no means the best or most appropriate available; and that, over and above everything else, there were some enormous technical and practical difficulties in implementing the programme that would in any event probably have rendered it impractical.

Thus it is questioned whether price stabilization is a suitable objective for international policy. A more suitable objective, it is argued, would be the stabilization of export earnings of developing countries, and this would require a different policy response, for example compensatory financing. As to the objective of maintaining 'equitable' prices, never fully articulated in the commodities programme, this is dismissed on the grounds that it would amount to a form of income transfer or aid, and that it would be an inefficient (and inappropriate) way to provide aid. Furthermore it is questioned whether buffer stocks could achieve the price stabilization (or price maintenance) objectives, except perhaps at costs far in excess of the estimates put forward in the UNCTAD proposals. The technical and practical difficulties of implementing such a complex and over-arching scheme are left to the imagination.

These criticisms, which abound in the academic and other writings emanating from the North, certainly have their merit.[26] They are not, however, the overriding consideration. The fact is that there was no imperative political consideration that would have induced the industrial countries to adopt such a programme, which would have been costly to them, potentially open-ended, and was intended for the benefit of only the developing countries. Where such political imperatives exist, ambiguities of objectives, inappropriateness of means, and technical difficulties and complexities are no barriers to action, as is witnessed, for example, by the case of the EEC Common Agricultural Policy. This ambitious programme was from the outset, therefore, doomed to lead to a dead end.

Other issues

Agreement in principle to proceed with preferences (GSP) was reached at the New Delhi conference of UNCTAD in 1968, but it was only in the 1970s that implementation really got under way. The US was the last of the developed countries to implement preferences, which it did in 1976. While, in general, the schemes provide for duty-free treatment of manufactured goods exported by developing countries, they are subject to exceptions and limitations (tariff quotas, ceilings, maximum country amounts, and, in the case of the US, to products for which developing countries do not demonstrate competitiveness!) that greatly limit their usefulness. Textiles and clothing, the manufactured product of greatest export interest to developing countries, are excluded.

There has been a good deal of debate about how useful the GSP has been to developing country exporters. According to UNCTAD studies, US$28 billion of exports from developing countries received preferential treatment in 1982, and about one-quarter of these exports may be attributable to GSP-induced trade expansion. The benefits, however, were not evenly distributed, with roughly a dozen of the industrially more advanced developing countries supplying 80 per cent or more of total preferential imports.[27] Other writers are not so sure, arguing that because of the exceptions and limitations, the schemes as implemented are a far cry from the GSP originally envisaged, and have not been effective in facilitating expansion of developing countries' exports. According to Kreinen and Finger, 'detailed studies of the GSP schemes have placed an upper limit on their value in promoting LDCs' exports at US$100 million a year.'[28] This seems a much more modest estimate of the value of the GSP. In addition, there is the uncertainty surrounding the GSP, the fact that the rules are not binding and can be (and have been) unilaterally changed by the donor countries, and the tendency in practice for the rules to be tightened in those cases where developing countries' exports begin to make significant inroads into the developed countries' markets.

Another factor limiting the usefulness of the GSP is that over the years, following the successive rounds of tariff negotiations under the GATT, tariffs have come to play a much reduced role in the trade policies of the developed countries, with non-tariff barriers (not covered by the GSP), increasingly being the major tool of trade policy. All in all, one can probably agree with those writers who argue that the importance attached to the GSP by the developing countries (and the energies they have expended in promoting its cause) has not been warranted by the results achieved.

On the transfer of technology, the Nairobi conference decided to establish an inter-governmental expert group to elaborate a draft code, and to convene a conference to negotiate a final text. In view of the continuing difference between developed and developing countries as to whether the code should be binding, the expert group was to 'formulate the draft provisions ranging from mandatory to optional, without prejudice to the final decision on the legal character of the code of conduct.' The negotiating conference was duly convened in October 1978, and made considerable progress in agreeing texts. On the vital question of the legal character of the code, however, no agreement could be reached. The developing countries maintained that 'an international legally binding instrument is the only form capable of effectively regulating the transfer of technology', while the developed countries took the position that the code should consist of voluntary and non-binding guidelines which 'neither alter nor in any way supersede national or international law nor the responsibilities of States thereunder or as set forth in international treaties or agreements.'[29] There was therefore an unbridgeable chasm between the two groups, with the developed countries absolutely refusing to countenance any change in the existing international order in this area. The negotiations eventually fizzled out, and the attempt by the developing countries to introduce an international code on the subject of technology transfer failed.

A summing up

We may conclude from the discussion so far that, notwithstanding the great fanfare and hooting of horns that accompanied the demands of the developing countries for a new international economic order, at the end of the day, when things had quietened down and stock been taken, precious little had been achieved in meeting any of these demands. The reasons for this outcome are not difficult to discern. In retrospect, it now seems clear that the new-found strength of the developing countries following the launching of the oil weapon and the accompanying raw materials crisis was at the time greatly exaggerated on all sides. The industrial countries, led by the United States, quickly recovered their composure and soon realized that no significant shift in the fundamental balance of international economic forces had really taken place (or need take place, if appropriate policy responses were forthcoming). The developing countries probably continued for a longer time to believe that a significant shift had taken place, though it is always difficult to distinguish between the rhetoric and the underlying appreciation of the situation. But given the fact that the oil and raw materials crises were quickly seen as temporary and passing, it was inevitable that the efforts to bring about basic changes in the structure of international economic relations would fail.

The response of the industrial countries to the crisis was to distinguish between the short-term and long-term aspects, and to take action appropriate to each case. The short-term problem was largely one of financing burgeoning balance-of-payments deficits and of adapting to the sudden fall in real purchasing power. The long-term problem was that of making the necessary adaptations to facilitate the substitution of other forms of energy for petroleum and, even more importantly as it turned out, to economize on the use of energy and of raw materials generally. In fact, having put their minds to it, this latter policy was carried out so effectively that by the 1980s such economies had been achieved in energy and raw materials use, that the boot was now firmly on the other foot, and the situation more one of glut than of shortage. In fact, it now seems clear that one of the long-term responses was a reorientation of the priorities of industrial research with the aim of maximizing savings in energy and raw materials use. The result is that economic growth in industrial countries now requires proportionately much less energy and raw materials inputs than previously, with corresponding reductions in the demand for the output of these sectors on which developing countries are so dependent for export earnings. In this respect, therefore, the effect of the response was to permanently reduce the dependence of the industrial countries on inputs derived from developing countries, to the disadvantage of the latter.

As far as the developing countries are concerned, it now seems clear that, given the underlying balance of economic forces, too much energy was expended in trying to force systemic changes on the unwilling industrial countries, and insufficient attention paid to the important question of how best to adjust to the short-term disturbances so as to least disturb long-term growth prospects. It should have been apparent that behind the rhetoric and the diplomatic and political manoeuvrings that so dominated the international economic scene during these years, the economic impact of the events of this period was the underlying reality, and that the manner in which countries responded to these events would have an important bearing on how relative economic power was distributed, and hence would be a critical factor in the potential for eventually bringing about changes in the world economic order. We may usefully conclude here therefore with a brief review of how various groups of countries responded to the events of this period and of the economic legacy left by these events.

Following the rise in oil prices the oil exporting developing countries were in the position of seeing their export earnings register massive increases, which in the short term they were unable to convert into increased imports. The result was that they generated large surpluses in their balance of payments. For the oil exporters as a group, the cumulative total of this surplus during the years 1972-77 amounted to some US$310 billion. The other side of this surplus was the corresponding deficit generated by the rest of the world. Bearing in mind that about 80 per cent of oil exports went to the industrial countries, they were the ones to carry the bulk of this deficit in the first instance. The major part of the task of recycling these surpluses to make them available to finance the deficits was carried out by the commercial banks, although some direct investments, as well as some direct loans, also played a role. It was not long, however, before the industrial countries were able to make the necessary adjustment to the new situation. For some, for example West Germany and Japan, the adjustment was so rapid that balance-of-payments deficits were quickly converted into surpluses, while for others the adjustment took somewhat longer, but was soon achieved. An important factor in this adjustment process was the sharp recession induced in the industrial countries during 1973-75, and the resulting fall in the volume of imports into these countries (augmented by a fall in prices of non-oil primary commodities). Equally important was the rapid increase in demand for imports of manufactures into the oil exporting counties precipitated by the massive increase in their export revenue. This demand (together with import demand into other developing countries, which were able to maintain relatively high growth-rates of income and investment) provided major new markets to sustain export growth in the industrial countries, and contributed in no small way to the rapid turn-around in their balance of payments. The importance of this factor is reflected in the very rapid rate at which exports from the industrial countries to OPEC countries grew during these years (between 1972 and 1977 the growth of these exports averaged 44 per cent per annum), and by the marked increase in the share of total exports of the industrial countries destined for OPEC countries (from 3.6 per cent in 1970 to 9.1 per cent in 1978).

It is now apparent that the oil exporters were for the most part profligate and intemperate in the haste with which they went about the task of spending their new-found wealth. The speed with which large new capital projects were conceived, planned and executed could not but give rise to a great deal of waste, over-pricing, and excess profits, to the overwhelming benefit of the main contractors and suppliers who happened to be based in the industrial countries, and who were thus able quickly to recapture the surplus revenue accruing to the oil exporters. Lacking the institutional depth and social and political cohesion necessary to use the sudden flood of new-found wealth effectively in promoting long-term economic growth, there was a tendency in many of these countries towards widespread inefficiency, corruption and wanton waste. The spectacle of dozens of merchant ships standing idle for months off the coast of Nigeria, filled with cement they were unable to unload because of a lack of port facilities, of having no clear idea as to what purpose the cement was to be put if it was ever unloaded, and of the frightening cost to Nigeria of this rather bizarre affair, was only one of the more sensational examples of this general lack of prudence shown by the oil exporters in husbanding and using their new-found wealth effectively for genuine economic development. The huge sums spent on arms also contributed to this waste and to the precipitate recycling of funds back to the industrial countries, leaving little of permanent benefit in terms of development potential in the newly rich oil states.

All this is not to suggest, of course, that nothing was done to improve the economic conditions and development potential of the oil exporters following the sudden rise in their export revenues. That is far from the case. What we are emphasizing here is the waste, imprudence and lack of foresight on the part of the oil exporters, and the manner in which the industrial countries were as a consequence quickly able to recapture the wealth brought about by the higher oil prices. Clearly, the thinly populated oil states of the Gulf region were so awash with cash that even with the waste they could still establish a full array of physical and social infrastructure to set the stage for long-term development. It was the heavily populated oil exporters (Indonesia, Nigeria, Venezuela, Mexico, Algeria, etc.) that most seriously failed to exploit the economic development potential that the boom made possible. And even more disturbingly, many of these countries were to emerge from the boom to find themselves in the debt trap.

The oil importing developing countries were able to maintain relatively high rates of economic growth during the 1970s in the face of oil price rises and other shocks, by running substantial current account deficits. For these countries as a group, the deficit rose from US$9 billion in 1973 to US$34 billion in 1975 and to US$45 billion in 1979. The financing of this growing deficit underwent important changes during the decade, reflected in particular by increasing reliance on borrowings from private capital markets, especially in the form of eurocredits made available through the commercial banks. Such credits were at floating interest rates, the interest-rate risks being transferred from the banks to the borrowing countries.

While the inflow of foreign credits was effective in sustaining growth-rates and maintaining development potential, it was also taking place on slippery ground. During the 1970s a number of voices were raised drawing attention to the danger hidden just below the surface from the debt build-up resulting from this borrowing. As we have already noted, the issue was an important item on the agenda at the third UNCTAD conference in 1976. Since then the debt build-up had continued at an even faster clip, against what must have seemed to many as a favourable background. According to an OECD report,[30] the explanation for the increasing 'privatization' of financial flows to developing countries lay in the

parallel evolution of international financial markets and creditworthy developing-country borrowers. The major increases in lending to developing countries by the international banks were effected against a record of strong economic growth, improving current-account balances and rising export volumes and prices...[furthermore]... interest burdens remained relatively small and inflation consistently reduced the real burden of the accumulating debt stocks.

But this rather optimistic assessment of the debt problem is contradicted by the same report when it points out that the lending technique itself 'appears to have reduced the incentive to base lending decisions on objective risk assessment, since the fees and margins of lenders and participants . . . depended on volume rather than attention either to prudent exposure limits or to the economic policies of borrowing countries.' Thus, with the large profits to be obtained up front clouding all prospect of prudent behaviour, there was a natural tendency to overlend (and overborrow). Not surprisingly, when the direction of the wind suddenly changed, the chickens would be coming home to roost, with serious consequences for the banks, but with devastating consequences for the developing countries, which were to find themselves caught in what can only be described as a debt trap, from which there would be no easy escape.

Notes

1. One arrangement that was soon to become institutionalized to deal with this and other problems of economic co-ordination is the annual economic summit of the major industrial countries, the so-called G-7 meeting.
2. See Chapter 2 above.
3. Manfred Tietzel, *Primary Commodities in the North-South Dialogue* (Friedrich-Ebert-Stiftung, 1979), p. 11.
4. Anthony Sampson, *The Seven Sisters* (Bantam Books, New York, 1975), p. 7.
5. See M. A. Adelman, *The World Petroleum Market* (Johns Hopkins University Press, Baltimore & London, 1972), p. 208, for details on payments per barrel through 1970. For Iran, for example, it peaked at 89.0 cents per barrel in 1957, fell to 74.5 cents per barrel in 1962, and was 80.8 cents in 1970. For Saudi Arabia it peaked at 88.2 cents in 1957, fell to 75 cents in 1960, and by 1970 was back at the 1957 level.
6. The figures in this paragraph are taken from Frank S. McFadzean, 'The Economics of the Energy Crisis,' appearing as chapter 7 in Hugh Corbet and Robert Jackson (eds.), *In Search of a New World Economic Order* (Croom Helm, for the Trade Policy Research Centre, London, 1974). According to McFadzean's projections made before the 1973 price increases, oil consumption in the main industrial regions of North America, Western Europe and Japan was expected to increase from 34 mbd in early 1970 to 75 mbd by the middle of the 1980s, at which time they were expected to be dependent on the Middle East and Africa for 90 per cent of their imports. Plans then afoot called for Saudi production capacity to rise to 20 mbd by the 1980s, at which rate the enormous Saudi reserves, the largest in the world, would be exhausted in 18 years!
7. Estimates of production costs at the time ranged from 10 to 30 cents per barrel. See Adelman *op. cit.*. See also Michael Tanzer, *The Political Economy of International Oil and the Underdeveloped Countries* (Beacon Press, Boston, 1969), p. 12.
8. For a more detailed account of this phase in the development of relations between the oil producers and the companies, including an analysis of some of the factors which made these developments possible, see Philip Connelly and Robert Perlman, *The Politics of Scarcity: Resource Conflicts in International Relations* (Oxford University Press, for The Royal Institute of International Affairs, London, 1975), pp 68-80.
9. Robert Solomon, *The International Monetary System, 1945-1981* (Harper &

Row, New York, 1982), chapter XVI for a discussion of some of these causes. See also Barry Bosworth and Robert Lawrence, *Commodity Prices and the New Inflation* (Brookings Institution, Washington, 1982).

10. See D. H. Meadows *et al, The Limits to Growth*, Report for the Club of Rome (Potomac Associates, New York, 1972).

11. In fact, the industrial countries accounted for about one-half of world exports of all primary products, compared with two-fifths for the developing countries, with the socialist countries accounting for the other one-tenth. On the other hand, the industrial countries accounted for 76 per cent of total world imports of primary commodities, and are heavily dependent on imports from developing countries for industrial raw materials. At the same time, industrial countries are major exporters of foodstuffs to developing countries. The pattern of dependence in the primary product sector is therefore quite complex.

12. Robert F. Meagher, *An International Redistribution of Wealth and Power: A Study of the Charter of Economic Rights and Duties of States* (Pergamon Press, New York, 1979), p. 5.

13. The reader is referred to W. M. Corden, *The NIEO Proposals: A Cool Look*, Thames Essay No. 21 (Trade Policy Research Centre, London, 1979), Appendix A, for a select bibliography; see also Lars Arnell and Birgitta Nygren, *The Developing Countries and the World Economic Order* (Frances Pinter Publishers Ltd, London, 1980), pp 175 ff for a more general bibliography. Meagher, *op.cit.*, is the best source on the legislative history of the Charter of Economic Rights and Duties of States, and is an excellent source on the NIEO as well.

14. Quoted in Meagher, *op.cit.*, p.3.

15. In effect, we are dealing here with what economists call a zero-sum game, where the gains of one side represent the losses of the other, and where there is therefore no scope for mutually advantageous compromises.

16. Meagher, *op.cit.*, p. 51. The issue which caused the greatest difficulty in these negotiations revolved around jurisdiction over compensation disputes. The developing countries insisted that local laws should apply, while the industrial countries were equally insistent that 'international laws' should be applicable, meaning that in the event of nationalization, compensation should be, in their words, 'prompt, adequate, and effective.'

17. These called, among other things, for the indexing of the prices of raw materials to those of manufactured goods, for commodity agreements in order to stabilize commodity prices, for the preparation of an integrated programme for a comprehensive range of commodities, for buffer stocks financed by international financial institutions, and for improved compensatory financing mechanisms.

18. Action called for included the effective participation of developing countries in the decision-making relative to the reform of the international monetary system, the establishment of a link between SDRs and development financing, more effective participation of developing countries in the decision-making process of the IMF and the World Bank, improved access to IMF resources, and measures

to mitigate the debt burden of developing countries.

19. See B. Gosovic and J. Ruggie, 'On the Creation of a New International Economic Order: Issue Linkage and the Seventh Special Session of the UN General Assembly,' *International Organization*, (Spring 1976).

20. See *Proceedings of the United Nations Conference on Trade and Development, Fourth Session*, Volume III, p. 3.

21. See *Ibid.*, Vol. II, p. 17 for the text of the resolution on debt.

22. We should perhaps qualify this somewhat since some action on the aid front, particularly in the smaller developed countries, was probably spurred on by these demands or in any event by the atmosphere thereby created. Except in areas where developing countries could take action themselves to put into effect principles which they advocated (for example on issues relating to the exercise of national sovereignty), it is doubtful whether the rules and principles set forth in the NIEO have greatly influenced international behaviour.

23. See Meagher, *op.cit.*, p. 139.

24. See Graham Bird, 'The IMF and the Developing Countries: Evolving Relations, Use of Resources and the Debate over Conditionality', Working Paper No.2 (Overseas Development Institute, London, March 1981), p. 17. See also p.160 of the present work for a reference to the impact of the revaluation in the price of gold on the reserves of developed countries.

25. Ironically, while the US was conspicuously active during the common fund negotiations in watering down the scope of the fund from the original intentions, it was alone among the major developed countries subsequently to decline membership in even this watered-down version. By so doing it contributed further to dimming the prospects of the fund.

26. See Mordechai E. Kreinen and J. M. Finger, 'A critical Survey of the New International Order,' *Journal of World Trade Law*, Vol. 10 (1976) for a useful summary of these criticisms. See also Robert L. Rothstein, *Global Bargaining: UNCTAD and the Quest for a New International Economic Order* (Princeton University Press, Princeton, New Jersey, 1979), Chapters 2-4, for a wide-ranging critique of the politics and the economics of the programme. A point made by Rothstein that is worth noting here concerns the fact that among the developing countries themselves there were varying degrees of support for the programme, reflecting divergences in their commodity interests and the resulting differential impact that the programme was likely to have on their respective economies. This made it all the more unlikely that the developed countries would feel obliged to support it, given their underlying misgivings.

27. See *The History of UNCTAD 1964-84* (United Nations, New York, 1985), p. 110.

28. Kreinen and Finger, *op.cit.*, p. 497.

29. *Proceedings of the United Nations Conference on Trade and Development, Fifth session*, Vol. III, p. 216.

30. OECD, *Twenty-Five years of Development Co-operation: A Review* (Paris, 1985), p. 167.

6. The Counter-revolution of the 1980s: the Age of the Radical Right

Background to the economic revolution

The 1980s ushered in a major shift in the orientation of economic thinking and policy-making in the developed world, a shift that made itself felt in the far corners of the globe. It permeated thinking and action world-wide and had profound implications for the North-South dialogue and for the manner in which North-South relations were henceforth conducted.

This shift was the aftermath of a breakdown of the economic policy consensus that had brought in its train more than two decades of almost uninterrupted economic growth and prosperity in the industrial North. The most important pillar of this consensus, and the key to the ensuing prosperity, was faith in the ability of governments to maintain rates of economic growth consistent with full-employment at stable prices by managing aggregate demand, using essentially Keynesian tools. The consensus was underpinned not only by the fact that the resulting prosperity tended to filter through to wide strata of the populations of these countries via the operation of market forces, but also, and especially, by the fact that it supported the emergence and spread of a social security system providing unemployment benefit, health, education, old-age pensions and other social benefits to the population at large. Demand management and the social security system went hand-in-hand, the latter complementing the former in playing the role of automatic stabilizer in the maintenance of steady non-inflationary growth.

Up to the late 1960s, the results achieved were such as to give little reason to doubt the efficacy of the assumptions on which this prosperity was based, given the long, almost uninterrupted, period of steady economic growth, low inflation, and low unemployment experienced by the industrial countries as a whole during the 1950s and 1960s. The experience of the 1970s, however, gave rise to grave doubts concerning the continued validity and relevance of the underlying model. Inflation, previously well under control, was now high and rising, and became an increasingly worrying problem. For the industrialized countries as a group, the rate of inflation averaged 12.3 per cent per annum during 1973-75, and, after falling somewhat, accelerated again to reach a level of close to 13 per cent by the turn of the decade, and this after averaging rates of only 2-3 per cent per annum during the 1950s and 1960s.[1] In some industrial countries, for example the UK, Italy and the US, inflation rates during the 1970s were much higher and more worrying.

Accompanying this upsurge in inflation was a distinct tendency towards a slow-down in the rate of growth of GDP. From averages of 4.7 and 5.8 per cent per annum during the 1950s and 1960s, respectively, the rate of growth of GDP for the industrial countries as a group fell to 3.2 per cent per annum during the 1970s. There was also a marked tendency towards rising unemployment, particularly in some of the major European countries, for example France, Germany and the UK, where unemployment had previously been kept to very low levels.[2] The result was the emergence of a new phenomenon, the co-existence of high and rising inflation with low and falling GDP growth-rates, soon christened stagflation. This phenomenon went against the grain of established thinking concerning the relationship between unemployment and inflation, thinking which provided a large part of the theoretical underpinning for the contemporary macro-economic policy framework.

The problems posed by this turn of events in the industrial countries were put very succinctly in a report to the OECD by a group of independent experts published in 1977. The report states:[3]

In the quarter of a century following World War II, the industrial world enjoyed growth to an extent unprecedented in economic history. In part, this was due to the process of post-war reconstruction, rapid and widespread technological progress, stable supplies of raw materials and energy, and the rise in volume of international trade. This potential for rapid growth would not have been realized, however, had it not been for the favourable economic climate created by governments - first by their assumption of responsibility for the achievement of high employment, and second through their commitment to economic integration in the framework of an open multilateral system for international trade and payments.

During recent years, by contrast, the industrial economies have experienced substantial slack in the use of their productive potential, and both unemployment and inflation remain disquietingly high in all but a few countries. Adjustment among the industrialized countries to the new situation created by large OPEC financial surpluses has been unsatisfactory. And there is some danger that the edifice of free trade, so carefully built, may begin to disintegrate.

In the light of these developments, public confidence in the ability of governments to manage the economy has waned, and belief in the likelihood or even desirability of continuing economic growth in the industrialized world has weakened.' (Italics added)

In the ensuing debate a number of underlying factors were put forward to explain the onset of this malaise.[4] Some thought the trade unions were to blame, having become too strong, operating under the cover of laws which provided them with excessive protection and which sometimes allowed them to hold whole industries to ransom and to bring entire economies to a standstill. Others drew attention to trade union practices that introduced excessive rigidities into the work place, denying industries the capacity to display the requisite flexibility in adaptating to changing technological and market conditions. Much was also made of the importance of unemployment insurance and other features of the social security system in making labour less mobile and less responsive and adaptable to changing circumstances.

Then there was the more general question of the role of government in the economy, with many arguing that government had become too big, too all-embracing, and too pervasive, to the extent that it was now a major factor in stifling initiative and dampening growth potential. This argument was supported by reference to data on the share of national income taken in taxes and spent by government. These data show that over the two decades leading up to the early 1980s, general government expenditure as a percentage of GDP increased, for the industrial countries as a group, by 21 percentage points, to represent by 1982 just under 50 per cent of GDP, having grown during these years on average about 2.9 per cent per year faster than the value of economic output.[5] Expenditure on social services (education, health, housing and community services) and on social security transfer payments (e.g. pensions, family allowances, unemployment compensation), together with interest payments on the rising public debt, accounted for the predominant share of rising government expenditure. The OECD report remarks:[6] 'These changes testify to the significant increase in the role of the public sector and, in particular, governments' greater role in the redistribution of income and the collective welfare state responsibility for the financial risks associated with economic perturbations, old age and sickness.'

While there were significant differences between individual industrial countries in the share of government expenditure in national income, they all displayed this upward trend, though even here there were important differences, with the share rising least noticeably in the case of the US. It is also worth noting that among the industrial countries there does not appear to have been any obvious relationship between economic performance and either the share of government expenditure in GDP or the rate of increase of this share, thereby casting somewhat in doubt the relevance of this factor. But this is another matter that need not detain us.

Much has also been written about the emergence of structural maladjustments during the 1970s as a factor in the economic malaise, and of the resulting need for major programmes of industrial restructuring. The restructuring process, it was argued, was being hemmed in and rendered difficult to achieve by inherited rigidities and inflexibilities in the economy, and these needed to be removed or alleviated if the process was to proceed successfully, structural maladjustments corrected, and the economy put on a proper long-term growth path in keeping with the new realities. The rigidities and inflexibilities included some of the aspects mentioned earlier, 'such as' the role of the labour unions, the impact of the social security system, and the heavy weight of government in the economy. This latter point referred not only to the question of the share of government expenditure in national income, discussed above, but equally importantly, to the role of government in regulating and controlling economic activity. Many voices thus began to be heard arguing that this role had become overbearing, that government was now meddling too much in various aspects of economic activity that need not concern it, and that this over-regulation by government was stifling private initiative and preventing the economy from achieving its full potential for growth. This aspect was considered particularly important in view of the demands of new and emerging technologies requiring, according to this line of thought, unprecedented levels of flexibility and initiative which could not be achieved in a highly regulated environment.

The ultra-conservatives take over

Given the reality of the economic malaise, which had become the growing preoccupation and concern, these arguments, plausible and immediately appealing, fell on sympathetic ears, and were to have a major impact on public thinking and public policy.[7] In fact, they were to lead to what can only be described as a revolution in the economic policy matrix in the industrial West. As usual in the post-war world, the US was to be the pacesetter in this policy revolution, at least in the popularization of the doctrine and the spreading of the message, followed on its heels by the UK. In the US the new doctrine would come into full bloom during the presidency of Ronald Reagan, the darling of the far right, who conducted his presidential campaign largely on the slogan that government was too big and should be reined in. In the UK at about the same time, Margaret Thatcher, the in-coming Conservative Prime Minister, came to office fully converted to the virtues of the new doctrine, of which she became a passionate advocate and a resourceful exponent. Her task in this regard was an especially difficult one, given the extent to which the economic policy framework based on Keynesian full-employment doctrines had permeated and dominated all strata of economic thinking and expectations in the UK.

In the US, the new thinking had begun to take hold and to influence policy actions even before the accession of Reagan to the presidency. It was under the Carter Administration that deregulation first began to raise its head as an explicit policy objective, intended to expose the industries concerned to greater competition, with beneficial effects for consumers. It was also under the Carter Administration that a determined attack on the inflation problem through a strict monetarist approach to macro-economic policy was first attempted, reflected in the appointment of Paul Volcker to the chairmanship of the Federal Reserve Board and in the use that began to be made of monetary targets as the major control variable in the quest for macro-economic stability. These were the beginnings of the sea-change in economic policy that was to sweep the American body politic during the 1980s. The fact that they started under President Carter serves only to underline the fact that the time was ripe for radical changes in policy direction, and that it only required someone on the scene to capture the new mood.

Ronald Reagan came to the White House fully prepared to do so. He brought with him what seemed to many a strange new ideology, inherited from the ultra-conservative far right, together with great skills as a communicator able to reach the soul of the American heartland. He was therefore able to lead a virtual revolution in US economic policy making. The theoretical foundations of the new policy framework were provided by what came to be known as supply-side economics. The essence of this new doctrine is its assertion that an appropriate supply response is not assured by the adoption of Keynesian aggregate demand policies, but that such response requires purposeful specific policies directed to the supply side of the economy. In fact an increase in demand, it says, where the natural incentives to economic growth are being stifled, will result simply in inflation. The economic malaise, stagflation and slow productivity growth characteristic of the 1970s were attributed to the neglect of appropriate supply side policies. And what is the recommended policy response? First and foremost, a lightening of the tax burden, particularly on corporations and on individuals in the higher income brackets, with emphasis on reductions in the marginal tax rates. The purpose of this policy of tax reductions is to provide greater stimulus to investment, savings and work incentives, and thereby to expand the capacity of the economy to produce goods and services efficiently.

In its extreme form, the theory asserts that a tax reduction along the lines envisaged need not (or would not) result in a reduction in government revenues and an increase in the deficit, in view of its powerful stimulating effect in raising output and income, and hence the tax base. Thus, according to one of the foremost exponents of the new economics, 'Those who argue against tax cuts because they are inflationary or who demand matching spending cuts are not true supply-siders.'[8]

Other related policy responses include a general reduction in the role of government in the economy. This involves reducing government expenditures, particularly in the areas of social welfare, health and education, income support payments, etc., which are considered to have gone too far and to have introduced undesirable rigidities, and in any event are better left to private initiative. There was also need for reductions in government regulations affecting business. Such regulations were considered to be too pervasive to the extent of stifling business. Then of course there was the focus on monetary policy as the basic tool for macro-economic stability, replacing the previous Keynesian emphasis on fiscal policy. Strict monetarism, based on targets for monetary growth, would now be the order of the day, with interest rates being left to find their own levels. Over and above everything else in this new policy environment is the primordial importance that was attached to the role of the market, to private initiative and to private enterprise as the key to the promised land of economic progress and prosperity. This was the economic programme proposed and pursued during the Reagan years.

In the UK, it was the Thatcherites, on the extreme right of the Conservative Party, who would be spearheading a similar revolution on their side of the Atlantic. Here the revolution would need to go even deeper, since government was, in relative terms, much bigger and more pervasive, taxes much higher, the social welfare system more firmly established and more far-reaching, the trade unions more securely entrenched and more powerful, and the population more tradition-bound and set in its ways. But revolution there was, and under the determined and resourceful leadership of Thatcher the 'new' economics found fertile soil in the UK. Taxes were reduced, strict monetarism introduced, the power of the trade unions curbed, and deregulation advanced. Moreover, the British were to add a new dimension and a new catchword to the rhetoric of the revolution - privatization, a shibboleth that would soon be exported far and wide to become the guiding principle of policy-making worldwide. It must be noted for the record, however, that only limited progress was achieved in dismantling or curbing the social welfare system during the years of the Thatcher revolution.

As is not unusual in these matters, the US lead, supported and carried forward with such enthusiasm and fanfare by the British under Thatcher, soon began to set the standard for government policy in the industrial North, and while there would be considerable variation among the individual countries, the trend was clear, and soon there would be much talk in these countries about tax cuts, deregulation, freedom of markets, reducing the role of government in the economy, monetarism, and privatization. Only a few countries, like Switzerland and Japan, and to some extent West Germany, which had always gone their own way, and had been pretty successful, remained relatively aloof from this new trend, though not for any lack of sympathy with the basic philosophy behind it.

This new policy framework, with the philosophy and way of thinking which underpinned it, was to be a major factor in determining the course of North-South relations in the years ahead. The triumph of the ultra-conservatives, with their free-market no-nonsense approach to the poor in their own countries, was hardly the harbinger of a sympathetic approach to dealing with the problems of the South. And this lack of sympathy would soon be translated into concrete action. But first the policy framework itself would set the stage for putting the squeeze on the South, from which it would emerge chastened and greatly weakened, drained of any fighting spirit. And it was through pressures arising from the burden of debt that the squeeze would be tightened, and the new approach to policy make itself felt.

The debt build-up and the balance-of-payments squeeze

The 1970s witnessed a rapid increase in developing countries' external debt. For non-OPEC developing countries, external debt increased from US$130 billion in 1973 to US$612 billion in 1982, almost a five-fold increase, representing an average annual growth of 19 per cent. A number of OPEC countries not in capital surplus also borrowed heavily during this period (including Algeria, Ecuador, Indonesia, Nigeria and Venezuela), and accumulated debts totalling US$80 billion by 1982.[9] For the non-OPEC countries, the increase in the debt arose largely from the desire to maintain growth-rates and the development momentum in the face of the external shocks encountered during these years, in particular the increase in oil prices and the adverse impact on their export earnings of the induced recession in the industrial countries. In this respect they were fairly successful. During the 1970s non-oil developing countries achieved an average GDP growth rate of 5.5 per cent per annum, rather above the annual rate of 5 per cent averaged during the 1960s, and substantially above the rather modest rate of 3.3 per cent per annum achieved by the developed countries during the 1970s.

The significant feature of the debt build-up during the 1970s is the role played by the private banking sector in making funds available to developing countries at variable interest rates - usually LIBOR (London Inter-Bank Offered Rate) plus a margin. Of course, not all developing countries were able to borrow in this market, access to which was restricted to countries considered creditworthy by the banks. This criterion excluded most of the poorer countries, and meant that lending was concentrated in a few middle-income developing countries. Thus, while the share of private bank debt in the total external debt of developing countries increased considerably during the 1970s (to the extent that by the end of the decade, two-thirds of the total external debt was indexed to LIBOR), the bulk of this bank debt was being carried by a relatively small group of 10 or 12 countries. For the rest of the developing world, and particularly for the poorer countries, the more traditional forms of external finance derived from bilateral and multilateral official sources, continued to predominate. It is interesting to note, however, that notwithstanding these differences in sourcing, foreign debt grew during the 1970s at roughly the same rate in all three major regions of the developing world, by approximately 18.5 per cent per annum in Africa and Asia, and by 21 per cent per annum in Latin America.[10]

It has been widely argued that, for the most part, this borrowing by developing countries during the 1970s was warranted, given the conditions of the time and the use made of the borrowed funds in sustaining growth-rates and in maintaining the capacity to grow.[11] This view is supported by reference not only to the fairly satisfactory GDP growth rate achieved, but more particularly to the relatively high export growth registered by the non-oil developing countries during this period. As a result, between 1973 and 1980 the ratio of debt to export earnings increased only moderately, from 112.7 per cent to 121.9 per cent, and the debt service ratio (the ratio of debt service payments to export earnings) also showed only a moderate rise (from 15.9 per cent to 17.6 per cent between 1973 and 1980).[12]

This is not to argue, however, that the best use has always been made of borrowed funds during these years. Far from it. It is an incontestable fact that in a number of cases policies were pursued that led to large capital flight, with the borrowed funds being immediately re-exported abroad, leaving the country with the debt and no assets to show for it (the newly exported capital not being traceable to nationals and hence not identifiable as national assets). Countries where capital flight associated with foreign borrowing was most notorious included Venezuela and Mexico among the oil exporters, and Argentina among the oil importers. Such capital flight was invited by the extraordinary policy of maintaining at the same time significantly overvalued exchange rates and a fully convertible currency. It has been estimated that capital flight from these three countries between them amounted during 1981 and 1982 to something of the order of US$36 billion, accounting for nearly one-third of total debt in both Venezuela and Argentina and to approximately one-fifth in Mexico. And these are no doubt only the most dramatic and well documented cases. One can only guess at what the magnitudes might be in countries like Nigeria (an oil exporter), Zaire or the Philippines, among others. The availability of easy credit from bankers eager to off-load their wares must have provided an irresistible temptation in many cases. And significantly, the great bulk of this capital flight took place after the tide had turned, high interest rates had become the order of the day, and it was clear that the days of easy credits would soon be over. It was like organizing a purposeful last minute escape before the gates were firmly shut.

Nevertheless, for the non-oil developing countries as a group, the debt picture through the end of the decade did not seem unduly alarming, given the underlying conditions of the period. These conditions included sustained world economic growth and high inflation rates in the industrial countries, particularly in the US, together with moderate nominal interest rates, resulting for much of the period in negative real interest rates on the external debt.[13] This was therefore a period favourable to borrowers, who became accustomed to low real (and moderate nominal) interest rates.

There was to be a rude shock, however, as the climate changed radically, bringing in its wake a triple squeeze that was to hit the non-oil developing countries severely. First, the doubling of the price of oil in 1979-80; second, a steep rise in interest rates as a result of the vigorous anti-inflation policy pursued in the United States using a wholly monetarist approach; and third, the induced recession resulting from the anti-inflation policy in the US and elsewhere in the industrial world. All three were to have a disastrous and immediate impact on the non-oil developing countries' balance of payments, the first by increasing the oil import bill, the second by increasing the cost of debt servicing, and the third by the negative effects it would have on export earnings, both in reducing export volumes and in precipitating a fall in commodity prices. Cline calculates that between them these three factors were responsible for a balance-of-payments loss of some US$141 billion for non-oil developing countries during 1981-82.[14]

For the group of mostly middle-income developing countries that carried the bulk of the bank debt, the critical factor in the squeeze was the steep rise in interest rates. From an average level of 6.6 per cent in 1976, the applicable interest rate on bank debt registered an almost three-fold increase, to 17.5 per cent by 1981. This, together with the downturn in export earnings, made the debt crisis inevitable. The problem was exacerbated by the peculiar version of Reaganomics being applied, which combined a tight anti-inflationary monetary policy with loose fiscal policies, resulting in high interest rates and an overvalued dollar. Since most of the developing countries' debt was denominated in dollars, the effect of the overvalued dollar was to make the debt burden even more onerous.

The IMF, the debt strategy and the debt trap

When the debt crisis broke, with the announcement by Mexico in August 1982 that it could no longer meet its debt service payments, it was immediately apparent that a major financial crisis was threatening. The Mexican announcement was thus only the sounding of the trumpet, since it was also clear that the other large developing country debtors to whom the major banks, particularly the large US banks, had lent heavily, were equally in trouble. Because the banks play such a critical role in the economy, and because their loans are so heavily leveraged on a small capital base, any significant default on outstanding debt could precipitate the insolvency of the banks and threaten the financial and economic stability of the major industrial countries in which the banks are based. And the exposure of the major US banks to some of the large debtors such as Mexico and Brazil was so great that extensive default on these loans would almost certainly bring these banks down and seriously threaten US and worldwide financial stability.[15] Not surprisingly, when the debt crisis broke, the international financial community, with the US in the lead, acted promptly to protect the banking system from the threat of default. Efforts focused on the major debtors whose default could do the greatest damage, particularly

Argentina, Mexico and Brazil, who between them owed US$31 billion to the nine largest banks, whose capital totalled only US$29 billion.

The IMF was to play a key role in the emergency rescue operation mounted to stave off default and avoid serious disruption to the financial system. Since the resources available to the Fund had fallen substantially in relative terms over the years (see below), the role of the Fund would be less that of provider of liquidity (the function that it was originally established to perform), and more that of bailiff and policeman acting on behalf of the creditors. In this capacity the role of the Fund was to extract the maximum possible debt service payments from debtor countries, with little regard to the effect that this would have on their economies. This operation was carried out by a carefully calibrated process of organizing just enough liquidity to the debtors via new bank loans (so-called 'involuntary' lending), reschedulings, World Bank lending, IMF loans, etc., to make it not worth their while to declare outright defaults (with all the costs to them that this would entail), and instead to continue co-operating with their creditors in servicing the loans. These policies were associated with the names of successive US Treasury Secretaries, first the Baker Initiative, then the Brady Plan.

The key to these initiatives was the policy package of austerity measures which it was the role of the Fund to impose on the debtor countries. The main objective was to secure a rapid reduction in the current account deficit, and this was to be accomplished by the vigorous application of standard deflationary measures of which the main elements consisted of tight monetary policies, high interest rates, cut-backs in government expenditures accompanied by increases in taxes and devaluation. These measures were duly applied and the current account deficit soon reduced or eliminated. Thus, for the 16 developing countries which together accounted for nearly 80 per cent of debt to the banks, the deficit fell drastically from US$54.4 billion in 1981 to US$4.5 billion in 1984.[16] But, as may be expected, the effect of these policy measures was to put the economies of the debtor countries into reverse gear, sending them reeling in a downward spiral towards economic depression. But the primary objective of the policy package was the collection of the debt and the protection of the interests of the creditors, and in this it largely achieved its aims.

From the point of view of the banks, the strategy for dealing with the debt problem can be said to have been quite successful. First, the chaos and possible ruin that they would have had to face from any major default on the part of developing debtor countries was averted. Second, they were able to earn substantial profits from the very manner in which the debt crisis was managed, given the high lending margins, of between 2 and 2.5 per cent, that were imposed during the restructuring negotiations, compared to margins of much less than 1 per cent applicable before the onset of the crisis.[17] And third, with the passage of time, the growth of profits (thanks partly to the debt crisis itself), and the diversification of the banks' loan portfolio away from developing country debt, the exposure of the banks to the developing countries would soon be substantially reduced, making them much less vulnerable to the debt problems of these countries.[18] For the banks, therefore, the debt crisis would soon be behind them, thanks largely to the energetic and resourceful role played by the IMF in keeping the debtor countries just afloat, their heads just above water, while supervising the extraction of the maximum possible debt service payments from them.

From the debtor developing countries' point of view, however, the outcome looked rather different. The sudden and massive policy-induced deflation to which they were subject meant a great deal of disruption to their social and economic life, and a major set-back to their long-term economic development prospects. It was in Latin America and in Africa, the two regions where the debt problems were most acute, that the disruptions were greatest. For developing countries as a whole, *per capita* GDP fell by an average of 1.4 per cent per annum between 1980 and 1984. For Latin America and the Caribbean, however, the fall averaged 2.7 per cent per annum during these years, and in Africa south of the Sahara the fall averaged 3.9 per cent. For 1983, the first full year of the debt crisis, a fall of 4.5 per cent in *per capita* income was registered in Latin America, and one of 4.9 per cent in sub-Saharan Africa. Of course, in some individual countries the downturn was even sharper (in Latin America and the Caribbean falls of more than 10 per cent in per capita income were recorded in two countries in 1983, and another ten countries recorded falls of more than 5 per cent; in Africa three countries recorded falls in excess of 10 per cent, and another ten in excess of 5 per cent).[19]

These are massive, perhaps unprecedented, falls in income at the level of nation states. One can well imagine the havoc that this brutal economic nose-dive must have caused. In the short term, the impact was felt most acutely in high urban unemployment, reduced earnings, economic deprivation and shortages of essential goods, and while most sections of the community had to bear part of the sacrifice, the heaviest brunt of the adjustment was borne by the poorest groups. This was the inevitable consequence of the Fund's more recent approach to policy conditionality, where the traditional recipe of tight fiscal and monetary policies and currency devaluation is now invariably supplemented by structural adjustment policies giving free rein to market forces and requiring the lifting of all constraints on full market pricing, including the elimination of subsidies on essential foods and other basic necessities, with effects which bear particularly heavily on the poor. The poor were also those most affected by the reductions in government expenditure on health, education and social welfare, key elements in the Fund's package of conditionality. But the effects went beyond the short term, since these are expenditures which finance the basic investment in human capital, without which there can be no development.

Education is perhaps the most obvious example of investment in human capital so essential to economic development. For developing countries generally, and particularly for those who emerged from colonial rule only in the preceding two decades or so, a functioning, broad-based education system was still in the process of being established and remained delicately poised and fragile. An education system is built up of a series of layers, from the primary school through the various stages of secondary and higher education. For all these layers there are students and teachers, and it is the quantity and quality of the teachers that will determine the quantity and quality of the students, from whom in turn will be recruited the teachers to keep the system functioning and growing. It seems clear that in many cases the brutal manner in which expenditure on education was cut, and the low income and status to which teachers were reduced in the ensuing market-oriented adjustment process, have so weakened the educational infrastructure in these countries as to greatly damage the prospects for rebuilding it. This would be a disaster for their development prospects in the medium to long term.

The sharp cut-backs in imports which became necessary during the 1980s, owing to the external financial squeeze, also seriously undermined long-term development prospects. Developing countries typically depend on imports for a wide range of essential products to keep the economy going - most importantly in the present context, for machinery and equipment to maintain and expand the productive base of the economy. For some countries, imports declined in real terms by as much as 20 per cent per annum during 1981-84, and for the five major Latin American debtor countries as a whole (Argentina, Brazil, Chile, Mexico and Venezuela), imports declined by almost one-half between 1981 and 1983. Such sharp cut-backs in imports seriously reduced availability of essential supplies and equipment and led to what has been described as 'import strangulation' of the economy (falls in output and capacity utilization due to unavailability of imported inputs).[20] Such import strangulation also means inadequate maintenance of existing capital stock in transport, industry, agriculture and basic infrastructure, with adverse effects on production, and, particularly in the poorer countries, shortages of essential imported inputs such as drugs, medical equipment, textbooks, and other items necessary to keep the basic medical and educational services functioning. In many cases the unavailability of fuel, inputs and spare parts has also adversely affected export potential, making it all the more difficult for such countries to escape from the balance-of-payments trap in which they have found themselves.

For developing countries, the 1980s have been described as 'the lost decade'. Except for the countries of Asia, particularly East Asia, which have been able to do quite well and to maintain a creditable economic performance, the term is apt. For developing countries as a whole, per capita income in 1988 was below the level of 1980, implying negative growth during the decade. But as can be seen from the data in Table 6.1, it was in the African and Latin American regions that performance during the 1980s was most disastrous (excluding from consideration here the high-income oil countries of West Asia who also suffered badly in relative terms, giving up most of the gains they made during the 1970s). It was especially bad in sub-Saharan Africa, with some of the poorest countries in the world, where per capita income fell by nearly one-fifth between 1980 and 1988. In comparison, the decline in Latin America was much less dramatic. One is left to imagine the social and economic trauma associated with such a prolonged period of economic decline, especially in a world newly accustomed to the idea of continuous economic growth as a normal fact of life. Especially, also, in view of the 20 per cent increase in *per capita* income which the developed countries achieved during these years of decline in the developing world, with the consequent enormous widening of the income gap between the 'haves' and the 'have-nots' that this implied.

A new role for the IMF

While drought in Africa compounded the difficulties which the countries in that region faced, the underlying problem there, as in Latin America, was the balance-of-payments crisis brought about by the factors mentioned above (the 1980-82 recession, the rise in interest rates and the rise in the price of oil); in other words, a sharp deterioration in the balance of payments brought about by external factors beyond the control of the countries themselves. It was to meet this kind of situation that the IMF was originally established; that is, to provide temporary liquidity to assist countries in adjusting to unplanned and unex-

Table 6.1

Per capita income in developing countries by major geographical regions, 1980 and 1988

(constant US $ 1980)

	1980	1988	Change	%
All developing countries	937	929	-8	-0.9
Latin America	2245	2056	-189	-8.4
North Africa	1259	1118	-141	-11.2
Other Africa	549	453	-96	-17.4
West Asia	2893	2189	-704	-24.3
South Asia	232	307	75	32.4
East Asia	919	1270	351	38.2

Source: UNCTAD, *Trade and Development Report*, 1990, p. 68.

pected disequilibrium in their balance of payments. In doing so, the Fund's purpose was (or should be) to permit the necessary adjustment to take place with as little economic disruption as possible, bearing in mind particularly that one of its primary objectives was 'the promotion and maintenance of high levels of employment and real income and . . . the development of the productive resources of all members as primary objectives of economic policy,' (Article I [ii] of the IMF's Articles of Agreement). Despite this, it was the Fund itself, in responding to the balance-of-payments crisis faced by developing countries in the early 1980s, that took the lead in imposing the brutal policy measures responsible for the sharp cut-backs in incomes and imports, massive unemployment, social deprivation, and widespread deterioration in capital stocks and in productive capacity that were the hall-mark of the adjustment process to which these countries were subjected.

It was a long road that the Fund had taken from the original conception in the minds of the American and British Treasury officials who sought an institution that could provide temporary liquidity to ease the pains of adjustment to balance-of-payments disequilibrium and thereby to promote the stability and growth of the world economy, to its present role of debt-collector on behalf of private banks and enforcer of harsh policy conditionalities pursued with a singlemindedness that leaves little room for independent manoeuvre in countries which fall prey to it. In the process its purposes have surely been transformed, in practice if not in its legal constitution.

In the earlier discussion we traced the evolution of the Fund from its inception, and saw the way in which from the very beginning it was never able to fulfil the role originally intended for it, largely because the European countries then in balance-of-payments deficit were not willing to have the Fund play the role of national policy maker, as the US, then the main creditor and determiner of Fund policy, was wont to insist. But times have changed; the Europeans and other industrial countries have now joined the US as joint creditors controlling the Fund, and with their joint support Fund conditionality now has free rein in (developing) countries which happen to be on the receiving end of Fund policy.

A telling aspect of the changing nature of the IMF over the years concerns the evolution of the size of quotas relative to trade or other relevant variables. The size of quota determines the extent to which a member can have access to the resources of the Fund. Since potential need for resources can be expected to grow in proportion to the size of trade, one might have expected the idea to be that the size of quotas would grow *pari passu* with trade. But this is not what happened. Instead, the growth of quotas lagged far behind that of trade. According to Sidney Dell, IMF quotas averaged about 16 per cent of total imports in 1948, but by 1980 the proportion had fallen to less than 3 per cent.[21] For the industrial countries themselves, this fall in the (relative) size of quotas was without significance, since they had long ceased to turn to the Fund as a source of liquidity, having evolved alternative arrangements for this purpose. It was the developing countries, therefore, which still depended on the Fund as a source of liquidity, that the quota policy affected (and this of course explains the reluctance to increase quotas).

As an alternative to increasing quotas, a whole series of new access facilities was introduced. Apart from the original Credit Tranches, these include (or have included) the Extended Fund Facility, Supplementary Financing Facility, Policy of Enlarged Access, Compensatory Financing Facility, Cereal Import Facility, Buffer Stock Facility, and the Oil Facility. All in all, members can now draw up to a cumulative total of over 600 per cent of quota, compared with a limit of 125 per cent of quota in the early years of the Fund. But the consequence of this approach to enlarging access to Fund resources has been devastating from the borrowers' point of view, since it has meant that access to low-conditionality resources is now minuscule in relation to needs (amounting to only 25 per cent of quota), while increasingly stringent conditionalities are imposed for access to the remaining 575 per cent of quota. The result is that low-conditionality resources are now virtually an extinct species, and any meaningful access to the Fund's resources now involves high conditionality. (This is not quite true, since access to some special facilities, such as the Compensatory Financing Facility and the Cereal Facility, which require special justification and are not included in the 600 per cent of quota mentioned above, carry low conditionality.) In this way the influence that the Fund is able to exert over members seeking any meaningful access to its resources has thus greatly increased.

Not only was this niggardly policy towards quota increases pursued to the detriment of developing countries, but equally niggardly has been the policy towards SDR allocations, with similar effect. Despite the Jamaica Agreement of 1976 under which the SDR was to become the principal reserve asset of the international monetary system, the developed countries have argued that there is no need for further SDR allocations since there is no shortage of liquidity. And for those countries of course there is certainly no shortage of liquidity. Increases in the price of gold since the breakdown of the Bretton Woods system have meant large increases in the value of their reserves (since these were the countries that held the world's stock of monetary gold), and this, together with the vast expansion of international commercial bank lending to which they have ready access, meant that their liquidity needs are fully met. Only developing countries without access to commercial bank lending would be unable to find low-conditionality short-term finance, and hence would remain dependent on the IMF for their liquidity. Writing just before the debt crisis broke, two well known North American experts noted that: 'As in the past, the bulk of the Fund's resources can be expected to be channelled to countries that, by and large, are excluded from ready access to private capital markets. Countries enjoying such access probably will remain reluctant to sign up for conditional Fund assistance.'[22] After the debt crisis broke, virtually all developing countries fell into the excluded category, and most of them 'reluctantly' had to sign up for conditional Fund assistance.

Dell, in his revealing review of the evolution of Fund policies referred to above, draws attention to the significant difference between the way in which the Fund approached the balance-of-payments disequilibrium created by the first oil shock in 1973 and that created by the second in 1979. In the former case, the IMF took the very sensible position that: 'Attempts to eliminate the additional current deficit caused by higher oil prices through deflationary demand policies, import restrictions, and general resort to exchange rate depreciation would serve only to shift the payments problem from one oil importing country to another and to damage world trade and economic activity.' It therefore called on oil-importing countries to accept the consequent short-term deterioration in their balance of payments, and made available the oil facility at low conditionality to assist countries in financing the resulting payments deficit. In contrast, in 1979-80, when the impact of the oil price rise on the balance was compounded by the effects of the interest rate rise and of the steep recession that was soon to follow, no reference was made by the Fund to the dangers of deflationary demand policies, nor was there any suggestion of the need to prevent damage to 'world trade and economic activity'. Nor, for that matter, was any attempt made to provide additional low-conditionality resources to meet the resulting balance-of-payments deficits, notwithstanding that the logic of the arguments put forward in 1974 applied with even greater force in 1979, given the deep recession that was developing.[23] But, apart from the general hardening of the policy stance in line with the new thinking in the US Administration which helps to explain developments here, there was also an important (unspoken) difference between the two cases which largely accounts for the unequal ways in which they were treated. In the former case a number of industrial countries were among those facing large unforeseen deficits in their balance of payments and requiring support from the IMF, hence the much more lenient and reasonable treatment, while in the latter case only developing countries needed to turn to the IMF for support, the industrial countries being by then awash with liquidity and having full access to the pool of resources by then available in the international commercial banking system.

As mentioned above, the new thinking in Washington was reflected in a general hardening of the Fund's access policy. Apart from the refusal to supply additional low-conditionality resources, thus forcing borrowing countries straightaway into the high-conditionality upper credit tranches, there was also a general tightening of policy conditions, which became harsher and more repressive, as well as more detailed and overbearing, extending beyond the traditional macro-economic variables relating to fiscal, monetary and exchange rate policies, to include structural adjustment policies at the sectoral and micro levels. There was also a hardening of IMF interest rate policy, with interest now being charged at close to market rates. All this served to make it much more painful to seek assistance from the Fund and to be on the receiving end of its policies. As Tony Killick *et al* have pointed out, 'the IMF has not set its programs within a cost-minimizing framework. It has treated the balance-of-payments objective as overriding, and has been reluctant to give weight to other government purposes when designing stabilization programs. From the point of view of a developing country, the Fund approach is *potentially* a high cost one . . .'[24]

One cannot avoid commenting here on the obvious asymmetry or lack of evenhandedness of the Fund in regard to the distribution of the burden of adjustment to balance-of-payments disequilibrium and in its dealings with its developed and developing member countries, a feature that became especially glaring with the advent of the new policy wave of the 1980s. We commented above on the asymmetries in the Fund's approach to the 1974-75 and the 1979-80 crises, and Dell has drawn attention to shifting US attitudes to the question of the distribution of the burden of adjustment. Thus in the early 1970s, the US argued strongly in favour of 'equity and efficiency' in the distribution of the burden of adjustment between surplus and deficit countries, pointing out that, 'If countries on both the deficit and the surplus side of a payments imbalance follow active policies for the restoration of equilibrium, the process is likely to be easier than if the deficit countries try to bring about adjustment by themselves.'[25] In the 1980s, however, the whole burden of adjustment would be thrown on the backs of the deficit developing countries, at great cost to them, and with not the slightest disposition to demand any corresponding adjustment from surplus countries or, for that matter, from the powerful industrial countries in deficit. As Albert Fishlow justly remarks, 'Inappropriate fiscal policy in the United States that contributes to high interest rates may be criticized by the IMF, but it goes unpunished and undebited for the difficulties that it has imposed on the adjustment of others.'[26]

To return to our main theme, the power of the IMF over developing country borrowers was made all the more formidable since, in the aftermath of the debt crisis, all other potential sources of credit, bilateral or otherwise, required an IMF stamp of approval (in effect, that an IMF high-conditionality agreement be in place) before any credit was extended. This was a continuation and development of policies started as far back as the 1950s (see Chapter 2), but was to assume particular importance in view of the tight financial squeeze which large numbers of developing countries now faced.

The enormous influence on economic policy-making which the IMF was now, by force of circumstance, able to exercise in the developing world can be gauged by the fact that between 1980 and 1984 more than 60 developing countries were parties to stand-by arrangements or extended facility agreements with the Fund requiring compliance with stringent policy conditions. And, as mentioned above, the scope of the Fund's conditionality package now became more intrusive and all-embracing, going beyond the traditional areas of macro-economic policy-making involving the broader aspects of monetary, fiscal and exchange rate policies that had long characterized its stand-by agreements, to include as well an increasing preoccupation with the setting of performance targets at the micro level. In this way the Fund's concerns would go beyond issues of macro-economic stability to include the details about 'supply-side' policies as well. According to Raymond Mikesell, 'Although the texts of stand-by and extended facility agreements are not made public by the Fund, public statements issued by the Fund indicate that a wide variety of supply-side policies are included in the "Letters of Intent" of the members receiving IMF assistance.'[27] Manuel Guitan, a member of the Fund's staff, states, 'It is also common to have a number of important policy understandings in the formulation of an adjustment program . . . They normally include: public sector policies on prices, taxes and subsidies, . . . interest rate policies, . . . exchange rate policy, . . . and income policies. Action in these policy areas is of direct interest to the Fund because they foster savings and investment - the basis for expanding supply and for the sound development of any economy.'[28] While the rationale for extending the scope of conditionality was undoubtedly a laudable one (i.e. to respond to a concern that Fund policies should promote not only macro-economic stability but also economic growth), it meant in practice that the Fund would have free rein to impose on the debtor developing countries the extreme versions of the free-market ideology which dominated official US thinking and policy-making. Thus supply-side economics, Reagan-style, would now become standard fare in the policy matrix of debtor countries under IMF tutelage.

Fund conditionality now overlapped with that which the World Bank imposed in connection with its programme of structural adjustment loans (SALs). It was the Bank's conditionality, however, focusing more specifically on the micro-economic aspects of policy-making, that provided the fullest scope for promoting the market-oriented supply-side economics currently in vogue. The SAL programme was introduced in 1980 as a form of Bank lending geared to the realization of specific policy changes and institutional reforms. According to Stanley Please, a former staff member and consultant to the World Bank, the policy areas on which the SAL programme focuses include: the relative roles of the public and private sectors in economic activity; the way markets are permitted to develop or are organized by governments; the process and criteria by which the level and structure of agricultural prices are determined; and the industrial policy framework within which industry operates as determined by tariffs, import licensing systems, and investment promotion schemes.[29] These issues go to the very heart of development policy, and it is not difficult to guess the direction of World Bank policy requirements in these areas. They focus above all on reforms needed to give free play to market forces, with emphasis on such issues as deregulation, privatization, cutbacks in the role of the state in the economy, import liberalization, removal of price controls (typically on basic necessities), elimination of budget subsidies, and on interest rate policy (with a strong bias against preferential rates for particular sectors). For better or worse, the World Bank's SAL programme provided a unique opportunity for promoting the new economic ideology in the developing world.

With the two institutions co-ordinating their individual country policies and working in tandem, countries coming under their sway soon found themselves overwhelmed and left with few policy choices. This was especially so for small- or medium-sized developing countries, sometimes stretched so thin in their dealings with the IMF that little time is left for consideration of other policy issues, not in the IMF programme. This latter point is brought out in Tony Killick's review of Kenya's experience in dealing with the IMF. Kenyan officials, he says, point to the considerable cost of Fund credit 'because of what they regard as the excessive amount of high-level manpower tied up in the preparation of a credit application, the subsequent negotiations, and the monitoring of results.'[30] And Kenya is by no means the most disadvantaged of the IMF's client states, so far as the availability of high-level manpower is concerned.

An aside on devaluation as a tool of policy

We may pause here to pose the question: what is the justification for prescribing devaluation as a standard ingredient in IMF/World Bank support programmes in developing countries? It is well known that devaluation as a means of correcting a balance-of-payments deficit will work if foreign demand for domestic exports and domestic demand for foreign imports are both sufficiently responsive to price changes, or price elastic. But for primary exporting developing countries both elasticities are notoriously low. For exports this is a result of the fact that overall demand for food and raw materials is not particularly sensitive to price, but depends much more on such factors as population size, the level of income, and the level of economic activity. For imports, low price elasticity follows from the fact that there is little scope for price substitution between domestically produced and imported goods, the latter consisting of products which may well be essential to the economy but which simply cannot be produced locally. Hence if the prices of imported goods rise following a devaluation, only from the operation of the income effect (the lowering of real incomes resulting from the higher prices of imports, assuming constant money income) will there be any reduction in import demand. As a result of these two peculiar features of the trade structure of low-income primary producing countries, devaluation can be very hazardous as an instrument of trade policy in these countries.

To focus first on the export side, if devaluation works as expected and production costs and export prices are lowered, what effect does this have? To begin with, there is a deterioration in the terms of trade. But this is not all. Since the export products are price inelastic, when prices are reduced foreign demand is not increased by much. As a result, export earnings fall, and the country is now exporting more of its products and earning less in foreign exchange, a perverse result well understood in the theoretical literature. Of course this only occurs directly if the country in question accounts for such a large share of the world market for its export product that its actions will have a noticeable influence on price. On the other hand, an individual small producer could hope to slightly undercut its competitor and steal some of his market without noticeably affecting market price, thereby increasing export earnings almost in proportion to increases in export quantities. But where there are many small producers all facing similar balance-of-payments deficits and all under pressure to devalue with the same purpose in mind, the result is the same as if the action were taken by the large producer, and they all will find their export earnings shrinking as a result of the devaluation.

This result is by no means a mere theoretical curiosity. Take coffee. Between 1980 and 1987 coffee exports of developing countries increased in quantity from 3,527 million to 4,130 million tons, or by 17 per cent, while their total earnings from coffee exports *fell* from US$11,654 million to US$9,131 million, or by 22 per cent. Tea and cocoa, two of the other main primary commodity exports of developing countries, tell much the same story, if less dramatically. In all cases export prices have fallen substantially over these years, while export quantities have increased.[31] And of course, when account is taken of the increase in the price these countries have to pay for their imports, and hence of the deterioration in their terms of trade, a clearer idea is obtained of the squeeze they face.[32]

The observations we are making here are by no means novel. Almost thirty years ago Ragnar Nurske commented as follows:

> To ask the less developed countries to increase their export quantities of primary products in the face of a price inelastic and not an upward shifting demand schedule would be to ask, in effect, for an income transfer from poor to rich countries through a change in the terms of trade in favour of the latter. If one of several countries exporting the same primary commodity were to cut its export costs and prices, its export proceeds could indeed increase, but only at the expense of a fall in the other countries' export proceeds. The balance of payments adjustment process alone (whether through exchange rate variations or domestic price changes) would lead the latter to cut their export prices too, and all will be worse off at the end than they were at the start.[33]

It is also pertinent to note here that the stimulus to expand supply comes not only from the policy of devaluation, pressed on developing countries by the IMF, but also from World Bank loan programmes, including its structural adjustment programmes, which over the years have targeted the primary commodity export sector of these countries for expansion and for promotion, notwithstanding the contradictions such policies raise in view of the elasticity problem discussed above. In this regard it is revealing to quote from a recent study by Stephen Weissman, for the US House of Representatives, of the effectiveness of the World Bank's structural adjustment policies in promoting economic growth in sub-Saharan Africa. He says:

> it is evident that certain adjustment policies had significantly favourable effects. In Ghana such measures as devaluation of the currency, increased producer prices for cocoa, and the rehabilitation of export infrastructure helped lead to major increases in the volume of cocoa, gold and log exports . . . The relative success of structural adjustment in promoting moderate growth could nevertheless fade if other circumstances change . . . Also, initially favourable world prices for key agricultural exports have recently slipped. Ghana's cocoa returned US$2406/ton in 1986 but was projected to fall to US$1700/ton in 1989. With world consumption increasing by only 2% a year, and world supply growing by 6-7% a year, cocoa supplies have been accumulating for several years.[34]

This then is the logic of the policies being pressed on developing countries by these institutions. Nurske's remark about asking 'for an income transfer from poor to rich countries' seems apposite here.

Concerning imports, the point that needs to be stressed is that the compression of real income required to bring about a reduction in imports following a devaluation requires a set of fiscal and monetary policies which is not always easy to administer in primary producing developing countries. The major problem arises from the income distribution effects of such policies, often characterized by large wind-fall gains to some sections of the community and heavy income reductions to others, and the fierce battles that are often fought on the political front to maintain income (or at least relative income) positions. Such battles often make it difficult to maintain the required policy stance, with the result that money incomes tend to rise in line with the rise in import prices, and a cycle of inflation and further devaluation follows. It may also be noted that in view of the key role of imports in these economies, a rise in import prices quickly reverberates throughout the economy, raising prices generally (though of course not necessarily uniformly), and thereby heightening the inflationary potential. In view of this, it is not surprising that adjustment programmes in which devaluation has played such a prominent role have been associated with inflationary spirals.

Beyond conditionality: the politics of the debt strategy

Returning to our main theme, it now seems relevant to raise the question: what is the purpose of IMF conditionality and on what basis is it justified? Sidney Dell, who has carried out a thorough review of the evolution of IMF conditionality, observes that, 'Originally the imposition of conditions on a potential borrower was considered to be justified largely in terms of the need to ensure prompt repayment of drawing so as to safeguard the revolving character of the fund's resources.'[35] But can the kind of conditionality we have seen imposed in recent years be justified on these grounds? For most developing countries that seek IMF assistance, IMF credits represent only a very small proportion of their total debt. Of 61 developing countries having IMF credits outstanding in 1987, for 34 of them these credits represented less than 5 per cent of total outstanding debt, and for another 18 the proportion lay between 5 and 10 per cent. Thus only for nine of the 61 countries did the share exceed 10 per cent.[36] And given the high priority that all countries necessarily attach to meeting their repayment obligations to the IMF, it is scarcely plausible to suppose that this formidable array of armour in the guise of conditionality can really be justified on these grounds. The real explanation must surely lie elsewhere.

We discussed earlier the role the IMF has played as debt collector on behalf of the banks, and it is undoubtedly this proxy role, not at all provided for among the purposes of the Fund, that better explains the severity of conditionality in recent years, rather than the need to 'safeguard the revolving character of the Fund's resources'. But the question goes further than this. Consider, for example, the almost religious zeal with which the IMF announces and insists on its standard package of austerity measures (almost without variation between countries except perhaps as regards the specific percentage targets to be achieved). It is as if the country had committed a grave sin by having got into balance-of-payments difficulties in the first place, and that only by undergoing severe punishment can the necessary repentance and cleansing of the soul be achieved. Hence the merciless character of the measures that are insisted upon. But going even beyond this is the idea of playing God, of the 'IMF knows best' syndrome. Thus the client states are told that the essential purpose of all the bitter medicine is to promote the recovery and healthy growth of the patient. And we are to believe that the purpose of conditionality is not only to 'safeguard the revolving character of the Fund's resources', but equally (perhaps more so) to promote the development and growth of its client states.[37] But is this a plausible interpretation of the purpose of Fund conditionality in actual practice?

There is a large literature on IMF policies, much of it critical. There is no need to review this literature here or to go over the ground it covers. But at least two conclusions seem clear. First, the shock therapy administered by the IMF to its developing country clients aims in the short term to achieve a reduction in balance-of-payments deficits essentially through a contraction of the domestic economy, and it usually succeeds in achieving this limited objective, with all the social, political and economic costs and human suffering that this entails. Second, there is no evidence that Fund programmes have contributed to achieving positive longer-term objectives such as bringing down inflation rates, increasing savings and investment, or setting the economy on a path to successful long-term growth. Among the large number of developing countries that have over the years been the objects of IMF stabilization programmes (repeatedly, for some countries) there is scarcely a single example of that kind of success. Indeed, the present sorry state of most developing countries that have been through the IMF wringer stands as vivid testimony to the contrary.[38]

As we have indicated earlier, the particularly harsh conditions imposed during the 1980s have seriously disrupted the development potential of the countries affected and substantially lowered their long-term growth path. All indications now are that the 1990s will be little different from the 'lost decade' of the 1980s for those countries that faced the balance-of-payments squeeze and were the victims of the debt crisis. They will, for some time yet, be reeling under the devastation and upheaval they were forced to undergo. But apart from permanently lowering the growth-rates and the long-run growth path of those countries immediately affected, the IMF-led strategy for dealing with the crisis was also to have far-reaching effects on the development climate in the South and on the course of North-South relations.

The shock treatment that developing countries were forced to undergo, described by one author as 'the political economy of overkill',[39] with its extreme demand deflation, high unemployment, sharp reductions in wages and incomes, severe import compression, heavy cut-backs in social services etc., was a traumatic experience that left a deep impression on the consciousness of the developing world. The noose that the international financial community held around the necks of these countries, and the measured way it was manipulated to keep the victims alive but struggling for air, greatly intensified the impact of this experience in the deeper recesses of consciousness, and brought forth the curious phenomenon, well documented by psychologists in their study of people held hostage by terrorists, of the victims embracing the ideological paraphernalia of the oppressor and espousing their cause.

The cause is spelt out most frankly in a telegram issued in February 1985 by US Secretary of State George Shultz to US AID officials, setting out matters to be raised with host governments 'in connection with aid projects'. It reads in part:

> Policy dialogue should be used to encourage LDCs to follow free market principles for sustained economic growth and to move away from government intervention in the economy. This allows the market to determine how economic resources are most productively allocated and how benefits should be distributed. To the maximum extent practical governments should rely on the market mechanism - on private enterprise and market forces - as the principal determinants of economic decisions . . . In most cases, public sector firms should be privatized. [40]

This reads very much like the recipe the IMF and the World Bank have been promoting in their dealings with the developing world. And the message has evidently sunk in. After a decade of tight financial strangulation and heavy political pressure, there is scarcely a developing country today that does not embrace the free market, private initiative, de-regulation, trade liberalization, privatization, foreign investment, and so on. If nothing else, the debt crisis and the strategy followed to deal with it have brought forth a host of converts to the cause of the market solution. And in the process Reaganomics, which once seemed far-fetched and unlikely even in that bedrock of capitalism, the USA, spread its wings and took hold in the developing world. In the words of Tony Killick, 'the emphasis now is on development through the more efficient allocation of resources. There is little apparent interest any more in structural and institutional changes as essential components of development. The market is to determine the distribution of the gains from development, according to the Shultz telegram.'[41]

It is hard to resist the conclusion that one of the chief purposes of the debt strategy as it actually evolved, and of the harsh conditionalities that were imposed, was to teach the developing countries a lesson, to put them in their place, to so frighten and weaken them and make them so obviously dependent on the favours and subject to the dictates of the industrial North, that it would be a long, long time before they would ever again have the effrontery to attempt to confront the North with demands for a restructuring of the international economic order. If indeed this was one of the main purposes of the strategy, then it is safe to conclude that it succeeded brilliantly. The trauma that the debt-ridden developing countries went through, the energies that they had to devote to negotiating and renegotiating debt relief and policy conditionality packages, and the struggle they had to engage in to stay barely afloat, left them drained and exhausted, bereft of any will to confront and to challenge. And their experience serves as a warning to those countries not immediately affected. We have therefore seen an eclipse of the will to fight on the part of the developing countries, and their caucus group, the Group of 77, has lost its sting, if not its *raison d'être*.

Notes

1. See OECD, *The Challenge of Unemployment, A Report to Labour Ministries* (Paris, 1982), Table B, for a summary of the trends in inflation in the OECD countries over the years.
2. See OECD, *op. cit*, for a discussion of the unemployment problem in the industrial countries during the 1970s. For a summary of the relevant data, see Table L of that report.

3. See *Towards Full Employment and Price Stability*, Summary of a report to the OECD by a group of independent experts (OECD, June 1977), p. 9.

4. The literature on the subject is extensive. The two OECD publications referred to above contain useful material on this subject. For a more comprehensive and analytic approach to the problem the reader is referred to Gottfried Haberler, *The Problem of Stagflation: Reflections on the Microfoundation of Macroeconomic Theory and Policy* (American Enterprise Institute, Washington, D.C., 1985). See also Michael Bruno and Jeffrey Sachs, *Economics of Worldwide Stagflation* (Harvard University Press, Cambridge, Mass., 1985), which contains an extensive bibliography.

5. OECD, *The Control and Management of Government Expenditure* (OECD, Paris, 1987), p. 17.

6. *Ibid.*

7. It is unnecessary to take up here the somewhat obtuse and theoretical question of whether the policy revolution was a result of the argument as such or if the underlying factors gave rise to the malaise. But we shall have some comments bearing on this issue later on.

8. See Bruce R. Bartlett, *Reaganomics: Supply Side Economics in Action* (Arlington House Publishers, Westport, Conn., 1981), p. 9. Chapter 1 provides a good brief statement of supply-side economics.

9. These figures are taken from William R. Cline, *International Debt: Systemic Risk and Policy Response* (Institute for International Economics, Washington, D.C., 1984), Chapter 1, and are based on data published in IMF *World Economic Outlook*, 1982 and 1983.

10. See Carlos Massad, 'Debt: an overview', in *Journal of Development Planning*, No. 16 (United Nations, New York, 1985), p. 4.

11. See for example Cline. *op.cit.*, Chapter 1. See also UNCTAD, *Trade and Development Report*, 1982 (United Nations, New York, 1982), pp. 38-42. See also the OECD Report referred to in Chapter 6.

12. See Cline, *op.cit.*, Table 1.1.

13. Cline calculates that, using US wholesale price increases as the deflator, real interest rates on international debt were negative on average for the entire 1970s to the tune of about -0.8 per cent (Cline, *op.cit.*, p. 11).

14. Cline, *op.cit.*, p.13.

15. For example, exposure in one major debtor country, Brazil, represented approximately 75 per cent of the capital of two of the largest US banks (Citicorp and Manufacturers Hanover), while exposure in Mexico equalled or exceeded 60 per cent of capital for Manufacturers Hanover, Chemical Bank, and First Interstate. Exposure in five Latin American countries alone exceeded 150 per cent of capital for Citicorp, BankAmerica, Chase Manhattan, Chemical, and Crocker National, the very cream of the US banking system. (See Cline, *op.cit.*, p. 23).

16. Rimmer de Vries, 'International debt: a play in three acts', United Nations, *Journal of Development Planning*, No. 16 (1985), p. 186.

17. One study estimates that in the period immediately after the debt crisis broke the banks were earning an additional US$1.75 billion per year from the extra profits of rescheduling. See UNCTAD, *Trade and Development Report*, 1988, p. 98.

18. It has been estimated that between 1982 and 1987 the ratio to capital of the debt owed to US banks by 15 highly indebted developing countries fell by a half, from 130 per cent to 65 per cent (*Loc.cit.*).

19. See UNCTAD, *Handbook of Trade and Development Statistics*, 1988, Table 6-2 for data on GDP growth rates for individual countries.

20. UNCTAD, *op.cit.*, p. 6.

21. Sidney Dell, *On Being Grandmotherly: The Evolution of IMF Conditionality* (Princeton University, International Finance Section, Essays in International Finance, No. 144, October 1981), p.16.

22. Rimmer de Vries and Arturo C. Porzecanski, 'Comments, Chapters 1-3', in John Williamson, (ed.), *IMF Conditionality* (Institute for International Economics, Washington, DC, 1983), p.70.

23. See Dell, *op. cit.*, p.22. The quote is from the *IMF Annual Report*, 1974, pp.25-26. See also in this connection Sidney Dell, 'Stabilization: The Political Economy of Overkill', appearing as Chapter 2 in John Williamson (ed.), *op. cit.*

24. Tony Killick *et al*, 'The IMF: Case for a Change in Emphasis', Chapter 2 of Richard E. Feinberg and Valeriana Kallab, (eds.), *Adjustment Crisis in the Third World, US - Third World Policy Perspectives*, No. 1 (Overseas Development Council, Transaction Books, New Brunswick and London, 1984), p. 60.

25. Quoted by Dell, *op. cit.*, p. 22 from the *Economic Report of the President 1973*, and from a memorandum submitted by the US Government to the IMF Committee of Twenty in November 1972.

26. Albert Fishlow, 'The Debt Crisis: Round Two Ahead?', Chapter 2 of Feinberg and Kallab, (eds.), *op. cit.*, p. 47.

27. Raymond F. Mikesell, 'Appraising IMF Conditionality: Too Loose, Too Tight, or Just Right?', Chapter 3 in John Williamson (ed.), *op. cit.*.

28. Quoted by Raymond Mikesell, *op. cit.*, p. 51, from Manuel Guitan, 'Fund Conditionality and the International Adjustment Process', *Finance and Development* (IMF, Washington, June 1981).

29. Stanley Please, 'The World Bank: Lending for Structural Adjustment', Chapter 3 in Richard E. Feinberg and Valeriana Kallab, (eds.), *op. cit*, p. 84.

30. Tony Killick, 'Kenya, the IMF, and The Unsuccessful Quest for Stabilization', Chapter 16 in John Williamson (ed.), *op. cit.*, p. 408.

31. These data are taken from UNCTAD *Commodity Yearbook*, 1989 and earlier years.

32. A good indication of the trend in prices which these countries have to pay for their imports is the export prices of developed countries, their main source of imports. Between 1980 and 1987 these prices increased by 10 per cent, and by 1990 by 27 per cent.

33. See Ragnar Nurske, 'Trade Theory and Development Policy,' Chapter 9 in

Howard S. Ellis and Henry C. Wallich, (eds.), *Economic Development for Latin America*, (Macmillan & Co, London, 1963) p. 244.

34. Stephen R. Weissmann, 'Structural Adjustment in Africa: Insights from the Experiences of Ghana and Senegal', *World Development*, Vol. 18, No. 12, 1990, p. 1624.

35. Sidney Dell, 'Stabilization: The Political Economy of Overkill', in John Williamson (ed.), *op. cit.*, p. 27.

36. Based on data in Table 21 of World Bank, *World Development Report*, 1989.

37. This is certainly the view of Ernest Stern, a Vice-President of the World Bank, writing about the complementarities between the Bank's SALs and the IMF programmes, when he flatly states that 'both institution share the same ultimate aim - to foster broadly based growth in incomes and employment in their member countries'. See Ernest Stern, 'World Bank Financing of Structural Adjustment', Chapter 5 of John Williamson, (ed.), *op. cit.*, p. 100.

38. Ghana is perhaps the example that proves the rule. Since the mid-1980s, Ghana has been swallowing liberal doses of IMF medicine and has often been cited as an example of success of the treatment. It would certainly come as some surprise to the Fund to learn that Ghana has recently achieved the dubious distinction of being proposed by the responsible UN organ (the Committee for Development Planning) for inclusion among the least developed countries.

39. Dell, *op. cit.*.

40. Quoted from Tony Killick, 'Twenty-five Years in Development: The Rise and Impending Decline of Market Solutions', *Development Policy Review* (Sage, London, Beverly Hills and New Delhi, Vol. 4, 1986), p. 101.

41. *Ibid.*, p. 102.

7. Reversal of the Tide and the South in Retreat

We turn now to a discussion of the evolution during the 1980s of the North-South dialogue in the light of the developments described in the preceding chapter. These developments, it goes without saying, were hardly propitious for the pursuit of dialogue along the lines we have been discussing, starting with the gradual build-up of the 1950s, followed by the organized pressures of the 1960s, and leading to the dramatic initiatives and confrontations of the 1970s, which for a time seemed to hold out for the developing countries the hope of bringing about beneficial changes in the international economic order. Indeed, as we shall see, this build-up would eventually reach a false crescendo and then gradually peter out and disintegrate, to be followed by a major reversal of the tide, with the pressure now coming from the North instead for a roll-back of concessions made in the past and for reverse concessions from the South.

The big business, free market, free enterprise philosophy which held sway with the rise to power of the ultra-conservatives during the 1980s went against the grain of Southern demands. As we observed earlier, many of these demands called for government action to control or regulate markets or their behaviour. This was exacly the kind of government action that the new conservatives professed to be most thoroughly against and to find so inimical to economic progress. There could be no sympathy from this quarter for entertaining such demands. But the aversion of the new conservatives to the idea of the South making demands went even deeper. The new philosophy held individual initiative and self-help as its cardinal principle, from which follows the responsibility of the poor for their own poverty (and conversely, the wealth of the rich being the just reward for their own efforts). In this light, there would be little sympathy for the plight of the poor in the rich countries themselves, not to mention the poor in the poor countries. In the new climate, the basis for dialogue would vanish. In the North there would be growing antipathy to dialogue, and the South, weakened and under pressure from the debt trap, would lose its will to fight. And the stage would then be set for the reversal of which we spoke.

One factor not mentioned earlier, which contributed in its own way to the turn of the tide in North-South relations, is the collapse of communist rule in Eastern Europe and the Soviet Union, the economic and political disintegration of the Soviet Union, and the consequent removal from the international scene of that country as a major world power. These developments brought in their train the end of the Cold War, of the East-West conflict, and of any hope for third world countries of being able to play off to their advantage one side against the other in the geopolitical confrontation between the two ideological and military factions. This was the converse of the important role the budding East-West conflict had played in the early development of the North-South dialogue, as discussed in Chapter 3. And while it is recognized that the Soviet Union and its system had long ceased to provide (or to appear to provide) a credible economic alternative for developing countries in search of rapid economic development, it is nonetheless true that Soviet military power and geopolitical interests remained important factors in the matrix of world power relations, and allowed developing countries considerable room for manoeuvre in their relations with the industrial North (or, in the present context, the West). The removal of this power from the international scene narrowed the space available to developing countries to manoeuvre, reducing their options and leaving them with little alternative but to accept the dictates of the now all-powerful West, led more firmly than ever by the US.

The Cancun Summit

The first real test of whether there was to be any serious pursuit of dialogue between North and South, following the rise to power of the ultra-conservatives in the two Anglo-Saxon bulwarks of the industrial North, was to take place in connection with the convening of the Cancun Summit in October 1981, nine months after the Reagan Administration came to office. This meeting came about as a result of recommendations contained in the report of the Brandt Commission (or to give it its proper name, the Independent Commission on International Development Issues). This was a self-appointed body established during the 1970s, under the chairmanship of the former West German Chancellor Willy Brandt, in the search for ways to help resolve some of the issues raised by the demands for an NIEO. The Commission's report contained a large number of recommendations for international action in specific areas, and in addition called for a political summit of heads of state and government of a representative group of developed and developing countries to discuss how various ideas for the promotion of closer economic interdependence between North and South may be pursued.

The idea of attending such a summit would hardly appeal to the new US President and his right-wing supporters. But given the auspicious sponsorship of the Commission's report by its renowned and highly respected chairman, and given furthermore that the US's important southern neighbour, Mexico, had offered to host the meeting, political sensitivities could not be ignored, and the invitation was not easily dismissed. In the event Reagan agreed to attend, and the summit was duly held, attended by the leaders of 22 countries broadly representative of North and South (with eight countries from the North and 14 from the South being represented). No formal communique was issued at the close of the meeting, but a vaguely worded summary of the proceedings in the name of the two co-chairmen (one from the North and one from the South) made it clear that there was little meeting of minds on any of the substantive issues. In fact, it appears from the summary that on only one such issue was a measure of agreement reached, and that was, curiously enough, on 'the need to complete procedures for bringing the Common Fund into operation', an issue that was already largely moribund and one which clearly faced an even more uncertain future in view of the new ideological climate in Washington. On other substantive issues the wording was vague and non-committal, and in the critical area of monetary and financial issues, there was merely a reference to the matters discussed and an indication of some of the 'Points raised by some participants in the discussion'. The latter read like a litany of the issues in this area which preoccupied the developing countries and on which they had been most vocal in seeking redress. There was no hint of even a sympathetic hearing from the North on these issues.[1]

On one important (procedural) issue, some apparent progress was made by the Cancun Summit. This concerned implementation of the 1979 General Assembly resolution sponsored by developing countries calling for the launching of 'global negotiations', within the United Nations framework, on international economic co-operation for development. The idea was to try and regain some of the momentum of the 1970s which had largely petered out without achieving many concrete results. But while there was considerable support among the industrial countries for pursuing the idea, progress had been blocked by US opposition. The US softened its opposition at the summit to the extent of agreeing 'the desirability of supporting at the United Nations ... a consensus to launch Global Negotiations on a basis to be mutually agreed and in circumstances offering the prospect of meaningful progress.' As US officials were quick to point out, however, the language agreed left almost everything to be decided, and gave the US full scope subsequently to reject arrangements it opposed. The US position was further protected by the very next statement in the summary, which noted that 'Some countries insisted that the competence of the specialized agencies should not be affected.'² There was little doubt, therefore, that notwithstanding the apparent success of the summit in confirming readiness to move forward on global negotiations, the agreement on this issue was paper-thin, and scarcely masked the gulf that separated US thinking from the main aspirations of the developing countries in seeking to launch these negotiations. Not surprisingly, subsequent attempts to start the negotiations were bogged down in procedural manoeuvres and posturing, and by the time they finally got under way, the whole climate had changed, the will of the developing countries had begun to break under the burden of the debt, and the negotiations ended up as a dull, formalistic, low-level diplomatic debating exercise without intrinsic interest.

The failure of the Cancun summit to make any impact, or to provide any hope for progress, on any of the issues then on the North-South agenda, notwithstanding the meeting's auspicious sponsorship, was a clear indication of the dimming prospects for North-South relations and of the receding hope of meaningful dialogue between these two economic spheres. Subsequent developments would quickly confirm this indication.

UNCTAD under attack

Over the years, ever since its coming into being in 1964 against the bitter opposition of the US and its allies in the industrial North, UNCTAD had been the symbol of the developing countries' determination to press for beneficial changes in the international economic order. It also served as the main platform for the articulation of their demands and from which to push their case. For the developed countries, which reluctantly came to accept the existence of UNCTAD, the reaction was to regard it as something between an active irritant that was barely tolerated and a relatively innocuous distraction that was a small price to pay as 'conscience money', and as an outlet for developing countries' frustrations. The more hard-line, market-oriented developed countries (particularly the US, West Germany and Japan), had always tended to view UNCTAD in the former sense, the smaller Northern European countries and France predominantly in the latter, with the other developed countries falling somewhere in between. With the rise to dominance of the ultra-conservative, free-market, non-government-interference school of thought during the 1980s, it was to be expected that the balance in the developed countries would shift towards the former end of the spectrum, and that UNCTAD would come under growing pressure and increasingly be regarded as an active irritant to be curbed and kept on a tight leash. The North's growing impatience, and the South's resolve collapsing under the increasing pressure of the debt, combined in the 1980s to remove the ground from beneath UNCTAD in its traditional role of vanguard for the South in its confrontation and dialogue with the North.

It is something of an irony that the efforts of developing countries and of the UNCTAD secretariat to use the momentum created by the mood of the 1970s to push for the strengthening of UNCTAD were to open the door to actions that would lead to exactly the opposite result. We refer here to the major initiatives on institutional matters put forward by the Group of 77 and by the UNCTAD secretariat at the fifth UNCTAD conference in Manila in 1979. In a document submitted to the conference, the secretariat drew attention to the evolving role of UNCTAD, 'to the point where [it] has become *de facto* the principal instrument of the General Assembly for negotiations in the field of trade and international economic co-operation for development, particularly in the context of negotiations on the establishment of a new international economic order.'[3] This evolving role, according to the secretariat document, involved an increased emphasis on negotiations and called for new methods of work requiring greater operational flexibility and managerial autonomy for UNCTAD as an organizational unit. Increased resources were also required to enable it to carry out its growing responsibilities effectively. The policy document prepared by the Group of 77 for the Conference ran along similar lines.[4]

As a result of these initiatives, a resolution on institutional issues was adopted at the Manila Conference calling for the strengthening of UNCTAD very much along the lines proposed. The resolution invited the General Assembly to 'take the necessary action for strengthening UNCTAD', based, *inter alia*, on the 'Clear recognition of UNCTAD as a principal instrument of the General Assembly for negotiations on relevant areas of international trade and related issues of international economic co-operation'. The resolution goes on to call for consultations with the UN Secretary-General designed to achieve greater autonomy for the UNCTAD Secretary-General in matters of management and budget. In addition, it called for the rationalization of meetings, documentation, etc., for improved efficiency, and for the establishment of an *ad hoc* inter-governmental committee 'on the rationalization of the machinery of UNCTAD' to make proposals for further action. These two ideas were introduced by the developed countries in the course of negotiating an agreed text for the resolution.

While in the succeeding years little progress was made in implementing the main ideas that motivated the resolution in the first place (the strengthening of UNCTAD and the granting of greater operational flexibility to the UNCTAD management), the section of the resolution calling for proposals and follow-up action on 'rationalization' was fully implemented. The inter-governmental committee was soon established, and in a couple of years was able to agree a draft resolution on the subject which was duly adopted by the Board (resolution 231 [XXII]). This was a comprehensive resolution dealing with a host of house-keeping matters, intended to impose greater control and order on the operations of the UNCTAD machinery. It dealt with such issues as the frequency of meetings, the timeliness, scope and length of documentation, translation and interpretation, and mechanisms for consultations between the secretariat and delegations. It also dealt with the question of integrating the ideas then being discussed in the General Assembly on programme planning, monitoring and evaluation into the work of UNCTAD. While on the surface the resolution could be viewed as an attempt to impose a reasonable measure of discipline and orderliness on the work of UNCTAD, below the surface it could clearly be seen as an effort to constrain and rein in the organization. This was evident in paragraphs 21 and 22 of the resolution, which went so far as explicitly to discourage (virtually to ban) the convening of groups of experts chosen by the UNCTAD Secretary-General and serving in a personal capacity - a technique that had proved over the years a powerful means of gaining visibility and political clout for views and proposals the secretariat wished to promote. All in all, the resolution was to serve as the point of reference from which the activities and influence of UNCTAD would in the coming years be further and further constrained.

At the sixth session of UNCTAD held in Belgrade in June 1983, the institutional issue came up as usual as an item on the agenda. Separate draft resolutions on the subject were submitted by the Group of 77 and by the developed countries, but these were so far apart in scope and purpose that there was virtually no prospect for useful negotiation. The Group of 77's draft dealt with the usual issues, calling for a comprehensive trade organization and for the strengthening in the meantime of UNCTAD, including the implementation of the previous resolution on the subject, while that of the developed countries, heavily influenced by US thinking, dealt exclusively with questions of programme planning, monitoring and evaluation. Given the gap separating the two resolutions, no progress was possible, and the only decision the conference could take was to refer the two resolutions to the continuing machinery of UNCTAD for further consideration.

In practice, the follow-up has largely been in relation to the issues that concerned the developed countries, particularly the US; in the period following the Conference a number of resolutions were adopted and actions taken on such issues. These related to programme planning, monitoring and evaluation, and to documentation, the scheduling and frequency of meetings, and other house-keeping matters. The high-point of this activity came in October 1987, when the UNCTAD Board established a working group of 19 member states to elaborate a report 'on issues pertaining to possible further improvements in the methods of work of the intergovernmental machinery of UNCTAD'.[5] The working group, heavily dominated by the US, prepared a report containing detailed prescriptions relating to the methods of work of the UNCTAD machinery, the effect of which was to reduce sharply the number and length of UNCTAD meetings and the volume of secretariat documentation, and to impose tight constraints on the contents and scope of that documentation.[6] The report remarks significantly (p. 3) that 'The 30 per cent reduction in the number of weeks of meetings held in 1987, as compared with 1986, and the correspond-ing reduction of 25 per cent in the volume of UNCTAD documentation mark an encouraging trend.' The report of the Working Group was duly adopted by the UNCTAD Board, which called for the full implementation of all the report's recommendations.

The main vehicle the UNCTAD secretariat has always had at its disposal for elaborating views on issues and for promoting ideas for implementation was the documentation prepared for consideration at intergovernmental meetings. With the heavy limitation on documentation and meetings now imposed, and coming after the effective ban on the use of independent expert groups referred to earlier, the effect was virtually to put a gag on UNCTAD and seriously to undermine, if not to extinguish, its ability to promote, advocate or espouse views not in keeping with those of the US and its allies in the North. It is of interest to note here that in the discussions surrounding the elaboration of the report of the Working Group, the US went so far as to argue that in the preparation of documentation the secretariat should consult representatives of member states on the outlines and the approaches to be followed (and presumably obtain their approval) before proceeding with work on the document. Apart from wholly undermining the independence of the secre-tariat, this procedure would very likely also bring the work to a standstill, a result probably not altogether unwelcome to the US.

That matters could come to such a head, that the developing countries could sit back and remain silent while the organization they had fought for so ardently twenty years earlier was being quietly neutralized and put on the back-burner, was a sign of the profound changes that had taken place in the relationship between North and South in the years since the Nairobi conference.

A crisis on voting

Perhaps we could date the crisis and turning point in UNCTAD itself to an earlier event, in 1982, when, in an acrimonious and somewhat dramatic confrontation, the Group of 77 used its majority to vote through a Board resolution against the bitter opposition of the developed countries, actively led by the US. The issue was one of principle and not of substance, and concerned the right to have the UNCTAD secretariat service meetings devoted to trade negotiations among developing countries. It was argued in terms of high principles, though at bottom it was really a question of the right of developing countries to exclude Israel from their meetings. The matter had been seething for some time, and came to a head with the vote at the 25th session of the Board in October 1982, after prolonged, intense and difficult negotiations had failed to bridge the gap between the opposing sides. The voting quite embittered the atmosphere. During the negotiations, the US had been the main protagonist opposing the developing countries, but the precipitate termination of the negotiations, long and drawn out though they were, by calling for a vote, was deeply resented by the developed countries as a whole, especially since many of them believed that significant progress was being made towards a consensus solution. The result was to rally the developed countries in unified opposition to the developing countries, creating a stand-off and an atmosphere of crisis.

The tension and high drama caused by developments at this meeting led to dark rumours and vague hints of the US, perhaps followed by other developed countries, withdrawing from UNCTAD. Technically, of course, UNCTAD was an integral part of the United Nations and it would not be possible to withdraw formally from UNCTAD without also withdrawing from the UN itself. These hints could therefore be taken as a form of bluff. But there are several ways of skinning a cat, and if the US and other developed countries were to cease to participate actively in UNCTAD, it could become an empty shell. The hints and undercurrents therefore had some practical force.

From the point of view of the US and other developed countries, it was the resort to voting, using the assured majority of the developing countries to settle the issue in dispute, that was most bitterly resented. It will be recalled that in the original negotiations leading to the establishment of UNCTAD (see Chapter 4), the issue which was to cause the greatest difficulty, once the principle of creating the new organization had been conceded, concerned the question of voting in the decision-making organs of the new institution. It was only after intense, drawn-out and difficult negotiations that the principle of one-country one-vote, demanded by the developing countries, was accepted. This was accompanied by an informal understanding (linked to a formal procedure for conciliation) that voting would be used sparingly to decide issues in UNCTAD (see p.89). In fact, in the subsequent history, voting was indeed used rather sparingly, reflecting the practical exigencies of the situation, but where the situation seemed to warrant it, the Group of 77 had never felt inhibited from calling for a vote to adopt a resolution or otherwise decide an issue. But the use by the developing countries of their assured majority to push through resolutions and decisions had always been a sensitive matter. Where on particular issues the developed countries were divided or split (as was not infrequently the case), voting could be a useful tactic for exposing this division while getting the necessary resolution adopted or decision taken. In such cases the developing countries would escape the full acrimony of the developed countries, now divided among themselves. Where, as in the present case, the developed countries were wholly united, the situation was different, and resentment could be intense. Given the obvious impatience of the Reagan Administration with everything that UNCTAD stood for, it was evident that matters had come to a head, that a point of crisis had been reached. What role this crisis in itself was actually to play in subsequent developments is, however, rather difficult to tell, since, as it happens, these events took place in late 1982, just about the time when the debt crisis was breaking, as a result of which the developing countries would be increasingly on the defensive in their relations with the North.

Standstill at Belgrade

In respect of the negotiations on substantive issues, the sixth UNCTAD conference, held in Belgrade in June 1983, provided the first important occasion to test the waters in UNCTAD following the rise to power of the ultra-conservatives in Washington and the growing influence of the new philosophy throughout the industrial North. As was customary, the developing countries prepared beforehand the demands they were to present to this conference, in the so-called Buenos Aires Platform of the Group of 77. Prepared, as usual, in consultation with the UNCTAD secretariat, this document contained specific demands for action on all the substantive items of the agenda, usually in the form of draft resolutions, decisions, etc.[7] In view of the nature of the crisis then facing developing countries, brought about by the sudden deterioration in their balance-of-payments situation and associated with such phenomena as the collapse in commodity prices, the sharp fall in export earnings, the massive increase in debt service payments, and the contraction of liquidity and of external financing, their major concern was for action on financial and monetary issues. Proposals were therefore submitted for action in the IMF on a number of issues on which developing countries had always wanted movement, including additional SDR allocations and the link to development finance, the enlargement of quotas, conditionality, compensatory financing, decision-making, and surveillance over policies of developed countries. Action by the World Bank to expand its loan programmes and in easing its terms of lending was also called for, as were specific measures to ease the burden of official debt. There was also a call for a conference to negotiate a new facility on compensatory financing of shortfalls in export earnings. For the rest, the proposals were not particularly bold or far-reaching, except perhaps in the area of international trade, where ideas were put forward (doubtless inspired by the secretariat) intended to give UNCTAD a central role in the monitoring of protectionism and in encouraging the phasing out of uneconomic industries in the developed countries.

The ideas and proposals put forward by the Group of 77 provided the basis for the negotiations, and the resolutions finally adopted ran parallel to the drafts originally submitted by these countries. Most of the resolutions were adopted by consensus.[8] But in the key area of financial and monetary issues they turned out to be greatly watered down versions of the original proposals, especially the demands addressed to the IMF and the World Bank, which were put in such circumspect, deferential and qualified terms as to be virtually meaningless. And on really difficult issues, the resolution merely 'Notes the interest of the developing countries in the following questions and their desire that they should be further studied . . .' While these resolutions were adopted without dissent, interpretative statements made after their adoption often served to distance the developed countries from the language and intent of the resolution. An example is the statement made on behalf of the developed countries that 'no part of the resolution [on international monetary issues] was designed either to prejudge decisions yet to be taken in the Fund or to reopen decisions and conclusions which had already been reached.'⁹ This interpretation largely negated the purpose of the resolution.

Another feature of the conference worth noting was the assertive and combative manner in which the US was prepared to stand alone in opposition when it was unable to bring the other developed countries along with it. We saw an instance of this earlier in the case of the US casting the lone negative vote on the resolution on compensatory financing. On two politically oriented resolutions (on Palestine and Namibia), the US was also alone among the developed countries in casting negative votes. The US stood alone in formally dissociating itself from the carefully negotiated and tactfully drafted statement adopted by the conference setting out shared views on the world economic situation, and on approaches to the contemporary world economic crisis.¹⁰ On a resolution on international trade in goods and services, the US called for a separate vote on two paragraphs dealing with services, and stood alone in voting against adoption of these paragraphs.¹¹ And the US, while joining the consensus on the resolution calling for renewed efforts to implement the integrated commodities programme, later made a statement expressing its serious reservations about the objectives of the programme, in particular the need for price-stabilization commodity agreements, and its scepticism as to the programme's chances of success.

All of this - the watering down of the Group of 77's draft resolutions, the developed countries' subsequent qualifying statements, and the US's uncompromising hostility - suggested that something of a dead-end was being approached. In fact, the post-conference period was to see not merely a standstill on new measures, but pressure building up for a roll-back on understandings and agreements previously reached, and for a redefinition of the role of UNCTAD in North-South relations.

Redefining UNCTAD's role

The Board meeting in September 1984 provided the occasion for commemorating the 20th anniversary of UNCTAD and for reflecting on UNCTAD's past and future. A statement made on that occasion on behalf of the developed countries gave a clear idea of the new thinking. Stressing the importance of the concept of interdependence, where 'the smallest economic action by one country could have far-reaching effects on others,' it was less easy than in 1964, the statement said, to see the various world economies as polarized, some being at the core and others at the periphery. The need now was for a forum 'in which

States at all levels of development had a part to play and obligations to fulfil in seeking and recommending courses of action,' and for UNCTAD to evolve into an instrument 'for handling economic issues in the broadest sense, less from the North-South standpoint than from the standpoint of partnership and interdependence.' In other words, rich and poor, strong and weak, were henceforth to be treated formally as equals, the shark swimming freely in the same waters as the small fry without any special measures for the protection of the latter. Apart from rejecting the centre-periphery concept of North-South relations, which inspired Prebisch's thinking, this would abrogate the very principle on which UNCTAD had been founded, that is, the need for special and differential measures to be accorded to the developing countries to allow them to survive and prosper in a world of unequals. The statement also referred to the need for a review 'of the working habits and institutional framework' of the organization in the light of the changed circumstances, aimed to ensure 'that UNCTAD remained a valid and widely supported institution, dedicated to development *within the context of increasing partnership and mutual dependence.*' (Italics added.)[12]

The US also used this Board meeting to make known its own thinking on the subject, pointing out that it had 'serious concerns' about how UNCTAD was carrying out its tasks. The US believed that the main purpose of UNCTAD 'was to allow member States to discuss their concerns and share their views with others, reach common understandings on the nature of problems of concern, and only then to seek agreement on issues or parts of issues where agreement was possible or likely.' In other words, it was to be little more than a talking shop, and certainly not a vehicle to exert pressure for change. The UNCTAD secretariat was also criticized for undertaking tasks on which 'there was little prospect of eventual agreement and for which there was no apparent need.' There was much stress on the need for improvements in working methods and on the way in which business was conducted, and, above all, there was 'an interest in ensuring that UNCTAD was effectively an organization that decreased confrontation between developed and developing countries by seeking realistic solutions to specific economic issues.'[13]

The statement by the Netherlands to the same Board meeting, stressing the need for 'a more realistic attitude' to the North-South dialogue within UNCTAD, approached the issue somewhat differently. The emphasis here was on the new-found realization 'that there were limits to what Governments could achieve through interventionist policies' and on an increased awareness of the power of market forces. This applied at both the national and the

international levels, leading to growing doubts that 'all-encompassing strategies set out by national Governments and intergovernmental organizations,
were the most appropriate way to promote development, . . . and an increasing
recognition of the need to facilitate autonomous, market-oriented change.'
That is to say, if interventionist policies were being abandoned at the national
level, much less could they be justified at the international level, and all that
was necessary was to leave well enough alone and to allow full rein to the free
play of market forces. Thus, so far as UNCTAD was concerned, 'What was
needed at the moment was somewhat more dialogue and somewhat less
negotiation.'[14] In other words, there should be nothing but talk, and the
recognition by the 1979 Manila Conference 'of UNCTAD as a principal
instrument of the General Assembly for negotiations in relevant areas of
international trade and related issues of international economic co-operation'
would quietly fall by the wayside.

The new UNCTAD takes shape

The aggressive campaign by the developed countries to rein back and
neutralize an organization whose creation they had actively opposed from the
outset, but to which they were obliged to acquiesce, given the political
dynamics of the period, was now to take on a new twist and to achieve new
success when they (particularly the US) were able to secure the precipitate
retirement of the incumbent Head of the organization, Sri Lankan economist
Gamani Corea. He had held the post for nearly ten years, had been an active
participant in and prime mover of the array of policy measures being promoted
in UNCTAD, which the US and other developed countries now wanted to see
behind them (including the much despised integrated commodities programme),
retained a certain independence of mind, and had established as well a personal
and intellectual standing among the developing countries, through which he
could exercise a considerable influence. It was therefore of some importance
that he should go if a new page were to be turned and a clean break made with
the past. He left office soon after the Board meeting of September 1984, at
which the views of the developed countries summarized above were expressed;
the pressure was so great for his hasty departure that it took place even before
a successor could be appointed, with the result that the organization was left
languishing for the better part of a year without an appointed Head. The path
that UNCTAD was to follow became quite predictable.

From now on, UNCTAD would operate within the parameters laid down by the US and its developed country partners. Confrontation would no longer be on the cards. The secretariat would be tamed and would play its part in holding the developing countries back. Gone would be the days when the secretariat put forward bold new ideas for policy action and encouraged the developing countries to press for their acceptance and implementation. In fact, with the rigid control that was placed on the quantity, aims and purpose of secretariat documentation (see p.180), there was soon scope for (and interest in) little other than humdrum, repetitive reports prepared for the regular meetings of the Board and the standing committees, of no great technical or policy interest. Overall, there has been a general standstill on action, and a noticeable lack of interest in the principal long-standing policy areas on the UNCTAD agenda, including the commodities programme, compensatory financing, financial flows, international monetary issues and debt. In the area of international trade, where the locus of action is in GATT rather than in UNCTAD, UNCTAD has been allowed to do some monitoring and analysis on questions of protectionism and market access, and to help developing countries to prepare for the Uruguay Round negotiations, about which more later. For the rest, the organization has been encouraged to find new outlets for its energies in providing technical assistance to developing countries, with emphasis on such issues as the computerization of customs documentation.

The low key style of the seventh UNCTAD conference, held in Geneva in July 1987, was an indication of the new mood. For the first time, the developing countries came to an UNCTAD conference without any draft resolutions and indeed without any specific demands. In fact, at the insistence of the developed countries (spurred on by the US), it was agreed beforehand that, breaking with tradition, the conference would not adopt any resolutions, but only a so-called 'Final Act', which turned out to be an agreed statement containing an assessment of economic developments and understandings about policy measures needed at the national and international levels, all carefully negotiated and involving no demands for action by developed countries. This conference marked a sharp break with the past.

The eighth conference, held in Cartagena, Colombia in February 1992, saw what must be the culmination of this process, ushering in the 'new' UNCTAD. At the initiative of the North, the question of institutional reform dominated the conference, and the final outcome represented a formal endorsement of all that the US had been pushing for over the years. Confrontation would henceforth be a thing of the past, and, at the urging of the North, developing countries would cease during the conference to caucus as a group on substantive issues, or to put forward common group positions. The document adopted by the conference makes clear that in future the emphasis would be on the exchange of experiences and on promoting international consensus through intergovernmental consultations and deliberations. Negotiations leading to resolutions, recommendations, etc., while not wholly excluded, should be preceded by a 'broad convergence of views', and should be launched only on the basis of 'a large degree of common understanding on the desirability of an outcome and its form.'[15] The transformation of the character of the organization was complete.

Least developed countries: a special case

UNCTAD's one long-standing activity that has always received the willing support of the developed countries, even after the backlash against UNCTAD that set in during the 1980s, concerns the special programme of support for the least developed countries. This term refers to a special category first recognized by the General Assembly in 1970, as being the poorest, economically weakest and most disadvantaged among the developing countries, in need of special attention and international help to assist them in overcoming their exceptional handicap. Twenty-five countries, with a total population of some 150 million, were originally identified as least developed, and UNCTAD was assigned the main responsibility for devising special programmes and for co-ordinating international action in their support. Among the developing countries themselves, the special programme in favour of the least developed had always occupied a somewhat ambiguous position, and had a tendency to be divisive. While the programme has always been formally supported by the Group of 77 as a whole, there has been throughout an undercurrent of antagonism between the least developed and the rest of the developing countries, based on the perception that special measures in favour of the former might be at the expense of the latter. No doubt this underlying antagonism, and the potential for schism among the developing countries that it created, were factors that helped to attract the support of the developed countries for the programme. But other factors were undoubtedly also at work, among which we might mention the relatively limited size of the group in terms of population, and hence the more manageable nature of the problem of providing meaningful assistance. This was particularly important for some of the smaller and more eager to help of the developed countries (for example the Scandinavians and the Dutch), whose only hope of making a meaningful impact was through a concentrated effort in a few of the smaller and poorer developing countries.

Over the years, a good deal of attention has been focused on the least developed countries, and much has been heard of special measures taken in their favour. While UNCTAD has been the focal point for the consideration of, and the call for, these special measures, they involved for the most part action to be taken elsewhere. Areas where special measures have been proposed and taken include the terms and conditions of external financing, debt relief, market access, and sundry others. To foster international support for the cause, two major United Nations conferences on the least developed countries have so far been held, both organized by UNCTAD and held in Paris at the invitation of the French Government. The first, in 1981, came up with a programme of measures with the resounding title of 'Substantial New Programme of Action for the 1980s for the Least Developed Countries (SNPA)', and the second, in 1990, adopted the more moderate sounding 'Programme of Action for the Least Developed Countries for the 1990s'.

It is difficult to come to any clear conclusion as to whether or to what extent the special measures proposed and adopted in favour of the least developed countries were relevant to their needs and have been effectively implemented. The dismal performance of these countries in the years since special international attention has been focused on them suggest at the very least that the programme has not been very effective. In fact, in the 20 years or so since the category was first recognized, its size has greatly expanded, with an additional 22 countries having joined the ranks of the least developed, bringing the total by the end of 1991 to 47 with a combined population of some 500 million.[16] The economic performance of the least developed countries has also been largely stagnant or downhill, and the gap between them and the rest of the developing countries has been widening.[17] There is little evidence, therefore, that the active support the developed countries have given to this programme of special measures has borne fruit.

Reappraisal and roll-back in the field of trade

Trade is the area in which developing countries have gone furthest in seeing their wishes met for special and differential measures in their favour. On the export side, the important example of this is the GSP, discussed in some detail in Chapters 4 and 5 (see pp.72, 86-7, 124). On the import side, article 18-B of the GATT, and the way it has been interpreted in practice, has been an important example. This is the Article containing the general balance-of-payments escape clause, permitting developing countries to impose wide-ranging import restrictions, in derogation of normal GATT obligations, in order to protect their balance of payments. Developing countries have used this widely as a means of allocating scarce foreign exchange resources with a view to promoting their development objectives. The generally relaxed conditions on which developing countries were able to gain membership of the GATT, without the need to make any major contributions in terms of tariff concessions as an entry fee, were also examples of the special treatment afforded these countries in the trade field. A related example of this was the minimal participation of developing countries in the various GATT negotiating rounds over the years. The tariff reductions which resulted from these negotiations, confined almost exclusively to industrial goods, were in practice negotiated and exchanged among the main industrial countries, after which, under the GATT system, they were multilateralized and made available to all GATT members. There was therefore little incentive for the active participation of developing countries whose main export products, consisting of agricultural and other primary commodities, were largely excluded from the tariff reduction exercise, and who, by virtue of the mfn principle, were in any event potential beneficiaries of the lower tariffs on industrial goods negotiated among the industrial countries. A further consideration that goes to explain their limited participation was the feeling that with their acute and seemingly permanent shortage of foreign exchange, their limited industrial base, and their utter dependence on the industrial countries for their supplies of industrial goods, there was little they could offer by way of meaningful concessions in the negotiations.

But over time things have been changing. The share of industrial goods in total exports of developing countries has increased markedly (from 10 per cent in 1955 to 47 per cent in 1980 and to 69 per cent in 1988), with a corresponding decline in the share of agricultural and other primary products, though this trend was by no means evenly reflected in the exports of all developing countries. In fact, a dozen or so countries account for the bulk of the increase in developing countries' exports of industrial goods, and a large number of developing countries remain, even in the 1990s, predominantly dependent on primary products for their export earnings.[18] Also, with tariffs in the main industrial countries now being minimal on most industrial goods, as a result of the substantial tariff reductions agreed during the past rounds of GATT trade negotiations, tariffs have ceased to dominate trade policy in these countries, having been replaced by an array of non-tariff barriers.[19]

While developing countries have been potential beneficiaries of the tariff reductions negotiated under the various GATT rounds, they have also been the main targets of the new wave of non-tariff barriers which have come to replace tariffs as the main trade policy instrument, and which operate quite outside the legal framework of GATT. The most notable example of this, and the one with the longest history (if we exclude agriculture, which was never really brought under GATT discipline), concerns the arrangements relating to textiles and clothing. This is the product group in which newly industrializing countries usually first achieve competitive strength, and that has traditionally always played the role of leading sector in export-led industrialization. This was so for the country that first blazed the path of modern industrialization, the United Kingdom, and it was also the case for the star performer of the 20th century, Japan. But, owing to protectionist pressures in the industrial countries, newly industrializing developing countries were never able to exploit fully their competitive strength in this sector, and since the early 1960s were obliged to be parties to *ad hoc* international arrangements limiting their exports of textiles and clothing to developed countries.[20]

The 1980s saw a movement towards reappraisal and roll-back of the various privileges and special advantages that developing countries had enjoyed in the trading system, and saw as well an augmentation and proliferation of the constraints and limitations to which their trade was exposed. This movement reflected to some extent the triumph of the ultra-conservative free market philosophy, and to some extent a conscious effort of the major industrial countries, particularly the US, to recapture some of the concessions won by the developing countries during the 1960s and 1970s.

The trade liberalization programmes imposed on developing countries by the IMF and the World Bank, in the context of their debt rescheduling and associated structural adjustment programmes, reflected the triumph of the free market philosophy in trade policies of developing countries. These programmes generally required the developing countries concerned drastically to reduce their tariffs, to eliminate quantitative restrictions and other non-tariff import barriers, and generally to free exchange rates and foreign trade as a whole from administrative control. In this way the Fund and the Bank were able to impose, on the developing countries affected, levels of trade disciplines much stricter than those to which they were subjected under GATT rules. There has also been pressure on individual developing countries to renounce unilaterally their right to resort to the balance-of-payments provision of Article 18-B, and a number of middle-income developing countries, including Korea and Brazil, have in fact done so, while Bolivia was forced to accept limits on its use of this provision in its accession negotiations for GATT membership.

The shift towards a more rigorous and less differential treatment of developing countries in the GATT framework is also revealed in the conditions these countries have had to satisfy to gain GATT membership. In the past, only minimal conditions concerning trade regimes and the level of tariff bindings had to be met, reflecting the currently accepted view that developing countries required greater flexibility in conducting their trade policies, as well as the general feeling that, for the reasons mentioned earlier, the cards were stacked against these countries and that it was therefore inappropriate to make any great demands on them as a price for GATT membership. During the 1980s, however, there was a significant change of attitude in this regard, and developing countries applying for GATT membership have had to satisfy much more stringent entry conditions in terms of tariff bindings and tariff reductions, among other things. According to Arthur Dunkel, GATT's Director-General, recent developing country applicants, such as Mexico, Bolivia and Costa Rica, undertook commitments that are more far-reaching than those operated even by some developed countries. Mexico, for example, as a condition of entry, established and bound a maximum *ad valorem* tariff of 50 per cent on the bulk of its imports and undertook to reduce substantially tariffs in the 20-50 per cent range. Mexico subsequently reduced its maximum tariff to 20 per cent, after which it was estimated to operate a low-weighted tariff of around 10 per cent.[21] The pattern set by Mexico was followed by other recent developing country applicants, including Tunisia, Venezuela, El Salvador and Guatemala, in addition to Costa Rica and Bolivia. This pattern contrasts sharply, for example, with the current situation in India, one of the original members of GATT, which has bound none of its tariffs, and whose average tariffs are currently estimated to exceed 100 per cent.

It is necessary to add that it cannot be taken for granted that the shift towards lower tariffs and increased trade liberalization, which this movement has brought in its train, necessarily involve a 'cost' to the developing countries affected, and indeed there is an important school of thought, led not surprisingly by the World Bank and its professorial consultants, that trade liberalization by developing countries is a (perhaps *the*) vital ingredient for successful economic development.[22] While there are grave doubts as to whether trade liberalization World Bank style is necessarily the best recipe for successful economic development - and in fact the cases usually cited by the World Bank and its acolytes as evidence of the efficacy of that approach, like South Korea, and Brazil in an earlier era, are hardly appropriate examples, since these are countries that practised extensive *'dirigisme'* in the foreign trade sector during the formative years of their industrialization drive - there seems little doubt that a good number of developing countries made inappropriate use of the freedom to protect that was not in the best interest of their development process. It is doubtful, for example, whether the very high tariffs prevailing in India over this extended period were in the best interest of its long-term industrialization and development prospects.

Preferences (i.e. the GSP) is another area where the 1980s have seen a trend towards reappraisal and roll-back of concessions and privileges earlier granted to developing countries. The GSP, of course, differs from GATT-based rights and privileges in that it is not binding in any legal sense, and can be unilaterally withdrawn or otherwise changed at the pleasure of the developed country granting the concession. So far, roll-back has taken the form mostly of 'graduation', where countries considered to have achieved a sufficient level of industrial development are wholly or partially denied GSP benefits. The US has been most active in applying graduation. The US has also been most active in another form of roll-back: threatening to withdraw GSP benefits in order to extract concessions from recipient countries, usually in respect of issues not covered by GATT trade rules, for example in relation to intellectual property, services or foreign investment.

More disturbing yet is the recent trend, spearheaded by the US, to seek to extract concessions from developing countries in areas not covered by GATT rules as a condition for their continued enjoyment of existing GATT-guaranteed benefits, in particular, access to markets for their exports of goods. This new approach, which began to emerge in the early 1980s, proceeded on two fronts: by strengthening Section 301 of the US Trade Act of 1974 in such a way as to make it a blunt instrument with which to force concessions from trading partners; and by calling for a new round of GATT trade negotiations which would go beyond the traditional goods sector to incorporate as well the 'new' areas of interest to the United States.

The background to this new wave of thinking by US policy makers is complex and involved, and cannot be gone into here. We may mention, however, some relevant considerations which had a bearing on the issue. These include the large US trade deficit, which had for some time been a cause of growing concern, and the feeling that began to take root that the US was losing its competitive edge in most industrial sectors. High interest rates, fiscal deficits, and an over-valued dollar, to which the economic policies of the Reagan Administration led, were clearly the important underlying factors behind the trade deficit and the associated belief that the US was losing ground in the trade field. Something clearly needed to be done, and since there was no disposition to change internal US policies, there was a tendency to place the blame for the deficit on the policies of partner countries, and there was much talk about forcing partner countries to open their markets, not only for goods but also for 'new' sectors such as services where the US felt they retained a competitive edge.[23]

Section 301 in the original 1974 legislation authorizes action against foreign trade practices that either violate international trade agreements or burden or restrict US commerce in an 'unjustifiable, unreasonable or discriminatory fashion'. While the wording was loose enough to open the doors to abuse, in practice it was used mainly to remedy treaty-defined violations of US trade rights, determined as such by appropriate multilateral procedures. With the amendment of Section 301 in the Trade and Tariff Act of 1984, and even more so in the Omnibus Trade and Competitiveness Act of 1988, however, all treaty-defined restraints were removed, and the section now became a crude instrument, backed up by the threat of massive tariff retaliation, to force withdrawal of any foreign 'unfair trade' practices (defined as such by no treaty whatsoever) determined by the US to be 'unreasonable' and impacting adversely on its trade. The Super 301, as the new legislation came to be called, was the unashamed use of the big stick, without any carrot, of demanding trade concessions from others using not the inducement of a counterpart trade concession (as was the practice in GATT trade negotiations) but the threat to suspend existing trading obligations if the demands are not met. And to make the threat more ominous, the legislation established a tight time schedule within which the Administration was obliged to come up with findings of unfair trade practices and either to have them removed or to take retaliatory action.

Apart from Japan, an industrial country with whom the US has a lopsided, complex and emotionally charged trading relationship, the main targets of the Super 301 legislation are those semi-industrialized and newly industrializing countries of Asia and Latin America that have begun to make a mark as exporters of manufactures, are highly dependent on export markets, and are therefore most vulnerable to pressure. And it is in respect to these countries that the legislation acquires its broadest sweep, for what is at issue here for the US is not reciprocal access to the markets of these countries for US merchandise exports, the usual stuff of trade disputes and trade negotiations, but concessions in various areas far removed from trade in the accepted sense of the term. Brazil and India were the first two countries (in addition to Japan) to be hit by the new legislation. In the case of Brazil, the US demanded the revision of Brazil's patent legislation, to provide greater patent protection to US pharmaceutical and chemical manufacturers. In the case of India, the demands concerned practices relating to the treatment of foreign investors, as well as the question of access to the Indian insurance market, a so-called service sector. In both cases the threat of trade sanctions was being used as a club to force changes in policies which the US unilaterally considered to be undesirable, notwithstanding the fact that such action would violate US commitments under GATT. In the case of Brazil, the threat led to the actual application of sanctions (a punitive tariff of 100% on selected Brazilian exports, worth US$200 million), in complete disregard of the fact that the action is GATT-illegal. An action was subsequently brought by Brazil before a GATT panel on dispute settlement. Countries placed on the 'Priority Watch List' for special attention under the intellectual property provisions of Super-301, with the threat of sanctions hanging over their heads, included, as of May 1989, Brazil, China, India, South Korea, Mexico, Saudi Arabia, Taiwan and Thailand.[24]

Developing countries and the Uruguay Round

As mentioned earlier, enhanced use of the strengthened S.301 went parallel with efforts to get a new round of GATT negotiations under way, which would encompass the so-called new issues. When the idea was first mooted by the US in late 1982, it was received with no more enthusiasm by the other industrial countries than by the developing countries. The EC adopted its traditional posture of reluctance towards a new round, always anxious to avoid the criticisms of its protectionist agricultural policy to which such negotiations inevitably gave rise. Most middle-sized industrial countries were not averse to a new round as such, though their idea of an agenda was rather different from what the US had in mind, their major preoccupation being how to rein in and control the growing tendency of the large powers (that is, the US and the EC) to ignore GATT principles.

The developing countries were from the outset very hostile to the call for a new round, and for good reason. They had for some time been the victims of a piecemeal chipping away of the GATT rules, leaving them to face a mounting burden of *ad hoc* restrictions on their exports. Restrictive measures affecting agriculture, and textiles and clothing, were followed by *ad hoc* restraints affecting a series of other export products, and their primary concern was to see these restraints removed or eased. Such restraints, which often go under the name of 'voluntary export restraints' (VERs), obliges the exporting country 'voluntarily' to limit exports to the importing country of the product concerned below some specified ceiling. The use of VERs grew dramatically during the 1980s, with the US and the EC between them accounting for the bulk of these export restraints imposed on developing countries. Product groups most seriously affected include steel products, footwear, electronic products and agricultural products, and developing countries hardest hit include Argentina, Brazil, Korea, Taiwan, Chile, Thailand, Uruguay, Trinidad & Tobago, Venezuela and Yugoslavia.[25] Abuses of safeguard measures and of anti-dumping legislation to restrain developing countries' exports were also of growing importance.

Developing countries had little faith, however, that a new round would lead to the removal or easing of these restraints. And it was clear that the attempt to expand the scope of the negotiations to include new issues could get them embroiled in new commitments in which they could only be losers, since in these new areas, which include patents and intellectual property rights, foreign investment and services (banking, insurance, telecommunications, etc.), all the advantages lay with the industrial countries. Their greatest fear, and the greatest danger they faced, was the prospect of linking commitments in these new areas to trade in goods. And if any doubts remained in anyone's mind as to their intentions in this regard, the threatening noises the US had begun to make, centred on its Section 301 legislation, would surely dispel them. As developing countries saw it, therefore, they had nothing to gain, and quite a bit to lose, from the proposed new round of negotiations.

It was not long before the US was able to convince the other industrial countries that they too had an interest in a new round of GATT negotiations that would focus on the new issues. Services were a rapidly expanding sector, playing an increasingly important specialized role in the economy, and at the same time the subject of growing cross-border links made possible through modern high technology (computers, information technology, telecommunications, etc.). It was therefore a subject that appeared well worth looking into to see whether there was scope for new international disciplines the better to channel and exploit the potential benefits from these cross-border links. But this was a game that would mostly be played by the industrial countries. Similarly, there was a broad congruity of interests among the industrial countries on the investment issue (or, as it soon came to be known, trade related investment measures or TRIMS), and on the issue of intellectual property rights (soon referred to as trade aspects of intellectual property rights or TRIPS), and certainly *vis-à-vis* developing countries, which, in respect of these issues, were necessarily always on the receiving end. The industrial countries, therefore, soon closed ranks behind the call for a new round along the lines proposed by the Americans. The shift in emphasis from trade in goods to the new issues would also get them off the hook, since they saw little scope for negotiating significant new trade concessions on goods. Tariffs on the main industrial goods had already been reduced to very low levels in the previous rounds of GATT negotiations, and in those cases where new non-tariff barriers had been erected there was no wish remove them. In fact, so far as the industrial countries were concerned, the only wild card in the pack related to agriculture, with the inevitable confrontation between the US and the EC threatening at all stages to spoil the negotiations.

Developing countries fought hard to block the negotiations, but under US pressure had to go along with the establishment in July 1985 of a Preparatory Committee 'to determine the objectives, subject matter and modalities' for a new round of negotiations. Led by India and Brazil, they fought a hard rear-guard action to limit the agenda to traditional items, excluding new issues. Again under US pressure, widely supported at this stage by the industrial countries as a whole, developing countries had to yield ground, and when after arduous negotiations the round was finally launched in Punte del Este, Uruguay in September 1986, the agenda included all the new issues demanded by the US. The only concession the developing countries were able to win in this regard related to services, concerning which it was agreed that the subject should be treated in separate but parallel negotiations (though the practical importance of this concession has never been entirely clear).

This is not the place for an analysis of the agenda of the Uruguay Round, nor for a review and assessment of progress in the negotiations to date.[26] It may be noted, however, that even apart from the question of the 'new issues', this is much the most ambitious of the negotiating rounds to date, with fourteen separate negotiating groups dealing with, among other things, such far-reaching issues as the review of the GATT Articles, dispute settlement procedures and the functioning of the GATT system. So far as developing countries were concerned, there was some reassurance in the fact that the Declaration launching the Round reaffirmed the principles of special and differential treatment, with particular reference to preferences, non-reciprocity and policy-exemptions, although in qualification it is also suggested that the better-off developing countries should participate more fully 'in the framework of rights and obligations' under the GATT. Another inclusion intended to reassure developing countries were commitments to implement a 'standstill and roll-back' of GATT-inconsistent trade policies, something they had been energetically demanding. But these commitments have been largely ignored, notably by the US, in proceeding none the less with its GATT-inconsistent S. 301 actions.

The Round was to have been concluded in December 1990, but the Ministerial Meeting formally convened in Brussels for that purpose had to disperse without achieving its aim, failure to come close to an agreement on agriculture being the primary (ostensible) reason for the failure to meet the deadline. Since then the negotiations have dragged on. In December 1991, Arthur Dunkel, the Director-General of GATT and the Chairman of the Negotiating Committee, formally tabled the 'Draft Final Act' embodying the results of the negotiations. This document, containing the 'complete and consolidated' package of draft agreements, covering all areas of the negotiations, has a somewhat ambiguous status, since the text in certain key areas, particular agriculture, was put forward by the chairman himself in the absence of agreement among the key players, in the hope that this procedure would force a successful conclusion to the Round. In the event, success was not easily forthcoming, and at the time of writing (September 1992) there is still no clear indication of what the final outcome will be. In the end, it will be up to the major industrial powers, particularly the US and the EC, to determine whether the talks will succeed or fail, and given the coincidence of interest between them on most of the major issues, much will ultimately depend on their willingness to come to an agreement on agriculture. On the new issues (TRIPS, TRIMS and services), there was always a wide measure of common understanding among the industrial countries,[27] and the texts in the Draft Final Act covering these areas are largely agreed among them. A uniting theme, which links all three new issues in the minds of the industrial countries, is their role in expanding the economic space in which the transnational corporations, the chosen instrument for knitting the world into a global economy under Northern domination, can operate free from interference from governments of developing countries.

Concerning TRIPS and TRIMS, the whole purpose of the exercise is clearly to hem in the freedom of action of developing countries in the important areas of technology transfer and the regulation of foreign investment in the interest of promoting their development, and at the same time to provide increased freedom of action for the transnational corporations. It is therefore the North-South dimensions of these issues that are relevant and that account for the presence of these items on the agenda. In the negotiations, developing countries can try and stem the tide and water down the language proposed, but in the end they can only look on with dismay at any 'progress' achieved in these areas. It is ironic that the relatively loose international intellectual property rights system, for example, which has been in existence now for 150 years and which served as the basis for the technology transfer, copying, learning and adaptation that permitted the currently developed countries (not least Japan, but also at an earlier stage the US, France, Germany, etc.) to catch up with the technological leaders and to achieve technological parity, is now to be made more restrictive in order to make it more costly and difficult for newcomers to enter the field. The demands being made by developed countries in this area, whose ultimate purpose may well be to entrench and perpetuate their privileged and increasingly dominant position in the international hierarchy, provide a signal example of the new push for roll-back and containment currently facing the South.

In respect of services the issues are wider, since the industrial countries have negotiating objectives among themselves in addition to the demands they wish to make on developing countries. But the way in which the issues are being defined leaves the developing countries at an obvious disadvantage, with little hope that their demands in the field of services can be requited. The proposals emanating from the US and other industrial countries envisage liberalization being confined to the capital- intensive, high-finance, high-tech service sectors in which these countries possess an overwhelming advantage, and they see no place on the agenda for labour-related services where the potential advantage of developing countries lies. The US, for example, has been pushing hard for the right of establishment for corporate entities as essential for ensuring market liberalization in the service sector, but dismisses out of hand the right of establishment for individual producers of labour services as being incompatible with immigration laws. The entire framework in which the issues are being defined by the powerful countries is heavily biased against developing countries. What will eventually emerge at the end of the day in respect of services remains to be seen, but we can already be sure that it will largely reflect the views and interests of the industrial countries, and those of the developing countries will be largely ignored.

Given the obvious threat that they face from negotiations on the new issues, in which areas would developing countries most wish to achieve a favourable outcome? Perhaps most important would be the strengthening of disciplines to curb unilateralism, excessive and abusive use of safeguards and anti-dumping, and the growing use of *ad hoc* extra-legal export restraints, all matters of the greatest concern to those developing countries beginning to break out of utter dependence on primary products for their export earnings. Important also would be a significant liberalization of trade in the textiles and clothing sector, as well as in agriculture. Unfortunately, however, these are not areas in which one can be too sanguine about the prospects. For the rest, only the fear of a total collapse of the international trading system in the event of the failure of the Uruguay Round could justify the continuing interest of developing countries in a successful outcome.

Environment and development: a new issue raises its head

Another indication of the remarkable changes in the currents of North-South relations that took place during the 1980s is the extent to which the initiative for defining the international agenda has shifted to the side of the North. In the 1960s and 1970s, the South defined the issues and mounted the pressure in calling for international conferences for dealing with issues they considered important, and the North was on the defensive, dragging its feet and agreeing reluctantly only under the onslaught of pressure from the South, the first UNCTAD conference being the most characteristic example of this kind. The boot is now on the other foot, and we saw an important illustration of this in the previous discussion concerning the broadening of the agenda for the new round of GATT trade negotiations. But perhaps nothing illustrates it better than the UN Conference on Environment and Development (UNCED) held in Rio de Janiero, Brazil, in June 1992. This was the most important UN conference on development-related issues for over a decade, and one of the largest international gatherings ever, attended at the level of heads of state.

The background to this meeting has a long history, and had its roots in the growing preoccupation in certain quarters in the industrial countries with the impact of the existing pattern of economic growth in these countries on the environment. There was, for instance, rising concern about the growing problems of waste disposal resulting from the accelerating pace of industrialization and from the emergence and spread of new industries generating ever more noxious and hazardous waste products, for example in the chemical, petro-chemical and atomic industries. Concern was focused on the environmental impact of existing practices, particularly in degrading the rivers, oceans and other waterways, and in the process undermining the vital ecological balance. There was also growing apprehension about the implications for the global environment of the expanding rate at which fossil fuels were being burnt, depositing waste gases in the atmosphere. The fear here, based on recent scientific findings, was linked to the so-called greenhouse effect, that is, the threat of global warming and of the depletion of the ozone layer, which could endanger life on the planet Earth. There was also the question of the deleterious impact on the environment of the intensified use of chemical fertilizers and insecticides in the highly industrialized agriculture increasingly being practised in the developed countries, and the harmful impact on the global environment of certain by-products of chemical processes, for example the escape into the atmosphere of chlorofluorocarbons (CFCs), associated with the use of refrigerating units and aerosol sprays.

Despite the clear reluctance of the political establishment in the industrial countries to heed these concerns, the negative implications of which for the existing pattern of economic growth were hardly welcome, the issue could not simply be ignored, and there was a burgeoning of increasingly active pressure groups hammering away at the need for something to be done and insisting that business as usual simply could not continue. In response we had first the trend towards the introduction of environmental legislation which began to take shape in the 1970s, but did not stem the pressure from environmentalists, especially in view of growing scientific evidence about the dangers faced. The 1980s therefore saw the growth of the green movement, particularly in Western Europe - politically active groups demanding radical changes in the pattern of economic growth, with the protection of the environment more firmly in mind, who soon became a serious political force in a number of Western European countries, notably West Germany, presenting a growing threat to the traditional political parties. It thus became increasingly necessary for the traditional parties to appear to be doing more to protect the environment and thereby to outmanoeuvre and contain the radical environmentalists.

The issue was the subject of a number of international conferences and, more significantly, gave rise to the Brundtland Commission, headed by the former Prime Minister of Norway, which prepared a report on the problems of the environment from a global perspective. The report focused on the need for a proper balance between environment and development, and introduced the concept of 'sustainable development' as an ideal to which policies should aim.

By this phrase was presumably meant a pattern of development which would not overburden the environment and which could in consequence continue indefinitely into the future. Whatever the exact meaning, the phrase caught the fancy of policy-makers and opinion-moulders in the North, and has since been bandied about with such panache and so constantly that it has come to achieve something of the status of a new paradigm. Soon every conference agenda or study outline on the international development circuit was paying homage to the need for 'sustainable development', and it was considered amiss to talk about development without the qualifying prefix. The phrase evidently filled a useful role in the search by policy-makers in the North for a means to deflect the attention of environmentalists from the need for the radical solutions at home which they had in mind.

Shifting the environmental burden to the South

It is not difficult to see why the phrase has been embraced so fervently and has proved so useful to policy-makers in the North. By shifting the emphasis from 'growth' to 'development' it obfuscates the issues that the environmentalists had primarily in mind, and shifts the spotlight in some degree away from the industrial countries. This it does by profiting from the close association the word 'development' has always had with the efforts of underdeveloped countries to raise their living standards and to enter into a phase of modern economic growth comparable to that which the developed, industrial countries have achieved, and by conveniently ignoring the fact that the rapid cumulative expansion of output and incomes that has taken place in the industrial North in the post-war years, whose impact on the environment was the subject of so much concern to environmentalists, has throughout been widely referred to as 'economic growth'. Hence, by a sleight of hand, a substitution of words, the problem is redefined, the North is no longer the main culprit in the environmental dock, and the developing countries, for whom 'development' is such an important catch-word, must now stand as co-accused.

On what grounds and by what method of reasoning are developing countries to be lumped together with developed countries when it comes to the question of saving the earth from the threat of environmental degradation and ecological collapse? The countries of the industrial North, in their zeal to achieve ever-increasing levels of consumption, bear the main responsibility for the extravagant use of the world's resources and for the great bulk of the industrial effluent, hazardous wastes, toxic chemicals, radioactive debris, fossil-fuel burning,

CFCs let loose in the atmosphere, and other environmentally damaging by-products of modern industrialization that now threaten the stability of the world's eco-system. While few question this, a way is now being found to ensnare the developing countries in the net of environmentalists' concerns and thereby to diffuse responsibility and shift the focus away from the North. So we began to hear how poverty itself can contribute to environmental degradation through the pressures of population growth, soil erosion, the clearing of tropical forests, etc., and it was not long before the latter phenomenon in particular was to take centre-stage, linked to the so-called greenhouse effect. It was discovered that the gases emitted by the earth's vegetation cover (of which tropical forests constitute the greatest proportion still in existence) acted as a neutralizing agent, counteracting the deleterious effects of fossil-fuel burning - the overwhelming proportion of which had hitherto been produced by the industrial North - on the protective layer of the upper atmosphere. Here, therefore, was an issue which enabled the Northern environmentalists to turn their attention on the developing countries in whose territories were to be found the remaining tropical forests.

It was along this line of reasoning that the environmental issue was globalized, ideas about an environmentally healthy planet as the 'common heritage of mankind' emphasized, co-responsibility (North and South) stressed, and what has come to be called 'earth patriotism' proposed as a new way of thinking on the international political scene. All this led to increasingly strident calls for co-operative action by all states to protect the earth from environmental collapse, and the convening of international meetings on the subject. Political leaders in the North, wishing to deflect attention from their own environmental sins, saw advantages in giving qualified support to the new twist in the environmental debate, and seized the opportunity of calling for a United Nations conference on environment and development in which the issues would be seen and discussed essentially in their global dimensions. The manner in which the promoters of the conference were able to define the issues in such a way as to place all countries on a largely equal footing in terms of responsibility for environmental damage is reflected in the following remark by the UN Secretary-General: 'The emergence of "earth patriotism" has led to co-operative efforts at the national and the international levels to ensure that future generations inherit a revived planet. It is now generally acknowledged that both greed and waste, among the economically privileged, and the desperate struggle for survival, among the poor, have despoiled the resources of the earth.'[28] Both, in their own way, are culprits, and stand equally charged.

Not surprisingly, the governments of developing countries have from the outset been wary of this new twist in the environmental debate, and had no desire to see themselves in the dock as co-accused. They were suspicious of the newly discovered concept of sustainable development that was being promoted with such fanfare. It had been difficult enough for them, throughout the previous 30 or 40 years of serious effort, to achieve any kind of development at all. They could therefore hardly look forward with any enthusiasm to the prospect of being asked to lower their sights to, and accept the constraints involved in, 'sustainable' development. Whatever this now hackneyed term may mean (the exact meaning has always been left suitably vague), there was little doubt that it carried the implication that additional constraints, and higher costs, were to be imposed on developing countries in their efforts to break out of the underdevelopment trap. A number of these countries were particularly irked by the growing pressure on them by Northern environmentalist groups to call a halt, for example, to land-clearing and other forms of commercial exploitation of their tropical forests, and for the maintenance of the integrity of these forests in their natural state, this being the act of self-sacrifice that these poor countries should make in order to save the wider environment 'for the common good of mankind', while the rich countries continue their extravagant burning of fossil fuels and continue to overload the environment with other noxious wastes generated by their excessive consumption habits. Some Northern environmentalist groups have even mounted campaigns for the banning or boycotting of trade in tropical timber and its products, an important source of foreign exchange in a number of developing countries.[29] This initiative comes in part from people living in countries where earlier generations unrestrainedly destroyed their forests in order to make room for urban civilization and to support their economic development efforts. This happened in an extreme way in the UK and to a greater or lesser extent in much of Western Europe. Even today, what is left of the European forests are slowing dying under the nefarious impact of the exhaust fumes from that symbol of modern consumerism, the ubiquitous automobile.

The forest issue is only one (though perhaps the most glaring) example of the way in which the debate on the environment has been turned around to try and restrain developing countries, in the name of the common good, from now doing all those things which the developed countries did with such abandon in the past in their efforts to attain their present levels of production and consumption. It is as if a referee has suddenly appeared and decided that all countries should be deemed to be starting from scratch in the race to save the environment, no allowance being made for the head start that some countries had enjoyed and the distance they had already covered.

All this is not to deny, of course, that for indigenous forest dwellers who have for centuries depended on the forest for their livelihood, and who have long adapted their ways of living to their natural habitat, the destruction of the forests can be a real tragedy. These are often the vulnerable groups who have lost out in the general process of commercialization and development. The awareness of their plight, which has come to the fore in the wake of the environmental debate, is therefore greatly to be welcomed, as are the opportunities which this provides them to better protect their interests, often by joining forces with Northern environmentalist groups.

On the meaning of sustainable development

This brings us back to the meaning and implications of the concept of 'sustainable development' which, from the point of view of developing countries, can now be seen to have an even more sinister and troubling aspect lying just below the surface. This was put very clearly and very bluntly by Gamani Corea, the former Secretary-General of UNCTAD, in a lecture delivered in Manila in April 1991.[30] To try and pin down the idea behind the concept, he wonders aloud whether there are any examples of 'unsustainable development' to serve as counter-examples, and asks whether the development models of the US, France, Germany, the UK, Japan, etc., are appropriate examples of unsustainable development. He observes that such development as has taken place in these countries to date has been sustained, and he sees no reason to doubt that it can be sustained if not allowed to get out of hand. But he suggests that such a model would prove unsustainable if copied by all the other countries now in pursuit of development. That is, the carrying capacity of the planet being limited, if the 4 billion people living in the poor countries today (and there will be many more in a decade or two) were to acquire a standard of living and consumption habits similar to those of the 800 million or so living in the rich countries, the planet would very likely simply collapse under the environmental strain. (To see this one needs only to contemplate the frightening thought of automobiles being available in the poor countries on the same *per capita* basis as that now existing in the rich countries of North America, Western Europe and Japan.) The logic therefore of all the talk about sustainable development is that there is hardly room for newcomers, and that the poor must remain poor in order to save the planet! This is the essential contradiction, barely hidden under the surface at UNCED, that the environmental debate poses as we move into the 21st century, and as the tensions and contradictions between rich and poor, developed and underdeveloped continue to simmer.

In the preparatory work for UNCED, the frame of reference was very much along the lines of thinking of the referee mentioned above. As counterpart, and to try and balance the picture somewhat, there was much talk about ensuring access by developing countries to the additional financial resources required to integrate environmental concerns into their development policies and practices and to meet the incremental costs to be incurred by them in complying with the international environmental conventions and protocols being contemplated. There was also talk about the need for making environmentally sound technologies available to developing countries 'on an equitable and affordable basis'. But what are the prospects of these needs being met? They clearly go counter to the direction in which the North's policies towards the South have been moving and crystallizing in recent years, particularly as regards the question of financing and the broadening of the GATT agenda to include the problems of intellectual property rights. One can therefore be forgiven for being sceptical about whether much can be expected on this score as counterpart for developing countries' involvement in the global environmental effort.

The outcome of UNCED fully confirms this scepticism. Little on offer in terms of financial aid was forthcoming, and it soon became clear that all the pre-conference talk about the massive new financing effort which the North would need to make to assist (and encourage) developing countries to play their part in the global environment effort had fallen on deaf ears. Thus, it has been estimated that, overall, the amount of new money committed by industrial countries amounted to a mere US$2.5 billion a year, compared to the US$70 billion a year that the organizers of the conference said was needed.[31] As one observer put it: 'The stinginess of aid pledges by the rich countries fell below the most pessimistic forecasts.'[32] The conference itself ended with the adoption of a number of wordy documents, including the voluminous *Agenda 21* action programme and a *Statement of Principles* on forest management. But these contain little in the way of commitment of any kind, and on forests, the most emotionally charged issue at the conference, developing countries successfully resisted all attempts to open the door to internationally imposed constraints on their freedom to manage their forests as they saw best and in their own interest. The conference also provided the occasion for the signing by governments of the previously negotiated conventions on climate change and on biodiversity. Right to the end, the US remained largely isolated in its reluctance to make any commitments, standing alone in refusing to sign the convention on biodiversity, and insisting on last minute changes to the convention on climate change, greatly weakening it, as the price for attendance at the conference by President Bush.

The drug issue: another example

Drugs are another issue that at the initiative of the North has recently been placed high on the international agenda and in respect of which the South has been forced to react and been placed on the defensive. By the North here is really meant the US, although here as elsewhere the US lead is fully supported by the rest of the North. The drugs problem is a very complex, tangled one, and it is very difficult for the casual (and even not so casual) observer to get anything like a proper understanding of the issues involved. From all accounts, colossal sums are being generated by the illegal drugs trade. Exact figures are obviously difficult to come by, but one often hears figures of hundreds of billions of dollars quoted as estimates of the value of the illegal drugs trade. Such figures would place illegal drugs among the world's largest industries. As every schoolchild (and certainly every convert to the recently ascendant free-market philosophy) knows, money is power. One can only imagine, therefore, the great power, economic, political and otherwise, exercised by those who control significant chunks of the great wealth generated by illegal drugs.

One gets the impression, from press reports and official pronouncements, that the industrial countries account for the great bulk of the consumption of these drugs. Be that as it may, it is clearly the consumption in these countries that has placed this issue on the international agenda. Developing countries are the main producers and sources of these drugs for the developed country markets. In most of the main developing country producers these drugs, now classified as illegal, have long historical roots in the local culture, and have been used for centuries as a narcotic (like tobacco or alcohol) and for medicinal and other purposes without creating any particular social problems.[33] With the growing demand in the developed countries however, they have increasingly been grown as cash crops, and production has no doubt been expanding to keep pace with demand. We should not fail to note here, however, that even more than for other cash crops, producers receive only a small fraction of the 'street' value or final selling price, most of which accrues to the various intermediaries involved in the trade.

The US has succeeded in having these drugs declared illegal virtually on a world-wide basis and has led a campaign to stamp out the trade in them. But with all the resources at its disposal for military defence and for the policing of its borders, it is apparently unable to prevent, reduce, or even to arrest the increase of, the illegal entry into its territory of these drugs, not to mention the impossibility of stamping out their consumption by means of the criminal law. It has therefore sought to place on the shoulders of the developing country producers the onus not only of preventing the export of these products from their territory but, even more significantly, of deterring production thereof as well. This is in countries where there has been a long tradition of production and use of these crops, and where, furthermore, in expanding production in response to market signals, producers are merely following the dictates of the market principles about which developing countries have had to listen to so much lecturing in recent years. Pressure of all sorts, financial, economic, political and even military, has been put on developing countries believed to be involved in the production of and trade in these products, and the US has even gone so far as to use, in the territory of these countries, chemical and biological agents, the wider environmental and other side effects of which are far from known, as defoliants to eradicate the crops. That the permission of the local governments might have been obtained for such grotesque action is only proof of the extent of the pressure that the US was able and willing to employ.

In spite of all this, the trade still seems to be booming. [34] One cannot therefore help wondering whether effort is being made in the right direction. Developing countries have long argued that the main responsibility for stamping out the evils of drug abuse lies with the consuming countries. To the extent that this arises from the import of drugs from abroad, this requires the proper policing of their borders. It is true that policing is a costly exercise, but these are the rich countries, well able to bear the cost. To the extent that the problem arises from demand in the consuming countries, then it is clear that effort has to be directed to eliminate or reduce that demand. Without demand their will be no trade, and the problem disappears. How to achieve this may not be immediately obvious, and may require a good deal of research and clear thinking. Obvious suggestions would include educational programmes and propaganda. Police methods, on which most efforts in the past have been concentrated, are perhaps less relevant for dealing with the problem of demand.[35] But the rich countries clearly have the resources at their disposal to undertake the required research if the problem is given the necessary priority.

But there has evidently been a reluctance to attack the problem at this basic level. Perhaps this is in deference to the free-market principle which recognizes the sovereignty of the consumer. It is clear in any event that so long as demand continues to exist and to grow, first principles of economics (much emphasized by the free-market enthusiasts) will ensure that production and trade will continue to grow and to prosper, and that the only remaining unknown will be the price at which the product will trade in the various markets, given the hurdles and obstacles that may have to be overcome to get the product there. And the greater the price at which the product is sold, the greater the incentive for traders and intermediaries to enter the business and to stimulate consumption and production, leading to ever larger profits and to the amassing of ever more stupendous wealth with which to exercise more power and influence, and thus at least to ensure the perpetuation of the trade. As we remarked earlier, the drugs issue is a very complex one, and it is not easy to fathom the meaning of all that is going on.

In UNCTAD and in the GATT, developing countries have often complained that chemicals, insecticides, drugs and other related products that for safety, health or similar reasons are banned or whose use is tightly controlled in the developed countries, in which they originate, are allowed to be exported freely or with inadequate warning to developing countries. They have been asking for many years now for the implementation of rules to protect developing countries from the importation of products so banned or controlled. They have pointed to the disadvantageous position in which they are often placed because of their inadequate familiarity with the technology and product characteristics involved, and have been requesting that the exporting developed country should assume a certain responsibility for warning potential importers of the dangers involved. But it has been an up-hill struggle, and meaningful results still remain to be achieved. The moral is clear. Where the interests of developed countries as exporters are concerned, nothing must stand in the way of unbridled export expansion, and certainly not the danger to the health and safety of developing country importers. Hence even the modest requests that exporters be obliged to provide a warning to importers on the dangers of the product is considered excessive and is tenaciously resisted.[36]

But the influence of the US and the developed countries being what it is, developing countries have been landed with the burden of policing the production and exports of products declared illegal drugs, sometimes imposing on them a heavy economic burden and not infrequently contributing to the proliferation of serious crime and other anti-social activities in their midst.

Notes

1. For the text of the summary by the Co-Chairmen of the meeting see the Annex to United Nations General Assembly document A/36/631.
2. This referred to US concern that the UN negotiations should not deal with matters in the competence of the specialized institutions, and above all of the Washington-based financial institutions.
3. Document TD/245, reproduced in *Proceedings of the 5th Session of the Conference*, Basic Documents, Vol.111, p. 498.
4. This document is reproduced as Annex VI to Vol. 1 of the *Proceedings of the Conference*.
5. Board decision 347 (XXXIV) of 15 October 1987.
6. The report of the Working Group appears as UNCTAD document TD/B/1154.
7. This document is reproduced in Annex VI to vol. 1 of the *Proceedings* of the 6th UNCTAD Conference.
8. An important exception was the resolution calling for the convening of an expert group on compensatory financing of export shortfall on which a vote was taken at the request of the United States, who cast the only negative vote, arguing that that was a matter to be discussed in the IMF and not in UNCTAD.
9. *Proceedings* of the 6th Session of the Conference, Part two. Summary of proceedings, p. 57.
10. The statement as adopted appears in the *Proceedings* of the Conference, p. 6.
11. It later explained its vote by its objection to the fact that the resolution made no mention of GATT in the area of services, noting that 'Throughout the current session, the Group of 77 had repeatedly taken the position that GATT had no role in services.'
12. Based on the summary of the statement reproduced in Annex V to the *Official Records*, Trade and Development Board, 29th Session, 10-27 September 1984, p. 102.
13. Based on summary of statement in *Ibid.*, p. 26.
14. Based on summary of statement in *Ibid.*, p. 32-33.
15. Quoted from the UNCTAD document 'A New Partnership for Development: The Cartagena Commitment', incorporating the results of the 8th session of the conference.

16. In December 1991 the ranks of the least developed were greatly expanded when no fewer than five additional countries, with a combined population of 60 million, were added to the list. These included Zaire, Zambia, Madagascar, Cambodia and the Solomon Islands. On the other hand, one country (Botswana), for the first time, graduated from the list.

17. Between 1960 and 1989, *per capita* income of least developed countries remained largely stagnant, while that of developing countries as a whole rose at an average rate of 2.4 per cent per annum (see the discussion in chapter 1).

18. At the end of the 1980s, there were some 55 developing countries for whom primary products (excluding petroleum) accounted for over 75 per cent of their export earnings, and for 15 of those countries the share exceeded 90 per cent.

19. The average tariff rate for developed countries as a whole was estimated by the GATT to have been reduced to about 4.7% following the 1970s Tokyo round of trade negotiations. But tariff escalation (i.e. higher rates on the more processed forms of a product) means that even quite low levels of nominal tariffs can mean high effective rates of protection. And in addition, for a range of industrial goods for which developing countries have a distinct comparative advantage and are internationally most competitive, for example textiles and clothing, footwear, leather goods, and various semi-processed materials and products, tariffs in industrial countries are still substantial and are at times quite high. See in this regard, J. Michael Finger and Sam Laird, 'Protection in Developed and Developing Countries - An Overview', *Journal of World Trade Law*, 21 (6), December 1987, pp. 9-23.

20. This started out as the so-called Short-Term Arrangement on Cotton Textiles, later rechristened the Long-Term Arrangement, and later still expanded to the Multifibre Arrangement covering synthetics and other fibres in addition to cotton. The textiles arrangements represent a legal derogation of fundamental GATT rules, particularly mfn, and is a blatant case of discrimination against developing countries.

21. As reported in the *Financial Times* of 16 November 1989.

22. See for example the various writings by Bela Balassa on the subject. A recent example is Bela Balassa, 'Interest of Developing Countries in the Uruguay Round', *The World Economy*, Vol. 11, No.1, March 1988.

23. See Jagdish N. Bhagwati, 'United States Trade Policy at the Crossroads', *The World Economy*, Vol. 12, No. 4, December 1989, for a good discussion of some of the background considerations behind US trade initiatives during the 1980s.

24. See GATT, *Review of Developments in the Trading System*, Sept. 1988-Feb. 1989, p. 114.

25. See UNCTAD, *Export Restraints and the Developing Countries*, Study prepared by Tracy Murray, Feb. 1990 (UNCTAD/ITP/27).

26. See L. Alan Winters, 'The Road to Uruguay', *The Economic Journal*, 100 (December 1990), pp. 1288-1303, for a more detailed discussion of these issues.

See also Chakravarthi Raghavan, *GATT and the Uruguay Round* (Zed Books; Third World Network; London and New Jersey, Penang, 1991).

27. At the Brussels meeting there was a last minute break-down of this common understanding in the area of services when the US, without prior warning, decided to withdraw telecommunications from the list of sectors it was willing to offer to liberalize. This sudden reversal of position threw the other industrial countries off balance, and was probably an important factor in the eventual derailment of the entire negotiations. In fact, subsequent backtracking by the US in the area of services, in particular its intended exclusion of the financial, maritime, audiovisual and telecommunications service sectors from MFN commitments, has become an important sticking point in the negotiations.

28. See Report of the Secretary-General on the work of the Organization, to the 47th session of the General Assembly, p. 11.

29. A recent GATT secretariat study sharply criticizes this tendency of the environmentalists to advocate the use of unilateral trade restrictions as a means of promoting environmental goals. The study provides a wide-ranging critique of such policies, including on grounds of efficiency and legal consistency of the trading system. On the specific subject of tropical timber, it draws attention to the deleterious effects of such restrictions on the exporting developing countries concerned, and points out quite rightly that even a complete ban on such trade would have 'at best only a very minor effect on the pace of global deforestation', the ostensible goal of the environmentalists. We therefore have here a clear case of do-gooders getting carried away with their own rhetoric. Using the logic of the market-place, the GATT study gives a somewhat different twist to the issue, arguing that 'countries which are home to large tropical forests are currently exporting carbon absorption (and biodiversity) services to the rest of the world free of charge', and that 'they should be offered compensation for reducing the rate of exploitation, rather than be threatened with restrictions on their exports.' This suggests a rather different approach to dealing with the issue of deforestation, but one that would shift the onus back to the industrial countries, who are mainly responsible for the carbon emission. It was brave indeed of the GATT secretariat to come out with these findings, which go against the thrust of the recent trend in the environment debate which has so caught the fancy of Northern environmentalist pressure groups. (See GATT, 'Trade and Environment', advance copy of part of GATT, *International Trade 1990-91*, Geneva, 1992.)

30. Lecture entitled 'World and Asian Development Perspectives in the 1990s', Asian Development Bank: Distinguished Speakers Series, Manila, 16 April 1991. The same theme was also taken up by Gamani Corea in an address to a Conference of NGOs on 'Challenge for a Planet in Crisis: Can the Enviroment be Saved without a Radical New Approach to World Development ?', Geneva, 21 March 1991. The reader may also be referred here to a recent article by Wilfred Beckerman ('Economic Growth and the Environment: Whose Growth? Whose

Environment?', *World Development*, Vol. 20, No. 4, 1992) for a discussion, highly critical, of the concept of sustainable development and of the use to which it has been put. He is especially critical of the current fashion of giving pride of place in the environmental debate to the global dimensions of the issue, seeing this not only as unjustified in itself, but more important, as diverting attention from the more urgent and pressing environmental problems the large majority of people in the developing countries currently face because of their poverty, including the lack of clean water and of proper sanitation facilities.

31. See *The Financial Times*, 15 June 1992, p. 7.

32. *Ibid.*

33. On the other hand the introduction to these cultures of alcohol, a narcotic drug perfectly acceptable to the industrial North (and hence sanctioned by the international community), often creates grave social problems in their midst, as in the case of the indigenous American Indians.

34. A recent article in the *International Herald Tribune* under the headline 'Years After "War" Began, Production Soars', makes this point vividly. The article was prompted by US President George Bush's second 'Summit' on drugs with the leaders of six Latin American nations held in San Antonio, Texas during the last week of February 1992, and puts the matter thus: 'Two years after President George Bush met with leaders of the world's top cocaine-producing nations and declared war on the South American drug trade, narcotics production across the region has surged to record levels and illicit profits are soaring, according to U.S. and Latin American drug officials' (26 February 1992).

35. An American legal scholar observes: 'There is no evidence that enforcement efforts have reduced drug consumption in any Western country. In the United States, anti-drug laws resemble the prohibition against alcohol of the 1920s, which was ineffective and undermined the criminal law.' See Sidney L. Harring, 'Death, Drugs and Development: Malaysia's Mandatory Death Penalty for Traffickers and the International War on Drugs', *Columbia Journal of Transnational Law*, Vol. 29, No.2 (1991), p. 366.

36. The history of the efforts by developing countries to make progress on this issue is instructive. These efforts started at least as far back as the 1970s, and the subject was included in GATT's work programme as early as 1982. No progress was made, however, and developing countries subsequently tried to have it included as an item in the Uruguay Round negotiations, launched in 1986. In this they were again unsuccessful. At the Montreal Mid-Term Review meeting in December 1988, developing countries again tried to have the subject included in the Uruguay Round negotiations, again without success, but this time they succeeded in having the matter taken more seriously, and it was subsequently decided (in June 1989) to establish a GATT Working Group with a mandate to draft an agreement on the subject by September 1990, a date subsequently extended to June 1991. By the latter date the Group was able to complete work

on a text acceptable to 'almost all members of the Group'. One country, however (the US), could not agree on the text, and the matter therefore remains in abeyance. In particular, the US wanted to exclude certain products, including cosmetics, alcohol and tobacco, from the rules concerning the need to provide the necessary warnings. We are therefore faced with the stark and ironic (to say the least) situation of seeing the US stoutly defending in an international forum the right of its exporters of alcohol and tobacco not to be obliged to inform foreign consumers of the grave danger to their health of consuming their products (although such warning has to be given to US consumers), while at the same time taking the lead in forcing developing countries to ban the exports and indeed even the production of what the US has succeeded in having declared 'illegal drugs' on the grounds that these substances are a danger to the health of consumers!

8.What Future for the Developing World?

In the four decades or so of post-war history, North-South relations seem to have come full circle, from the era of passive metropolitan-colonial relations, which prevailed at the end of the war, through the intervening period of decolonization, rising expectations and active pressure for change, when the North was forced for a while into serious negotiations and into making what turned out to be some shallow concessions, and back again, after this false start, to a new era of the South's abject dependence on the North.

In the meantime, the gap between North and South has widened. This widening gap reflects the immense strides that have been made in the North, as higher and higher levels of income and consumption have been attained and a rapidly expanding stock of social and physical capital accumulated, all made possible by a dynamic process of technological innovation and technical change standing at the centre of the phenomenon of modern economic growth. It reflects as well the relative stagnation in the South, and the inability of the South as a whole to participate meaningfully in this process of economic expansion.

In the light of these results the question arises: what sort of future now faces the developing world as we come to the end of the present millennium and approach the dawn of a new age? More particularly, are we witnessing a crystallization of the world into separate spheres, which will solidify and become a permanent and ever more marked feature of life on this planet, or do we see any grounds for believing that the seeds are being sown so that, in time, a process of catching up and economic levelling among nation states will eventually materialize? These are clearly questions of the first importance which, while they go beyond the scope of the present work, are nonetheless closely connected to the subject matter of our discussion, and therefore deserve our attention.

Failed bid to improve the international policy framework

The answer to these questions is clearly linked to the experience of the past 40 years and to the failed efforts of the developing countries to achieve meaningful economic growth and the accompanying economic transformation. In the previous chapters we discussed this experience largely in relation to the role

215

of the international economic system and the determined bid by these countries to bring about favourable changes in that system. As we have seen, they largely failed in this endeavour. How important a factor has this failure been in the larger failure of the development effort on which attention is now focused?

No one can doubt the transcendent importance of the international economic environment for the economic development of nation states. A receptive and responsive international environment is the very life-blood of modern economic growth. This is a fundamental truth to be learnt from the record of history. From its earliest beginning in England, through its spread to the European continent and elsewhere, modern economic growth has depended for its very existence on complex economic relations between nation states. Such relations are made necessary by the need to find markets for the products of modern industry, to find sources of raw materials, to find profitable means of employing surplus capital, and to find sources of investment capital and of new technology, to name some of the more obvious functions which such relations serve. The opportunities available for such economic intercourse between states constitute the international economic environment in which countries operate, while the international economic system defines the terms and conditions under which such intercourse may take place.

A favourable environment was one of the factors that permitted those countries which took part in the initial wave of modern economic growth to make such rapid progress in the latter half of the 19th century.[1] They had relative freedom of access to markets, freedom of movement of capital and technology, a stable and operationally effective international monetary system and rapidly expanding international demand for primary commodity exports.[2] And when, in the inter-war years of the 20th century, there was a breakdown in the international system, accompanied by a marked deterioration in the international economic environment, the disastrous effect that this had on economic growth and economic prosperity was patent for all to see. The great pains that were taken post-war to build a system of institutions to provide the basis for a favourable international economic environment in which at least the developed countries could prosper serve as a forceful indication of the importance of this matter.

One can therefore fully understand why the developing countries attached such importance to the question of the international economic environment and focused so much of their energies in seeking to bring about beneficial changes in the system. But in the end this proved to have been largely wasted effort. Very little was to be achieved in this respect, and eventually there would be a backlash which would turn the clock back to the starting point. In retrospect, it is not difficult to see why the results were so negligible. For the most part, the demands of the developing countries in their dialogue and confrontation with the North involved a zero-sum calculus, that is, the extension of benefits to them would entail a cost to the North, and were demands that could not be imposed without the agreement of the latter. National (and group) self-interest being what it is, it was to be expected that these demands would be heavily resisted. But we should also note that in the particular context of the North-South confrontation which burgeoned in the aftermath of the Second World War, the basic issues were clouded by other factors, including racial overtones, lingering perceptions of imperialist grandeur and cultural superiority, and an instinctive reluctance to countenance admitting outsiders into the exclusive club of the rich, the privileged and the powerful. These aspects added new dimensions to the problem and no doubt made beneficial changes in the system that much more difficult to achieve. As we remarked earlier, the issue was also influenced by the Cold War context in which the confrontation took place; this factor worked rather in the opposite direction, and was probably largely responsible for such marginal concessions as were made.

But with the hindsight of history we may well ask: what options did the developing countries really have, and were they justified in pursuing so vigorously this objective (unrealizable as it turned out) of bringing about changes in the international economic system, and in expending so much of their energies in doing so?

Domestic policies: the other dimension

Important as the international environment undoubtedly is, it is not the only precondition for the successful realization of modern economic growth. All writers on the subject will agree that a proper domestic environment in which economic development can blossom is an even more elementary pre-condition. What constitutes a proper domestic environment is a question extensively discussed in the literature, and while there is no unanimity of views on the specifics involved, there is little dispute on the broader aspects. Among these we may mention the importance of a stable governmental environment, with the minimum of major unforeseen shifts and turns in the policy framework, of a rule-based system where the whims and caprices of those in authority are suitably constrained, and of a sense of national integration in which there is an essential feeling of identity of interest and purpose linking political leaders to the community at large. These are perhaps the very minimum basic conditions without which not much in terms of modern economic growth can be expected. Beyond these one can perhaps identify a number of requirements which would be widely accepted as necessary pre-conditions (for example, a modern education system, physical infrastructure), but soon we enter terrain in which there is little agreement, indeed in which the dominant viewpoints have sometimes shifted considerably over the years.

This is not the place to enter into a discussion of this complex subject. Suffice it to say that without the appropriate domestic environment little will be achieved. So, did the preoccupation with the international dimensions of the problem during the 1960s and 1970s divert the developing countries' attention from a proper focus on domestic policy, and lose them valuable time in making necessary adaptations on the domestic front? We hinted at this question in a slightly different form in the discussion on the background to the first UNCTAD conference (see Chapter 4, p. 90), but the question raises its head more forcefully here in view of the subsequent failure to achieve any major breakthrough in the North-South dialogue. The question does not admit of any straightforward answer, and in any event the situation probably varies significantly from country to country. But it seems very likely that in many countries political leaders sometimes became so engrossed in fighting battles on the North-South front that insufficient time was devoted to thinking out and implementing a strategy for consolidating and cultivating the domestic base on which economic growth could proceed, and that opportunistic elements in some of these countries took advantage of the situation to entrench themselves in privileged positions and to postpone necessary reforms.

Having said all this, we return to the original question: what choice did these countries really have? In particular, given the existing, unreformed international economic system, would the necessary focus on the domestic policy front have made that much difference? Put in other terms, we might ask where these countries would be today if, instead of trying to change the system, they had taken that as given and focused their energies instead on how best to adapt their domestic environment to take advantage of such opportunities as there were.

We can throw some light on this question by referring to data on the performance of developing countries over the post-war years. As we saw in Chapter 1, there were considerable differences between these countries in development performance over these years, with some countries being able to do better than others in the prevailing international environment. In four or five countries, *per capita* incomes expanded on average over these years by the phenomenal rate of 7 per cent or more per annum, another thirty or so countries experienced reasonably satisfactory growth-rates exceeding 2 per cent per annum. The large majority had to be content with much more meagre rates of expansion, including a large number in the unhappy position of experiencing zero or negative growth-rates. Can we draw any conclusions about the role of the domestic policy environment from these differences in country performance?

If we could assume that all countries faced the same international environment, then differences in performance could presumably be explained by differences in domestic effort. However, such an assumption is not warranted. For political or other reasons, some countries have been greatly favoured in the manner in which they have been able to interact with and benefit from the international system, and as a consequence have not faced the same international environment as other less favoured countries. Perhaps the two most obvious examples of specially favoured countries are South Korea and Taiwan, which also happen to be the two most outstanding 'success' stories of the post-war era. For reasons connected with the Cold War and the pursuit of US foreign policy, these two countries were taken under the US umbrella and accorded special treatment by which they had liberal access to foreign capital and technology as well as to foreign markets, far in excess of that available to other developing countries. It is through the medium of capital, technology and markets that the international environment has its greatest impact on the development process.

The case of South Korea is particularly striking. During the 1950s and 1960s it received vast amounts of external financial assistance in grants, or grant-like, form. The importance of this financing to Korean economic development can be gauged from the fact that during these critical years, when the foundations for development were being laid, 85-95 per cent of Korean imports were being financed from abroad, Korean exports at the time being so tiny that they could finance only 5-15 per cent of import needs. This external financing was made available under conditions that did not give rise to a build up of foreign debt, which could subsequently bring the whole development process to a halt. This experience was in stark contrast to the situation facing most other developing countries, able to import only as much as their export earnings could finance (except for relatively minor amounts of external financing, which even then gave rise to foreign debt and to debt service difficulties). A further indication of the importance of the largesse made available to South Korea can be gleaned from the fact that during the 1950s and early 1960s capital inflows financed as much as 70-80 per cent of Korea's gross domestic investment, and represented over 10 per cent of its national income.[3]

For Taiwan the experience is rather similar if perhaps not as dramatic as the case of Korea. During the 1950s and early 1960s, exports covered on average about 60 per cent of import requirements, the remaining 40 per cent representing the current account deficit financed for the most part by official US assistance on grant or grant-like terms. In most of these years, the import surplus (or current account deficit) represented between 8 and 10 per cent of GNP, roughly the same as for Korea. External financing represented about 40 per cent of gross domestic investment. As in the case of Korea, the significant fact is that this heavy inflow of much needed foreign capital during these critical years when the foundations for economic development were being laid did not give rise to a debt build up that could have crippled Taiwan's subsequent development efforts.[4] It will be observed that in both Korea and Taiwan, where supreme political considerations were involved, approaches were followed similar to those under the Marshall Plan, when European countries were provided with generous financial assistance to enable them to recover from the ravages of war, and which did not leave them with a burden of debt.

These two countries are perhaps exceptional cases, but they do illustrate the point that all countries did not necessarily face the same international environment. We may also note that, apart from cases involving special political factors, chance and luck may also play a role in determining the extent to which individual countries can benefit from the existing international system. The existence on their territory of particular raw material resources, for which international demand is especially strong and rising (e.g. petroleum), may make all the difference. All this leads us to conclude that, however important domestic policy may be, the differences in growth recorded among developing countries in the post-war years cannot be attributed simply to differences in domestic policy responses, and that in all cases the international environment played a key role.

Nonetheless, even those countries that faced an especially favourable international environment, either by virtue of political considerations or by luck, must also adopt appropriate domestic policies if they are to convert the potential into actual progress. The spectacular success stories referred to above were evidently cases where this was done; the more dismal failures were probably cases where a lacklustre international environment was joined by an indifferent or poor domestic effort.

It is not difficult to identify countries where grave shortcomings in the domestic political system acted as a serious barrier to the pursuit of successful economic development. The more spectacular cases of the bleeding of the wealth and riches of their countries by political leaders intent on amassing personal fortunes in foreign bank accounts, real estate and other assets are clear examples of such shortcomings. In some of these cases (e.g. the Philippines, Zaire) figures of billions of dollars have been mentioned as estimates of the wealth political leaders have transferred abroad, denuding their countries of investment capital and leaving them under the burden of heavy foreign debt. One can only imagine the devastating effect on a country's development prospects of such acts of cynicism by political leaders. In a less spectacular form, such situations are probably more widespread than is recognized. They all reflect inadequate national integration and a lack of common purpose and sense of common destiny binding the political leaders to the nation state. There are the even more regrettable cases where countries come under the control of tyrants, whose rule is so arbitrary and destructive that only economic decline can ensue, Cambodia and Uganda being typical examples in this category. Finally, and more generally, there is the whole range of other experience to be found in the developing world, from relatively benign personal rule where corruption flourishes and the domestic environment remains uncertain, to more or less properly functioning rule-based systems where corruption is held in check, and where there is the required sense of national integration and national purpose, and the necessary stability exists for economic development to take root. It is not the purpose here to try to classify developing countries in terms of these categories. That is an exercise that might be worth undertaking elsewhere, one which could perhaps help us to understand better the political roots of economic success and failure. Suffice it to say here that there were significant differences among countries in the propitiousness of the political environment that prevailed, and that these differences undoubtedly help to explain the wide variation in their development performance.

It is important to note that the domestic environment is not necessarily independent of the international. It not infrequently happens that political leaders in the South come to power, and are maintained in power, with the support of the North. In such cases the resulting domestic political environment is very much the creation of the international system. Since such support is usually provided in order to promote specific Northern interests, it should not be surprising to find that it is in just those cases that the political leadership is likely to be most alienated from the interests of the community at large, that the diversion of the national wealth to personal ends is liable to be most blatant, and that, in consequence, the domestic environment is prone to be least propitious for economic development. Perhaps the history of Zaire can again be cited as the archetypical example of this kind of interdependence, where the feed-back from the international to the domestic environment has been far from positive. Any number of other examples in Asia, Africa and Latin America can also be cited. In the same vein, it is evident that the existence of massive corruption and diversion of wealth by political leaders in the South is only possible because of external facilitation, and in particular because of the collusion of the North in providing havens for these funds, complete with the necessary secrecy.

When it comes to pursuing what the North (particularly the US) regard as their own special concerns, for example fighting the illegal drugs trade, there is virtually no limit to the kinds of international co-operation arrangements that can be devised and put into effect. We have in mind here the demanding and legally complex cross-border co-operation arrangements for tracking down 'drug money', and the obligation which often arises in that context to confiscate funds and other assets deemed to have originated from the drugs trade. Switzerland in particular has been under strong pressure from the United States to assume responsibilities of this kind, and has felt obliged to enact relevant laws and to make an effort to comply, if reluctantly.[5] There has been no corresponding pressure, however, for international co-operation to deter the massive theft of public funds from developing countries by corrupt political leaders, nor to track down and confiscate such funds. The issue is evidently not high on the international agenda.[6]

Transforming the terms of reference of the policy debate

We have been discussing the domestic environment so far in terms of the political and governmental framework. Beyond this there is also the question of economic policy. Over and above providing the minimum basic conditions, governments must also formulate and implement policies designed to achieve their development objectives. This is also an essential part of the domestic effort, and we can again review the experience to see how effectively this has been carried out, and what role it plays in explaining economic performance.

Development policy is a subject on which there is no unanimity of views among writers. It is also one, as we mentioned earlier, where there have been important shifts in viewpoints among mainstream writers over the years.[7] In the language of science, there have been changes in the prevailing paradigm. In the first two decades or so after the war, the predominant view assigned to government the central role of chief planner and principal implementor of economic development. This was the counterpart of the then prevailing view, under Keynesian influence, of the activist role of government in the developed countries as animator and guarantor of macro-economic stability and full-employment growth. This was an era when it was widely believed that any serious attempt to promote economic development should include, as an essential ingredient, efforts by government at comprehensive development planning (see the discussion in Chapter 4). Such plans would provide the framework and the rationale for the investment and production decisions required to make economic development a reality. Furthermore, it was felt, governments would often need to get involved in the actual business of production, particularly in key sectors and industries sometimes referred to as the commanding heights of the economy. This was necessary either because the size and 'lumpiness' of such investments required a major effort beyond the capacity of the private sector, or because of the existence of external economies not included in the profit calculations of the individual entrepreneur, or because of a dearth of local entrepreneurs and a desire to keep key sectors and industries out of foreign hands.

In addition, because of market imperfections and structural weaknesses, governments would need to intervene actively in various ways to promote key sectors and industries, through protection or other means, including special allocation policies affecting key resources. Intervention would be especially necessary in dealing with the foreign trade sector, and would need to go beyond the usual trade protection policies to include foreign exchange allocation policies as well. Indeed, such policies were a standard feature of the development scene, reflecting the absence at the time of any influential advocacy among development economists of a purely market-determined exchange rate for developing countries, the prevailing view being that, given the nature of the markets for their primary commodity exports and the structural imbalances that they faced, devaluation was not an appropriate means of achieving exchange rate equilibrium. These countries would therefore often have to accommodate themselves to an overvalued currency accompanied by special foreign exchange allocation policies. A need was also recognized for the involvement of government in the allocation of financial resources to high priority industries and sectors through governmental influence on the banking system.

These were among the major tasks seen for government as primary mover and animator of the development process. This is over and above government's key role in providing education, health and other essential services, as well as the basic physical infrastructure (roads, schools, hospitals, etc.) without which economic development is not possible.

The above, in a nutshell, was the paradigm that dominated thinking during the 1950s and 1960s and into the 1970s, which set the tone for much development policy during those years. Not that there was ever any lack of controversy about development policy. Indeed there soon emerged a keen debate about the relative merits of import substitution and export promotion as policy objectives, and about how best to achieve these objectives. But by and large, the active role of government in promoting development was not seriously questioned.

The reaction that set in in the 1980s, originating in events in the developed world, spread rapidly through IMF and World Bank policy interventions, to dominate policy thinking in the developing world as well. To a large extent, policy in the developing world is therefore now based on quite a different paradigm. Comprehensive development planning is wholly out of fashion, and with the rising trend towards privatization, deregulation, removal of exchange controls, increasing reliance on market-determined exchange rates, trade liberalization, and market-determined interest rates, governments have begun to take a back seat, the market to reign supreme in the allocation of resources and incomes, and the private sector left free and unfettered and allowed to take the lead in promoting economic development. This is the direction in which the new paradigm leads, developing countries have already travelled long distances along this road during the past decade.

The new policy direction: is this the way to the Promised Land?

From the point of view of the outlook for development, what are we to make of this about-turn in policy direction? As we have seen, past performance was clearly unsatisfactory. But can we conclude that the old paradigm was to blame, and that now that we have a new paradigm, the way is clear towards the promised land of growth and prosperity? A number of considerations suggest that such a conclusion would be premature.

Firstly, there is the uncomfortable fact that since the new paradigm took root and began to dominate policy thinking, around the turn of the 1980s, development performance has on the whole been markedly worse than in the preceding decades, when the old paradigm held sway. This fact (without any necessary imputation of cause) clearly means, at the very least, that the efficacy of the new policy framework remains to be proven by actual results.

Second, it is necessary to recall (these things being so easily forgotten) that many of the elements of the old paradigm that have been unceremoniously thrown out were, at relevant stages of their development, very much a part of the policy mix of countries who have made an undoubted success of development. An obvious example is Japan. The strong activist role played by government in the modernization of Japan, following the Meiji restoration, is widely recognized. In the span of little more than half a century, up to the period of the Second World War, Japan was transformed from a backward, isolated, pre-industrial society into a major industrial power.[8] But it was in the post-war years that the Japanese economy recorded really spectacular successes, and the leading role played by government during this period is a good example of what can happen under the old paradigm. We have in mind, in particular, policies relating to the balance of payments and to industrial promotion.

During the 1950s and 1960s, when balance-of-payments deficits were the operative constraints on Japanese economic growth, the foreign exchange shortage was met not by a devaluation of the currency, as is demanded by the new paradigm, but by administrative controls on imports through 'the foreign exchange budget and the import deposit scheme' as part of a many sided policy framework aimed at industrialization and export promotion.[9] Among the measures utilized to promote this goal were preferential access to credit at favourable interest rates, customs exemptions, accelerated depreciation, and subsidies. Patrick and Rosovsky describe the import-competing industrialization policy pursued as 'a mixture of key-sector and infant industry approaches. Designation of a key industry brought favourable tax and depreciation treatment, loans on favourable terms, duty-free equipment imports, and protection from import competition.'[10] And in the words of Krause and Sekiguchi,

> The rationalization of domestic industry was accompanied by complete protection from import competition through the quota system - unnecessary imports were simply not permitted. In addition, more refined methods of export promotion were developed . . .. Since a licence to import scarce raw materials was very valuable, these licences were at times granted to encourage exports that would otherwise be unprofitable . . . for example , [u]ntil 1955, shipbuilders were given the windfall gains from the importation of sugar in order to subsidize their export of ships.[11]

During these years private investment by foreigners in Japan was strictly controlled in order to protect domestic firms. Government also played an active role in controlling (and promoting on favourable terms) the inflow of technology. Thus Japanese firms were encouraged to license or buy technology from abroad, and, 'Since foreign firms could neither export manufactured goods to Japan nor make direct investments there, they were frequently prepared to license their processes and products as the only way to share in the market.'[12] Control was exercised through legislation requiring government approval of all transactions involving remittances in foreign currency, and through its regulatory powers over these technology agreements, the government was able to ensure that Japanese firms did not overpay for technology.

It was not until 1968, after the balance-of-payments constraint had been fully transformed into one of export surplus, that a political decision was taken to liberalize imports and to open the Japanese economy to foreign competition. The Japanese experience, particularly as regards the all-important foreign trade sector, is therefore hardly one that can be cited by those who would argue for a hands-off, non-interventionist role by government as the way to go about promoting economic development.

South Korea, another country that has made a great success of development, also relied very much on the old paradigm as a guide to economic policy. Thus, from the 1950s to the 1970s, the problem of reconciling competing demands for acutely scarce foreign exchange, a major issue during those critical early years of development, was met not by allowing uncontrolled access to a market-determined equilibrium exchange rate, as now demanded by the free market enthusiasts and increasingly enforced by the IMF, but by a plethora of exchange controls, import programming, quantitative and other restrictions on imports, all within the framework of policy for promoting specific industries, and as part of overall development policy. This was accompanied by the liberal use of a wide range of *ad hoc* banking, interest rate and fiscal incentive measures to guide the allocation of investment resources to favoured industries and to promote exports.[13] Taiwan, another success story, is also an example where exchange controls, import restrictions, etc. were a standard feature of the policy mix during the formative years of development during the 1950s and 1960s.[14]

But perhaps the most telling examples of success stories following the use of this kind of policy mix are provided by the European countries after the war who, facing acute problems of reconstruction, made no pretence of relying on market forces to allocate scarce foreign exchange resources, but instead resorted wholeheartedly to exchange controls, import restrictions, and the like, to achieve their reconstruction and development objectives, despite IMF urging to the contrary.[15]

If these examples mean anything, they prove that the free-market solution, especially in relation to the foreign exchanges and the foreign trade sector, is by no means a necessary path to economic success. On the contrary, they suggest very strongly that at critical stages in the development process, the free market solution may be incompatible with the desired objectives, and may thus need to be set aside or supplemented by other mechanisms. While no one would wish to claim that the activist, interventionist policies pursued by developing countries in the past were necessarily the optimum for achieving development objectives - in many cases they may well have been overdone - there is the danger that the pendulum has now swung too far in the other direction, that free-market principles are now being called upon to perform tasks of which they are not capable.

In assessing the efficacy of the domestic effort, what seems to distinguish successful performers like Korea and Taiwan from the typical laggard is not the extent of government intervention and activism, but rather the domestic environment in terms of the criteria discussed above, and the specifics of policies - even more importantly, the rigour, purpose, and even-handedness with which these policies are implemented. It is one thing to recognize the importance of import-substitution industrialization and the need for a policy of protection and special support to bring this about. It is quite another thing actually to devise and implement policies that will achieve these aims, and, even more importantly perhaps, to be able to effect a smooth transition from import substitution to export expansion, without getting trapped in the cul-de-sac of high-cost import substitution. That Korea and Taiwan were able to make the transition effectively and thus to enter into a process of long-term economic growth, while many a Latin American country got stuck in the cul-de-sac, is a tribute to the efficacy of the domestic policy effort in the one case, and a sad commentary on its lack in the other. But it would be a mistake to suppose that the differences in performance can be explained in the simplistic terms of governmental interventionism and freedom of markets.

At the same time, it is not necessary to argue that the degree of governmental intervention and policy direction that took place in Japan or Korea is necessarily the best suited for all countries. It might well be that in the absence of a certain milieu such an activist role for government would be counter-productive. Such would be the case, for example, if the administrative cadre needed to staff the relevant government services is not available, or if corruption cannot be held in check. It is in this light that perhaps one can make some sense of the high-handed pressure brought to bear on developing countries in recent years to abandon all forms of state interventionism and planning and to rely exclusively on the market instead for the determination of the outcome on the key issues of resource allocation, pricing, investment targeting and income distribution, on which the prospects for economic growth ultimately depend. But while such a hands-off attitude of government might be a necessary response to a weak governmental structure unable to carry a heavy burden of state interventionism in guiding the economy, it is hardly the ideal way of navigating the difficult early years, when the foundations for economic development have to be laid. In any event, as we suggested earlier, the free market approach has undoubtedly been carried too far. We have in mind in particular the pressure to free up the foreign exchange market, and the resulting cycle of devaluation and inflation feeding on each other in a spiral which serves no useful purpose, and whose effect on the poorer fixed-income sections of the community can be quite devastating.[16]

It is also worth noting that notwithstanding the extent to which the unbridled free market philosophy has been hailed and trumpeted in developed countries in recent years, governments in these countries continue even today to play an interventionist role in their economies in areas beyond the reach of most developing countries. Thus most (perhaps all) developed countries continue to support an extensive social security system providing unemployment benefits, old-age pensions, free or subsidized medical attention, etc. where the allocation of benefits is de-linked from the operations of the market. The market does not determine resource allocation, and access, to education. Exchange rates are closely watched and are never left to the free play of market forces. Agriculture is heavily subsidized and highly regulated, with the market allowed only a limited role in the allocation of resources, the determination of prices and the apportionment of benefits. These governments also have programmes to subsidize investments in depressed regions, to support and subsidize the development of new technology, and to provide interest rate subsidies to their exporters. These examples go to show that, even now, after all this preaching, the market is still not allowed to operate with unrestrained freedom in these countries, and for good reason. It would be well for developing countries being urged to adopt the more extreme and unadulterated versions of the free market philosophy to bear this in mind.

Changes in the pattern of world economic growth: some relevant aspects

The discussion so far has been concerned largely with policy-induced repercussions on the international environment for development. But what about repercussions stemming from the process of economic growth itself? Here we have in mind the peculiarly dynamic role which technological innovation now plays in the growth process, the manner in which this has affected and brought about changes in the way the world economy operates and functions, and the implications of all this for those countries still to make a meaningful start in the development business.

We made reference earlier to one such specific repercussion having particular significance for developing countries, namely, the marked tendency for technological advances to result in reduced demand for primary raw materials relative to income growth, a tendency that has been accelerating since the 1970s and that shows no signs of petering out. The effect has been to close off or greatly reduce the option, hitherto available to newly developing countries, of relying on their primary commodities for the expansion of export earnings, so essential to economic development. One implication of this is that developing countries will need to become exporters of manufactures at an even earlier stage than formerly, if they are to be able to achieve an adequate rate of export growth. This is an added burden, given the difficulties in getting the industrialization process started and the problems of market-access for the traditional labour-intensive manufactures with which the process usually gets started.[17] But the essential issues are much wider, and will call for major adaptations by developing countries if they are to have any hope of not being left further and further behind.

More than ever before, technology is now the driving force of economic growth. For the leading industrial countries, economic growth is not achieved by investing in additional plant and equipment to expand production of existing products. Instead, it is a constant struggle to develop new and improved products, to devise more efficient and cost-effective ways of producing existing products, to develop new materials and new uses of existing materials, and so on, all of which requires not only investment in new plant and equipment but, even more importantly, a major effort in research and development, which now becomes one of the leading activities of the business enterprise. It is in pursuance of the constant need to push forward with technological innovation that competition between large firms is most keenly felt today. This is the sense in which we can say that technology is now the driving force that pushes the individual firm and determines the rate and pattern of economic growth.[18]

In this technological race no country is an island, and in order to stay abreast or one step ahead of competitors, intensive participation in international trade is essential. It is essential, on the import side, in order to have access to the fruits of technological innovation in other countries so that these can be used, copied, adapted and improved upon. It is essential, on the export side (apart from earning foreign exchange, creating employment, achieving economies of scale, etc.), in order to benefit from the pressures for technological improvements resulting from exposure to international competition. We therefore have a growing interdependence between technology, trade and growth, with trade, now more than ever before, a means for strengthening technological capacity, itself increasingly the main determinant of the pace and pattern of economic growth. This trend towards more intensive participation of countries in trade is reflected in the rising share of trade in world income and in the incomes of most of the major participants in world trade.[19]

This growing interdependence has been associated with the emergence of the phenomenon known as globalization, the essential aspect of which is the increasing tendency of large firms that market their products worldwide to locate production facilities abroad, close to their foreign markets; to source and locate production of parts and components in various foreign countries, bringing these together at various points at home and abroad for assembly into the finished product; to establish their R&D facilities at various locations at home and abroad; to obtain their short-term bank financing and even long-term capital needs in the international capital markets; and to establish links and various forms of co-operation arrangements among themselves in order to share the escalating costs of R&D, which even the largest and most powerful firms now find a heavy burden, and to share their world-wide marketing facilities, all designed to help cut costs and remain competitive. One can find in the automobile industry, for example, all these aspects of globalization being extensively practised.[20] There are many other major industries where similar developments are regularly reported, in some cases going so far as to cover the merger of major international firms based in different countries.[21]

Another factor to play an important role in forcing the pace of globalization is the rising threat of protectionism, and the desire of large firms to take out a form of insurance to assure their continued future access to international markets. This is done by 'nationalizing' production in the foreign markets, a practice most actively pursued by the Japanese, in view of the protectionist threats to which their exports are often subject in the markets of the other major developed countries.

The recent trend towards the strengthening of regional trade and other economic links among groups of developed countries is also relevant here. The outstanding example of this, of course, is to be found in developments in Europe, with the EC programme for the creation of a single market by 1993, and with the on-going pressures for the widening of the EC to include additional European countries. The recently negotiated EES (or European Economic Space) providing for closer economic links between the EC and the present European Free Trade Association (EFTA), important in itself, can also be seen as a first step in the eventual widening of the membership of the EC. The recently negotiated free trade agreement between the US and Canada is another important example of this trend, as are the negotiations to extend this agreement to include Mexico.[22]

The relationship between this trend and the globalization issue is two-fold. On the one hand, from the point of view of member countries of these blocs, one of the basic forces driving their creation is the need for a large common market to which they have free and unrestricted access and throughout which the potential for globalization (or the transnationalization of the activities of firms) can be exploited to its fullest. On the other hand, for countries outside these blocs, globalization is a means to gain access to and to exploit the large and unrestricted internal markets which these blocs represent.[23] The rapid increase in intra-EC foreign direct investments by EC-based firms in the run up to 1993, to the extent that such investment increased its share from a quarter to a third of the total stock of foreign direct investment in the EC between 1980 and 1987, is an indication of the extent to which globalization has been spurred on by the unification of markets.[24]

Two sectors have played particularly important roles in carrying forward this process of globalization. We refer to capital markets and to telecommunications and information. The last 10 years have seen the widespread removal of restrictions on international capital movements among the major developed countries. As a consequence, the capital markets of these countries are now largely consolidated into a global market, cross-border investments can now be effected by telephone or telex, and indeed it has become quite possible for a firm's ownership to change hands by a wired purchase order from a foreign national. This makes it possible for globalization to be carried one step further, since there can now be a high degree of international linkage in ownership and control, making it increasingly difficult to identify a company's national identity (for example, Jaguar, a uniquely British product, is now owned by Ford, a US company). Telecommunications and the computer, which stand at the very centre of this technologically driven growth process, are also of critical importance in facilitating the spread of globalization. Thus, by making it possible to organize large masses of information and to communicate this information instantly between any two points on the globe, technical developments in these two areas permitted the effective control of a business enterprise independent of the physical location of its various parts. It is this, more than anything, that has made globalization a practical and growing business.

Adapting to underlying structural changes

There is little doubt that we are witnessing basic changes in the way in which the world economy operates and functions. How do these changes affect developing countries and their prospects for joining the mainstream of world economic development? The aspect that comes most immediately to mind is the exponentially widening technology gap that separates developed and developing countries in a world in which technological capacity has become the critical factor determining trade performance and economic growth. In this world, technology capacity provides the platform for accelerating the pace of technological innovation, and thus for widening at an ever faster rate the technology gap between North and South.

It used to be argued[25] that late-comers had something of an advantage over early starters since the former could benefit from the accumulated experience of the latter and thereby reduce the time-lag and costs needed to catch up. But this was in a 19th century setting, when basic technology was much simpler, technological innovation was advancing at a much slower pace, the accumulated technological experience was much less, and the social, institutional and physical infrastructure needed to comprehend, digest and interact with the latest technological developments was much less demanding than at present. It is therefore far from certain how relevant this argument is today.

On the other hand, the revolution in communications brought about by modern technology opens up the possibility of wider and more ready access to knowledge worldwide. This certainly means increased awareness of the existence of the fruits of modern technology, embodied in new products, services, etc., thereby creating with minimum time-lag new demands in countries far removed from the centres of technological progress. It also creates the potential for an easier and wider access to knowledge about technology itself. But for those still in the initial stages of development, this potential becomes more difficult to realize as the technology gap increases, and as the infrastructure needed to digest and interact with modern technology increases both in size and in complexity, receding further and further from the practical means of these countries. To this we should add the growing attempts to put legal obstacles in the way, making it more difficult for developing countries to gain access to technical knowledge (see p .193).

If the nation state is still to be the relevant unit of analysis, we cannot fail to mention here the role of the brain drain in fortifying and perpetuating the technology gap. This reflects the fact that, for obvious reasons, the best brains in the developing countries will tend to migrate to developed countries and contribute to strengthening technological capacity there rather than in their home countries. It may be added that the 'obvious reasons' include not only the higher incomes to be earned in developed countries but, even more importantly from our present point of view, the existence there of all the increasingly complex infrastructure necessary for the pursuit of science and technology which, because of the growing income and technology gap, is sadly lacking in developing countries. It is as the Bible says: 'to him that has shall be given, and to him that has not shall be taken away even that which he has and given to him that has.'

Of even greater importance to developing countries will be the way in which they interact with and are affected by what we have referred to as the process of globalization, bearing in mind the expanding role of large, transnational firms in controlling the technology, the investment funds and the marketing channels through which modern economic growth is pursued. Since there is no way of avoiding the impact of these firms, the only practical question that arises is how best to seize the opportunities and minimize the hazards they present.

While in an earlier era foreign direct investment was regarded with suspicion by developing countries as something to be accepted in carefully measured doses, for fear of opening the door to excessive foreign control, attitudes have since changed. With the revolution in thinking during the 1980s, and with the obvious key role that the trans-national corporations (TNCs) play in this age of technologically driven economic growth,[26] developing countries now exhibit a much more positive attitude towards direct foreign investment, the means by which TNCs globalize their activities. And in an age where other forms of capital flows to developing countries have been rapidly shrinking (and in the case of private credits have become negative, taking the form of net outflows), much store has come to be placed on direct foreign investment as a means of helping to overcome the investment constraints and to bring these countries into the mainstream of world economic development.

Changed attitudes notwithstanding, there has been no rush on the part of the TNCs to increase direct investments in developing countries and to bring these countries into their globalization plans. In fact, since the beginning of the 1980s, developing countries' share of total foreign direct investment has fallen (even if in absolute dollar terms the amounts have risen), from 25 per cent in the early 1980s to 17 per cent by the end of the decade. Worldwide, these years saw a great upsurge in foreign direct investment, which grew at rates three to three-and-a-half times as fast as world exports and output. The bulk of the increase has taken the form of direct investment among developed countries, particularly the US, the EC and Japan, whose TNCs account between them for over four-fifths of world total foreign direct investment.[27] The outcome therefore reflects the dynamics of globalization described earlier.

Not surprisingly, the East Asian countries have been the major beneficiaries among developing countries of the recent upsurge of foreign direct investment, increasing their share in the total flows to developing countries from one-third in the early 1980s to over one-half by the end of the decade. Many of these countries have been able to benefit from the globalization strategies of the TNCs, drawing upon their technology and organizational skills to become producers and exporters of parts and components, from which some of them have been able to move forward to become manufacturers and exporters of their own branded products. Other newly industrializing countries, notably Mexico, have also been able to establish links with the TNCs as part of the latter's globalization strategies, and have thus seen their industrial exports stimulated, as well no doubt as an inflow of technology and organizational skills which can provide the basis for subsequent development.

Attracting direct foreign investment

But what about those developing countries that have been largely left out of this process, so far, as it happens, the large majority.[28] If this is now the only way forward, the question is how to join the bandwagon. A lot has been said in recent years about the need for developing countries to adopt appropriate policies to attract foreign investment, but clear prescriptions on how to do this are not so readily forthcoming. Indeed, apart from the usual injunctions on the subjects of favourable tax treatment and effective guarantees for repatriation of profits and capital, little clear guidance emerges from the rhetoric of those who have been most active in urging the adoption of policies to attract foreign investment, except perhaps for urging the pursuit of the hands-off, free-market, trade liberalization, non-government-intervention policies that have been so much on the ascendant over the past decade. Even after the widespread adoption of these policies by developing countries, not much progress has so far been achieved in attracting foreign investment.

In fact, it is simplistic and misleading to speak of 'policies for attracting foreign investment', as though these were something unique and peculiar and different from the broader policies for promoting economic development. That this is so can be seen from the fact that unless the domestic environment is conducive to economic development, there is no incentive for direct foreign investment (or any other investment for that matter), except perhaps in the special case where the exploitation of natural resource based export industries is involved. Thus, except in this special case, the domestic policy framework required to attract foreign direct investment is not very different from that required to promote economic development in general. The basic minimum requirements regarding the domestic environment that we mentioned earlier - relative stability of the governmental framework, and so on - apply equally here, as does the need for adequate physical infrastructure, education system, etc., without which economic development is not possible. Only after these requirements have been met, or allowed for, do we reach the stage where we may expect to encounter conflicting views about alternative policy approaches.

New markets and production locations are the TNCs' two most important objectives in their globalization strategies. Large and growing domestic markets are an excellent incentive for the establishment of local production by TNCs, which is itself the most usual rationale and justification for foreign direct investment. Countries where a meaningful process of economic development is already under way therefore have a head start in the business of attracting foreign investment. Once such production facilities are established, they may be later integrated into the wider global production strategy serving either as centres for producing for exports to other countries in their region, or for the production of specific parts and components to be assembled elsewhere. The policy of establishing facilities in foreign countries solely for the production for exports of parts and components as part of global production strategy is more unusual, but is of growing importance. To be attractive as a location, a country must have special advantages, and these include some of the same requirements as for promoting economic development generally, such as a stable political environment, adequate physical infrastructure, an educated and adaptable labour force, etc., quite apart from such special requirements as convenient geographical location, especially as regards access to the major international shipping lanes, and perhaps special political links with the home countries of the TNCs as well. The upshot of all this is that it is probably quite futile to exhort countries to adopt appropriate policies to attract foreign investment as if such policies were distinct and separate from more general policies needed to promote economic development.

The problem, therefore (assuming the minimum domestic political conditions are met), is, as before, to devise and implement an appropriate policy mix to promote economic development, and there is every reason to believe that the free-market enthusiasts, who now dominate policy-making, have gone overboard in pushing developing countries down the path of liberalization and government non-intervention in economic activities. Even the World Bank seems to be coming around to recognizing this, if a 1991 article by Lawrence Summers, the Bank's Vice-President and Chief Economist, is any guide. He argues that while the market message was relevant, it was only part of the story, and that:

> Getting the government out of economic activities is not the correct answer every time. Sometimes, governments will be called on to do more of what they must do, and to do it better - making the tangible and intangible infrastructure investments that underpin a healthy private sector and rapid growth, and ensuring social and economic justice .... We have concentrated attention in recent years on governments' errors of commission. It is time for more work on governments' errors of omission.[29]

Living with the growing power of the TNCs

As is evident from what has been said above, one of the significant features of this age of globalization is the rising power of the TNCs. The rising power of these behemoths of the modern world derives not only from the sheer size of the resources at their disposal (in 1988 only 14 countries worldwide had GDPs which exceeded total sales of the largest of the TNCs), but from the control they exercise over the resources, technology and know-how needed to carry forward economic growth, and from the extent to which they operate worldwide as one integrated enterprise, as if oblivious to the existence of national frontiers.[30] While in each individual country in which they operate they will be subject to the national laws, their are no international laws or conventions to control or circumscribe the transnational dimension of their activities. Given their enormous power and influence and the resulting competition among countries for their favours, the typical developing country is in a weak bargaining position in dealing with them. TNCs are thus able to play off one country against another, and practices which in national jurisdictions may be pro-scribed or tightly controlled are allowed free rein where the TNCs are concerned. For example, most governments have regulations to control combinatorial activities between enterprises, in order to foster competition and protect the interests of consumers. But such regulations do not apply to the transnational activities of the TNCs, who are able freely to combine and engage in restrictive practices designed to extract maximum monopoly profits from their dealings in third countries. In fact, governments of home countries (for example, the US under the Webb-Pomerane Act) encourage their TNCs to engage in such activities, while forbidding similar activities in the domestic market.[31] As one writer remarks, 'the asymmetry in treating monopolistic exploitation of citizens and that of foreigners, especially weaker foreigners, is glaring.'[32]

The crucial role of these firms, and the enormous powers that they wield for good and for evil, call out for a multilateral framework of rules to govern their activities. Such rules are needed not to provide a wider economic space in which these firms can operate unhindered (as currently being demanded by the US and other developed countries in the context of the Uruguay Round negotiations), but, much more importantly from the developing countries' viewpoint, in order to move towards a global order based on fairness and equality, in which all can have an even chance to participate and progress.

Reviving North-South dialogue?

We may now briefly summarize the main conclusions reached so far. First, both the domestic and the international environment need to be propitious for economic development to proceed successfully, and while much needs to be done in most developing countries to improve the domestic environment, this alone will not be sufficient if not accompanied by an improvement in the international environment. Furthermore, domestic performance itself is not independent of the international environment, and hence an improvement in the latter may well be an important factor for achieving an improvement in the former. Second, the marked deterioration in the international environment during the past decade has been the critical factor contributing to the noticeable worsening in the overall performance of developing countries in recent years. Third, there is no evidence so far that the new free-market thinking which has substituted for international policy action and which now dominates policy-making in the developing world is by itself able to turn these countries around and put them on the path to economic growth - on the contrary, the indications are rather the opposite. Fourth, underlying changes have increased the importance of greater integration into the world economy, but developing countries are being left standing, and there are no quick fixes for getting them on board. When all is said and done, we are left to speculate on the likely evolution of the international environment for an assessment of the prospects facing the developing world, and of whether the future holds out any hope for a reversal or even a halt to the growing gap in incomes and standards of living which increasingly separates the rich nations from the poor.

One has only to make simple calculations, with a compound interest table at hand, to get an idea of the staggering, almost unimaginable, gap that will separate the rich countries from the poor if the trends of the past 40 years are replicated during the next 40. As we saw in Chapter 1, the gap in average incomes between the richest developed and the poorest developing countries increased from about 50:1 in the early post-war years to about 130:1 by the end of the 1980s. A continuation of this pattern of differential in *per capita* income growth-rates would imply a gap of the order of some 350:1 in another 40 years. The magnitudes involved would correspond to comparing average annual incomes of US$70,000 in the rich countries with US$200 in the poor. Present policies and trends do indeed indicate a continuation, if not an accentuation, of the past pattern. There is little point in referring here to the statistical relation between population and *per capita* income growth, to imply the need for a reduction in population growth in developing countries, since it is only too clear that the relation between these two variables is a complex one, going well beyond statistical definitions, and that if anything is certain about this relation, it is that population growth will fall when the development effort succeeds and higher income levels are achieved. The relation between population and income growth is rather like the proverbial problem of the chicken and the egg.

In the present international climate, and in the absence of some dramatic new development which cannot be foreseen (but which in our unpredictable world is, of course, always possible), there is clearly no hope of reviving the North-South dialogue in the sense in which we have known it. The underlying basis no longer exists. The North, led as firmly as ever by the US, is now much too confident of itself, and much too complacent and self-satisfied with their achievements, both in successfully carrying forward the process of growth in their own economies and in successfully beating back past attempts by developing countries to bring about changes in the system, to contemplate wasting time even listening to the complaints of the South, much less to engage in dialogue about reforms to the system. The South, beaten and in disarray, is in no mood to put up a fight. The East-West conflict, which once served to increase the pressure for North-South dialogue, is no longer on the international agenda. The collapse of the communist system in Eastern Europe and the Soviet Union, and the resulting clamour in these countries to join the free-market bandwagon, has served to strengthen further the self-confidence and complacency of the North, making the idea of dialogue with the South that much more far-fetched.

Not only is dialogue now a thing of the past, but with the triumph of the free-market ideology in the 1980s, and all the philosophical trappings that came along with it, there has been a hardening of attitudes in the North, a growing reluctance to acknowledge their responsibility for the plight of the South. This is reflected in the manner in which the international environment for development has been allowed to deteriorate, and the indifference shown to the discomfiture this has caused (e.g. the debt crisis, the collapse of commodity prices, the drying up of capital flows to developing countries, protectionism).

Where do we go from here?

Given the clear implications of current trends, the question must now be raised whether a widening of the income gap between nation states of the order of magnitude mentioned above is realizable and sustainable on moral and political grounds, and if so, what kind of supporting international system is required to make this possible. We may first note that while the underlying dynamics of the growth process as it exists today is ineluctably dividing the world ever more sharply into separate and unequal camps of haves and have-nots, drifting further and further apart in terms of incomes and standards of living, there are at the same time other forces at work just as ineluctably drawing the world closer and closer together in other domains, for example in terms of common aspirations, mutual concerns, shared knowledge of each others habits, preoccupations, lifestyles, and so on. We have in mind the truly remarkable revolution in communications, transportation and international travel which has swept the world in the past half century, and which, far from

having yet spent itself, is even now gathering force. In the field of communications, in particular, the real revolution is only now just under way, and even
with the technology that is already fully developed and needs only to be more
widely deployed as the cost curves fall, the world is soon truly to become a
global village where it will be just as easy to communicate with someone half
way around the globe as with your next-door neighbour. The implications of
this revolution from the point of view of our present concerns are clear. Given
the potential thus created for rapid and worldwide diffusion of knowledge
about lifestyles and economic opportunities in each country, and for the
moulding of common aspirations of peoples otherwise widely separated
culturally and geographically, and given also the ease with which international
travel can now be undertaken at low cost, the pressure for the movement of
population from the countries of the have-nots to those of the haves will
become great.

This underlying pressure of international migration, and how it is played
out in practice, will be the Achilles heel determining how viable in the long run
is a world organized into nation states diverging ever further in income levels
and standards of living. The problem of illegal immigration is already a major
issue facing the developed world. In the US, estimates of illegal immigrants,
mostly from Mexico but also from other Latin American countries and further
afield, run into several millions, and the problem of how to stem the tide has
not been resolved. In Europe, illegal immigration is also a serious concern of
governments. The influx from southern-tier European and North African
countries, and, more recently, the threat from Eastern Europe have been the
great fear, though there has also been a threatening rise in illegal immigrants
from far-away third world countries. In Europe, interest in the problem is
particularly lively, not only because of Eastern Europe, but also because the
programme for a single European market by 1993 envisages free movement
of populations between EC member countries. The present skirmishing on the
immigration front - actual movements and immediate threats of movements of
populations, and official concerns and policy responses - is only a pallid
foretaste of what the future holds in store if present policies and trends continue.
Even Japan, geographically and culturally isolated as it is, may not be able to
escape the threat of an influx of immigrants.

In an earlier age, when the concept of the nation state was not so firmly
established, and when the movement of people between geographical locations
was determined more by technological possibilities and individual impulses,
migratory movements of peoples in response to geographical differences in

economic opportunities was a standard feature of life on earth. This age reached its apotheosis with the gigantic wave of European migration to the Americas, to Australasia, and to parts of Africa. In these countries, the indigenous peoples were overwhelmed by the migrants with their barely superior technology, and had to give way and suffer the consequences. Today, however, things are rather different. The nation state is now firmly established, with clearly defined geographical boundaries and with well recognized functions, which include defense of its borders from alien intrusion and protection of the interests of its citizens. Migratory movements are nowadays therefore heavily constrained by legal and administrative measures. Furthermore, the countries where the pull of economic opportunities now attracts migrants are those possessing the superior technology, and thus presumably better able to protect themselves from being overrun by aliens.

But as the pressure mounts (with the growing income gap and the ongoing revolution in communications and travel), it will become increasingly difficult on moral, political and military grounds to defend the borders against the onrush of immigrants. In the longer term, such defence would require that the North become virtually an armed fortress against invading migrants. We have seen some hints of what this may involve, with Vietnamese boat people trying to get into Hong Kong, Bangladeshis being smuggled across continents and oceans in the most wretched conditions in order to find an economic haven in Canada, Haitian boat people desperate to get to Miami, and the dramatic landing of tens of thousands of Albanians in Italy in search of economic asylum. To prevent the arrival of such hordes seeking refuge and a better life, it will not suffice to patrol the borders of the target state (since this is likely to leave that state with a messy problem on its hand), but to turn back the invaders on the high seas, or, as Italy has proposed doing, to patrol the foreign borders in order to deter would-be migrants from leaving in the first place. But this pattern may lead to a siege mentality, increasingly dissonant with the enjoyment by the rich countries of their ever rising incomes and of the freedoms to which such incomes should entitle them. It is not a stable situation. In fact, it holds out the prospect of becoming a magnification on a world scale of the kind of tense situation often seen in underdeveloped countries, where the rich and the privileged live barricaded in well manicured and heavily guarded compounds, surrounded by a hostile and resentful sea of poverty.

The ball now firmly in the hands of the North

In present circumstances, where the North is so firmly in control and there is simply no outside pressure to force their hand, what are the chances of a shift to policies more favourable to development? Such a shift could only come about if it appeared to the North, in their own cool judgement, that it was in their best interests to do so.

The instabilities and threats to the established order that could result from the build up of pressure for population movements from low to high income countries amount to the sort of prospect that it may be in the interest of the North to make sacrifices to avoid, and which could therefore cause them to institute policy changes to improve the economic outlook for developing countries, even at the expense of their own short-term interests. But to act in this way requires not only an ability to take account of longer-term implications of current actions, but even more important, a willingness to make concrete sacrifices today in exchange for what may seem ill-defined benefits in the distant future. And of course this is not the only way that one could go about meeting the problem. An alternative approach would involve making long-term plans to contain anticipated destabilizing influences resulting from the increasing income disparity. This might require mechanisms for co-ordinating international policy for keeping the lid on an increasingly discontented and restless South, backed up by a suitable mixture of sanctions, economic and otherwise, including the use and the threat of force, an area where the heavily armed North now has and very much intends retaining the overwhelming advantage. Perhaps it is something along these lines that US President George Bush had in mind when he spoke about the 'New World Order' now on the drawing board. And indeed this is the logic of the thinking that has dominated policy-making in the North over the past decade.[33]

There is also the question of how the growing international concern with the problem of the environment might affect the issue. Could this help to provide motivation for more favourable policies towards developing countries? The answer is not obvious. As we argued in the earlier discussion, the carrying capacity of the planet would be likely to be seriously overloaded should the existing pattern of economic growth in the North be replicated in the South. The implication of this is that the poor countries must remain poor if the rich countries are to be able to continue their present pattern of economic growth without fear of environmental collapse, and there is then a definite disincentive for the North to help promote the economic development of the South. It may be doubted, however, how important this factor would be in practice. There are just too many more immediately relevant factors and currents influencing policy thinking for this rather hypothetical consideration to play an important role, especially since the prospects for economic development in the South are already so dim.

It is more fruitful to focus on the question of whether any positive incentives for such help can be discerned. We recall the link between poverty and the environment that came up in the earlier discussion and that provided the rationale, as it were, for assigning co-responsibility to developing countries for the environmental degradation which now threatens the stability of the world's eco-system. Population growth, soil erosion and desertification are most often mentioned as ways in which poverty contributes to environmental degradation, though, from the point of view of ecological balance, it is the clearing of tropical forests that generates the greatest concern. Perhaps, then, concern with environmental protection may justify policies to promote economic development in the South. While this may well be a positive factor, it is unlikely to weigh heavily in the balance. Apart from population growth, which raises fundamental geopolitical issues going well beyond the immediate concern with the environment, the clearing of tropical forests is the only aspect that seems of any considerable importance in the wider global context. And its connection with poverty *per se* seems rather tenuous - indeed, the clearing of forests is more likely to be an indication of economic development in progress than of poverty as such. It may well be, however, that the North may be willing to make compensation payments to the South to dissuade them from cutting down their tropical forests. But to the extent that this is only compensation for the use value of the output of forest clearing (including the use of the cleared land for agriculture and other more immediately productive purposes), it is unlikely to make any net contribution to economic development.

As to the broader question of international policies to promote economic development in the South, clearly the most critical area where action involving sacrifices by the North is needed concerns financing and the transfer of resources to the South. The World Bank estimates that over the next two decades developing countries will account for 95 per cent of growth in the world's labour force, but for less than 15 per cent of capital investment.[35] Unless this imbalance in capital investment can be arrested by a deliberate policy of resource transfers, reversing the trend of recent years, it is difficult to see how the trend towards increasing income disparities between North and South can be slowed.

Recent developments in Eastern Europe and the Soviet Union are likely to add to the woes of developing countries from this point of view. With the collapse of communism in these countries, a dramatic shift has taken place in the preoccupations and concerns of the North. A high priority now attaches to helping these countries successfully carry through the process of conversion to market economies.[35] The years ahead are therefore likely to see a considerable focus of attention on extending aid to these countries, which can only be at the expense of third world countries. This will be so especially in the critical area of finance. It is now becoming clear that with the total collapse of the economies of these countries following the breakdown of the old system, massive amounts of foreign capital will be required to get these countries back on track as functioning economies based on market principles, where economic growth can resume. The enormous cost of restructuring the East German economy, a cost which is straining the resources of the large and powerful West German economy, but which nonetheless is being borne by the West Germans in the interests of national solidarity, gives an indication of the extent of the effort required. The implications for developing countries of this turn of events are not encouraging. Not only is there now greater overall demand for available investment capital, with a resulting tendency for capital to become more costly and expensive, but developing countries now find themselves pushed further back in the queue for this heavily rationed commodity.

An interesting phenomenon, and an indication of the extent to which the North is now firmly in the driver's seat, is the high prestige now enjoyed by the Bretton Woods institutions, notwithstanding their role in the recent past in putting the squeeze on debtor developing countries. It reflects, apart from anything else, the overriding power these institutions have come to wield, and the perceived lack of any practical alternatives to them. This prestige also reflects the enthusiasm now being shown worldwide for membership and active participation in these institutions, notably by the Eastern European countries and the former Soviet Union. Indeed, there is now the prospect that in the not too distant future they will become truly universal in membership, while remaining under tight Northern (particularly US) control. GATT membership has also been increasing rapidly, 19 countries having acceded to membership in the 10-year period up to March 1992, seven in the last 15 months of that period. When all is said and done, the international system created in the aftermath of the War, heavily criticised and deeply distrusted as it may be, and still unreformed in any important way, now reigns supreme and virtually unchallenged.

Granted that the North is now firmly in control, it remains true that the doors are not necessarily all shut. Markets are still accessible to a certain extent, foreign capital and technology are still available in some degree and under certain conditions, and the structural change accompanying world economic development both closes options and opens opportunities. It will therefore be up to each country to do what it can to improve its lot, given the international environment in which it must now operate. Except for the thinly populated oil exporters, the major objective will be to overcome the foreign exchange constraint. And, in view of the bleak future facing primary commodity exports, there is no alternative to reliance on exports of manufactures. Middle-income countries that are already semi-industrialized will have a head start in this respect, since they are better able to attract the foreign investment and the technology needed to press forward with industrialization and to achieve greater integration into the world economy, without which exports of manufactures will not expand. They are therefore in a much better position to prosper in the present environment.

The countries of East and South-East Asia are particularly well placed from this point of view, having already made great strides in forcing the pace of industrialization, in attracting foreign direct investment, in absorbing technology, expanding exports of manufactures and integrating into the world economy, setting the stage for a take-off into self-sustained growth. These are countries where, for reasons that are not always easy to understand, both the domestic and the international aspects seem to be more favourable. While the issues are much too complex for us to attempt an explanation here, there is little doubt that one important factor is the close geographical (and perhaps cultural) proximity of these countries to that most dynamic centre of post-war economic growth, Japan. They have thus benefited from growth-stimulating impulses emanating from that source: investments, travel, tourism, technology, methods of business organization, and so on, all of which have had favourable effects on the climate for development.[36]

A number of larger, middle-income Latin American countries also show signs of approaching this category. They have suffered a severe set-back from the debt crisis, but are already sufficiently semi-industrialized to have joined the ranks of exporters of manufactures, and with appropriate policies to push forward industrialization and to attract foreign investment and technology, they can hope eventually to join the mainstream of world economic development. The task will not be easy in the present international climate, but one can at least see some possibility of a way forward, if the debt problem can somehow be held in check.

For those developing countries still in the earliest stages of development, however, with abysmally low income levels, where industrialization has as yet made little headway, still dependent almost wholly on primary commodities for their export earnings, the prospects are grim. In their present state they offer little or no attraction for investment, foreign or domestic. The slow process of trying to build, in a hostile or unsympathetic international environment, the necessary social and physical infrastructure on which to base economic development will be a daunting task. Even with the most acute domestic effort on their part, it is difficult to see how, in the present international climate, these countries will avoid falling further and further behind.

Perhaps a glimmer of hope for these countries could emerge if we could perceive any likelihood of a return to a more expansionary phase in world trade for primary commodities, particularly the primary agricultural products on which these countries are so dependent for their export earnings. A more rapid expansion in world demand for these products in the years ahead could work wonders in helping these countries to expand export earnings and overcome the foreign exchange constraint which so limits their development potential. The outlook here is certainly not encouraging, given the nature of the underlying forces which continue to operate. But there is at least some basis for hope in this regard.

Eastern Europe and the former Soviet Union represent a large potential market. Under communism, imported consumption goods received low priority, and as a consequence, *per capita* consumption in these countries of such traditional primary commodities as coffee, cocoa, tea, bananas and spices, not to mention the newer exotic products (e.g. tropical fruits such as pineapples, mangoes, papayas, avocados), have been low by international standards. There is, therefore, in these countries a considerable latent demand for these products, which, if realized, could have an important impact and give a significant lift to developing country primary exporters. Before this demand can be made effective, however, the vast and as yet uncertain process of converting these countries into functioning market economies must get under way. This will take time, and may well be a slow process, but if and when realized, it could usher in for a while a new era of significant growth in primary commodity exports, which could boost prospects for the poorer developing countries. Hopeful as this possibility is, however, it is not likely to make an immediate impact.

The efforts now under way in the Uruguay Round negotiations to bring agriculture under stricter GATT rules and disciplines could, if successful, also help improve the prospects for agricultural exports from developing countries. The importance of this factor should not be exaggerated, however, bearing in mind that it is mostly temperate-zone products, exported by the developed countries, that are covered by those negotiations. For the poorer, less developed countries, the implications of a successful outcome to those negotiations could even be negative, in view of the adverse impact of the resulting higher food prices on the cost of their food imports. [37]

Another development which could favourably affect the outlook is the rapid economic expansion now taking place in East Asia, and the likely impact of rising incomes in these countries on their demand for primary products, though it has to be borne in mind that some of these countries are themselves producers of tropical products similar to those produced by other developing countries.

These are aspects of current developments that could be important in opening new horizons for the poorer developing countries. How important they will be in practice remains to be seen. It is clear, however, that given the present international policy climate, unless developments along these or similar lines come to the fore to provide these countries with an opening, they risk being by-passed by the rush of world economic development, and being left further and further behind.

For the rest, we can only wonder aloud whether it is really possible to envisage a future in which the world is permanently split into nation states separated along caste lines, into haves and have-nots, rich and poor, privileged and underprivileged. And if not, what are the forces that may come into play to steer us away from such an outcome?

It is difficult to see how an affirmative answer to the first question can be sustained. The contradictions and tensions inherent in such a world would be too great for it to be viable. As to the second question, we can only speculate. It is possible that as the contradictions inherent in present tendencies play themselves out and make themselves felt, enlightened self-interest will prevail, political thinking will evolve, and policy stances change, and what seems unlikely and far-fetched today may tomorrow become the order of the day. For example, it might be that in time, as income disparities widen, globalization proceeds, and the immigration pressure mounts, the fall-out will force a change in thinking in the developed countries about the geographical scope of governmental responsibility for development and economic welfare, from the present exclusive focus on the needs of the individual nation state to a wider international concern. Such thoughts lead inevitably to utopian ideas about world goverment that have always seemed too fanciful to be seriously pursued.

But these are the thoughts on which we must close as we reflect on the current impasse in North-South relations, and the seemingly inexorable process by which these two poles of humanity are drifting economically apart. If nothing else, they serve to remind us that, unyielding as current trends may seem, they may themselves contain the seeds of change, now hidden or difficult to discern, pointing in quite unexpected directions.

Notes

1. The question why these countries, and not others, were able to take advantage of the favourable international environment to promote modern growth success-fully has been dealt with in chapter 1.

2. On this see, for example, Ragnar Nurske, 'Trade Theory and Development Policy', Chapter 9 in Howard S. Ellis and Henry C. Wallich, *Economic Development for Latin America* (Macmillan & Co., London, 1963). See also C.P. Kindleberger, *The Terms of Trade: A European Case Study, op. cit.*

3. See Seung Hee Kim, *Foreign Capital for Economic Development: A Korean Case Study* (Praeger Special Studies in International Economics and Development, (Praeger Publishers, New York, 1970), especially chapter 2. As the author points out (p. 62), official aid financed over 90 per cent of the current account deficit during 1957-62, the peak years of dependence on foreign capital inflows. It was not until 1962 that use began to be made of private loans and that debt service payments began to enter the picture. See also Anne O. Krueger, *The Developmental Role of the Foreign Sector and Aid, Studies in the Modernization of the Republic of Korea: 1945-1975* (Council on East Asian Studies, Harvard University (Harvard University Press, Cambridge, Mass., 1979), for further discussion of the role of external financing in Korean economic development.

4. See Neil H. Jacoby, *U.S. Aid to Taiwan: A Study of Foreign Aid, Self-Help, and Development* (Frederick A. Praeger, New York, 1966), for a discussion and relevant data on the subject. See also in this connection Ching-yuan Lin, *Industrialization in Taiwan, 1946-72,* (Praeger Publishers, New York 1973), especially table 4-4 for some relevant statistics on the subject.

5. The co-operation arrangement between the US and Switzerland in this regard has even led to dispute as to how the confiscated funds should be shared between them.

6. Interestingly enough, at the 48th session of the UN Commission on Human Rights concluded in March 1992, a resolution on 'Fraudulent enrichment of top

State officials prejudicial to the public interest', was adopted, one of the preambular paragraphs of which recognized the special responsibility of developed countries to contribute to 'the restitution to despoiled peoples of the funds which their leaders have extorted from them.' But this was not an issue that developed countries were prepared to have put on the international agenda, and, led by the United States, they either voted against, or withheld their votes from, this paragraph of the resolution. The matter would therefore continue to get the blind eye from those who benefited from existing arrangements.

7. This is brought out clearly in a recent essay by Albert Hirschman, whose own writings contributed so much to the reign of the old paradigm. See the essay entitled 'The Rise and Decline of Development Economics' in A. D. Hirschman, *Essays in Trespassing: Economics to Politics and Beyond* (Cambridge University Press, Cambridge, 1981).

8. For the story of this transformation and of the role of the government in it, see, for example, Kazushi Ohkawa and Henry Rosovsky, *Japanese Economic Growth: Trend Acceleration in the Twentieth Century* (Stanford University Press, Stanford, 1973).

9. Lawrence Krause and Sueo Sekiguchi, 'Japan and the World Economy' in Hugh Partick and Henry Rosovsky, *Asia's New Giant: How the Japanese Economy Works* (The Brookings Institution, Washington, DC, 1976), p. 412.

10. Hugh Patrick and Henry Rosovsky, 'Japan's Economic Performance: An Overview', in Patrick and Rosovsky, *op. cit.*, p. 45.

11. Patrick and Rosovsky, *op. cit.*, p. 413.

12. *Ibid.*, p. 415.

13. See Anne O. Krueger, *op. cit.*, for a discussion of the use of these various policy instruments in the formative years of Korea's economic development. See also in this connection Charles R. Frank, Kwang Suk Kim, and Larry E. Westphal, *Foreign Trade Regimes and Economic Development: South Korea* (National Bureau of Economic Research, New York, 1975). See also A. K. Sen, 'Public action and the quality of life in developing countries', *Oxford Bulletin of Economics and Statistics*, Vol. 43, 1981, for a discussion of the powerful role of government and of state *dirigisme* in Korea's economic development.

14. See for example, Chin-yuan Lin, *op. cit.*

15. See the discussion in chapter 2.

16. Guyana is a good example here. Under IMF guidance, and after years of economic mismanagement and economic decline, Guyana shifted suddenly in the late eighties from a policy of extreme autarky to full trade liberalization, complete with a free floating exchange rate system. As a result, the exchange rate has been experiencing a free fall. In early 1987 the official rate was G$4.40 to the US$ and the black market rate G$28. Since then there have been several devaluations, and the official rate has been catching up with a fast-moving black market rate. By June 1990 the official rate was G$45 and the black market rate

G\$66. The two rates have since merged in a free float system, and by late 1991 this rate was above G\$125. In the span of just over four years, therefore, there has been a 30-fold fall in the exchange rate in a seemingly endless cycle of stagflation and currency depreciation. As pointed out by Thomas, from whom the above information is taken, this approach could 'drive the domestic entrepreneurial class to ruin. Thus . . . real incomes are falling because of higher import prices and general inflation; the cost of borrowing is unprecedentedly high . . .; and the onset of sudden 'competition' following on import liberalization measures have all favoured major deflationary dislocations . . . and essential public service inputs (health, education, sea-defences etc.) are declining. All this has led to falling morale, a reduction in social cohesion, . . . and a spread of the process of pauperization from traditional locations (unemployed, disabled, small landless peasants, isolated communities) to non-traditional areas (public employees, security personnel, teaching and health workers, young couples, etc.).' See Clive Y. Thomas, *The Cambio-System of an Independent Exchange Rate Float: The Case of Guyana,* (Institute of Development Studies, University of Guyana, October 1990). The quotes are taken from p. 55.

17. See our discussion on this point in chapter 7.

18. The importance of R&D as a factor in contemporary economic growth is illustrated by the following figures, which also provide a dramatic illustration of the immense and dynamic gap which now separates the developed from the developing countries: in 1989 (as reported in *La Tribune de Genève,* 4 November 1991), Swiss companies spent some US\$8 billion on research and development, equivalent to an expenditure of approximately US\$1,300 per head of population for Switzerland as a whole. This may be compared with the average *per capita* income of all developing countries of just over US\$1,000 in the same year. Thus in 1989 Switzerland spent more per head of population on research and development than the average income earned per head of population in developing countries as a whole, and in most developing countries individually.

19. Between 1960 and 1980 the share of trade in GDP virtually doubled for the world as a whole and for the developed countries in particular, in both cases from about 11 to 21-22 per cent. Since 1980 this share has tended to level off. See UNCTAD, *Yearbook of International Trade and Development Statistics*, Table 6.3.

20. To give just a few examples, Japanese car makers, both independently and in partnership with US firms, start building automobiles in the United States and announce plans to export more cars from the US than from Japan by the early 1990s; Honda, the Japanese carmaker, already the fourth largest US producer, announces plans to export 50,000 cars to Japan by 1991; Toyota makes a US\$850 million investment in the UK to produce cars for the EC market. The growing importance of the transnationalization of the R&D effort of the large TNCs is illustrated by the following facts cited in a recent OECD study: in 1988 some 28% of the R&D workforce of British drug companies was employed abroad; between

1987 and 1990 the Japanese electronics companies established 33 new R&D centres abroad - 21 in the US, six in Europe and six in Asia; Japanese companies are creating new basic research laboratories close to universities in the UK, with Sharp electronics planning to set up a large centre in the Oxford Science Park in 1992; in 1988 US companies spent an estimated US$6.2 billion on R&D in foreign countries, equivalent to 10.5% of domestic R&D outlays, about the same amount that foreign companies spent on R&D in the US. The report also examines the recent upsurge in cross-border inter-firm collaboration agreements, especially prominent in such high-tech sectors as information and telecommunications, new materials and biotechnology. See the OECD *Observer* of February/March 1992.

21. Again to give a few examples: BBC, a Swiss company, and ABB, a Swedish company, two of the world's largest engineering and electrical equipment producers, merge to form a single giant multi-national company; Bristol-Myers and Squibb, two of the world's largest drug companies (one originally British, the other US) agree to merge; in both cases economies in research and marketing are cited as the basic reason for the merger. In a somewhat different vein Philips Electronics, a Dutch company with the world's largest marketing network, enters into an agreement with Japanese companies whereby the latter would establish a joint research centre in the Netherlands; in return, the Japanese companies will be allowed to use the Philips marketing outlets to sell their products. (Some of these examples and those in the preceding footnote are taken from E. R. Moss, 'The New Global Players: How They Compete and Collaborate', *World Development*, Vol. 19 No. 1, January 1991).

22. The negotiations to extend the Canada-US free-trade area to include Mexico (creating NAFTA, or North American Free Trade Agreement) illustrates another aspect of these developments: the burgeoning drift towards the formation of huge cross-hemispheric regional blocs encompassing both developed and underdeveloped countries. Thus there has been much talk recently (including from the US President) of the whole of the Americas, North and South, forming one large free-trade area. There has also been much talk of an emerging Asian-Pacific bloc, centred on Japan. While the full implications of this new drift for the broader issues of North-South relations and for overcoming the development problems of the South are as yet unclear, it constitutes nonetheless part of this emerging trend towards the formation of regional blocs.

23. Our example in the previous note 20 above, about the Japanese car maker investing in a factory in the UK in order to supply the EC market, is a typical example of this.

24. These figures are taken from United Nations doc. E/C.10/1991/2, *Recent Developments Related to Transnational Corporations and International Economic Relations* (April 1991), p. 12.

25. See, for example, Alexander Gerschenkron, *Economic Backwardness in Histori-*

cal Perspective (Harvard University Press, Cambridge, Mass.), 1962.

26. An indication of the key role that TNCs now play in the world economy is suggested by the following figures for the United States: in 1988 at least 80 per cent of the country's total foreign trade was undertaken by TNCs, and foreign affiliates of US-based TNCs exported US$87 billion in goods and services to the US, accounting for about 19 per cent of all US imports; US-based affiliates of foreign TNCs accounted for an additional 34 per cent of imports, implying that 53 per cent of total US imports passed through the affiliates of TNCs. And in the same year, third-country exports by foreign affiliates of US-based TNCs were almost as large as all exports from the US. See United Nations, *op. cit.*, p. 30.

27. See the UN document cited above.

28. According to the UN study quoted above, 10 developing countries accounted for about three-quarters of total inflows to developing countries during the 1980s. These 10 include 5 in Asia (Singapore, Hong Kong, China, Malaysia and Thailand), 4 in South America (Brazil, Mexico, Argentina and Colombia), and one in Africa (Egypt).

29. Lawrence Summers, 'Research Challenges for Development Economists', *Finance & Development*, September 1991, p. 3.

30. This, of course, is not really true, since it is to their home governments that they look for succour and support, and they know very well where their primary loyalty lies.

31. Thus the Foreign Trade Antitrust Improvement Act was adopted in 1982, the purpose of which was to establish beyond doubt that the antitrust laws will not apply to export trade or transactions foreign to the United States. See report prepared by Professor Robert Pitofsky, entitled 'Legislative Environment to Corporate Policies in the United States', UNCTAD/ITP/67, p. 25.

32. P. Streeten, 'Global Prospects in an Interdependent World', *World Development*, Vol. 19, No. 1, January 1991, p. 129.

33. Lest the reader think that this is mere speculation on the author's part, he (or she) should read the influential US political scientist, Stanley Hoffmann ('A New World and its Troubles,' *Foreign Affairs*, Fall 1990), who gives clear expression to this way of thinking. Hoffmann sees the end of the Cold War as providing an opportunity for the establishment, not quite of a world government, but a 'halfway house' managed by the US, Japan and the EC, with Russian support, which would, *inter alia*, deny advanced technology to the Third World, ensure the latter's compliance with Northern-defined environmental standards and drug eradication programmes, and dole out aid (presumably permanently) for 'health care, energy efficiency, agricultural productivity and human rights', the idea apparently being that the third world is to become a permanent ward of the advanced countries, with no hope or intention of ever aspiring to equality.

34. Figures cited by Summers, *op. cit.*, p. 5.

35. The reasons for this are complex and will no doubt be the subject of volumes in

the years ahead. We may mention here, however, a number of considerations which are particularly relevant. Not the least among these is geographical proximity and the cultural and historical affinities which link Eastern and Western Europe with each other and with North America. These are bonds which unite in a way absent from North-South relations. The immigration factor is also of great importance in this context. Thus, given the geographical proximity and the affinities mentioned above, it will clearly be politically difficult to stem the tide of migration motivated by an increasing income gap between East and West. All the more reason, therefore, to try and prevent a widening of the income gap. And in a subtle sort of way, embracing the former ideological enemies and welcoming them into the fold is a way of building an even stronger foundation for a world order in which the South, with their large and growing numbers of poor and disinherited, can be held in check. It is therefore no accident that it was only with the collapse of communism in Eastern Europe that the possibility of a 'New World Order' seemed to attract the attention of the US President.

36. The effect here is something analogous to ideas we advanced earlier in trying to understand why the locus of modern economic growth in its initial phase was confined to the countries of Western Europe and their off-springs in North America and Australasia (see the discussion in chapter 1). In an obverse way it is also analogous to the suggestion made there to explain why Argentina, notwithstanding its apparent similarities to the North American model and a very promising initial start, found itself in the end left behind to join the ranks of the underdeveloped.

37. A recent OECD study calculates that while the OECD countries and the world as a whole would gain significantly if the agricultural measures proposed in the GATT talks are implemented, the countries of sub-Saharan Africa, among the poorest in the world, would be big losers. See the study by Ian Goldin and Dominique van der Mensbrugghe: 'Trade Liberalization: What's at Stake', (OECD Development Centre, May 1992), as reported in the *Financial Times*, 21 April 1992.

Acronyms

CIEC	Conference on International Economic Co-operation
CIPEC	*Conseil Intergouvernemental des Pays Exportateurs de Cuivre*
DAC	Development Assistance Committee (of OECD)
ECLAUN	Economic Commission for Latin America
EEC	European Economic Community
EEE	*Espace European Economique*
EFTA	European Free Trade Association
GA	General Assembly of the United Nations
GATT	General Agreement on Tariffs and Trade
GDP	Gross Domestic Product
GNP	Gross National Product
GSP	General Scheme of Preferences
IBA	International Bauxite Association
ICAs	International Commodity Agreements
IDA	International Development Association
IFC	International Finance Corporation
IMF	International Monetary Fund
ITO	International Trade Organization
LIBOR	London Inter-Bank Offered Rate
NIEO	New International Economic Order
ODA	Official Development Assistance
OECD	Organization for Econmic Co-operation and Development
OPEC	Organization of Petroleum Exporting Countries
R&D	Research and Development
SALs	Structural Adjustment Loans
SDR	Special Drawing Rights
SUNFED	Special United Nations Fund for Economic Development
TNCs	Trans-National Corporations
TRIMS	Trade Related Investment Measures
TRIPS	Trade Related aspects of Intellectual Property Rights
UN	United Nations
UNCED	United Nations Conference on Environment and Development
UNCTAD	United Nations Conference on Trade and Development
UNDP	United Nations Development Programme
UNIDO	United Nations Industrial Development Organization
USAID	United States Agency for Internatinal Development
VER	Voluntary Export Restraints

Index